Pro Unity Game Development with C#

Alan Thorn

Apress®

Pro Unity Game Development with C#

ISBN-13 (pbk): 978-1-4302-6746-1

ISBN-13 (electronic): 978-1-4302-6745-4

President and Publisher: Paul Manning
Lead Editor: Michelle Lowman
Development Editor: Douglas Pundick
Technical Reviewer: Marc Schärer
Editorial Board: Steve Anglin, Ewan Buckingham, Gary Cornell, Louise Corrigan, James DeWolf,
    Jonathan Gennick, Jonathan Hassell, Robert Hutchinson, Michelle Lowman, James Markham,
    Matthew Moodie, Jeff Olson, Jeffrey Pepper, Douglas Pundick, Ben Renow-Clarke, Dominic Shakeshaft,
    Gwenan Spearing, Matt Wade, Steve Weiss, Tom Welsh
Coordinating Editor: Kevin Shea
Copy Editor: Kimberly Burton-Weisman
Compositor: SPi Global
Indexer: SPi Global
Artist: SPi Global
Cover Designer: Anna Ishchenko

Distributed to the book trade worldwide by Springer Science+Business Media New York, 233 Spring Street, 6th Floor, New York, NY 10013. Phone 1-800-SPRINGER, fax (201) 348-4505, e-mail orders-ny@springer-sbm.com, or visit www.springeronline.com.

For information on translations, please e-mail rights@apress.com, or visit www.apress.com.

Apress and friends of ED books may be purchased in bulk for academic, corporate, or promotional use. eBook versions and licenses are also available for most titles. For more information, reference our Special Bulk Sales–eBook Licensing web page at www.apress.com/bulk-sales.

Any source code or other supplementary materials referenced by the author in this text is available to readers at www.apress.com. For detailed information about how to locate your book's source code, go to www.apress.com/source-code.

Contents at a Glance

Contents

About the Author

Alan Thorn is a freelance game developer and author with over 12 years of industry experience. He is the founder of London-based game studio Wax Lyrical Games, and is the creator of the award-winning adventure game *Baron Wittard: Nemesis of Ragnarok*. He has worked freelance on over 500 projects worldwide, including games, simulators, kiosks, and augmented reality software for game studios, museums, and theme parks. He is currently working on an upcoming adventure game, *Mega Bad Code*.

Alan has also spoken on game development at venues throughout Europe, and is the author of 11 books on game development, including *Learn Unity for 2D Game Development* (Apress, 2013), *Unity 4 Fundamentals* (Focal Press, 2013), and *UDK Game Development* (Cengage Learning, 2011). He is also a frequent contributor at the online video training library 3DMotive.com. More information on Alan Thorn and Wax Lyrical Games can be found at www.alanthorn.net and www.waxlyricalgames.com, as well as Alan's YouTube channel at http://goo.gl/xwDOU4 and on Twitter at https://twitter.com/thorn_alan.

About the Technical Reviewer

Marc Schärer is an interactive media software engineer creating cutting-edge interactive media experiences for training, education, and entertainment with his company, Gayasoft (www.gayasoft.net), located in Switzerland, using Unity since its early days in 2007.

Marc has a strong background in 3D graphics, network technology, software engineering, and interactive media. Starting programming at the age of 11, he later studied computer science and computational science and engineering at the Swiss Federal Institute of Technology Zurich before working with various teams in North America, Oceania, and Japan to create compelling interactive experiences.

With the rise of serious games, interactive education, and immersive experiences, Gayasoft's focus is on researching options and technologies for the next generation of interactive and immersive experiences, applying state-of-the-art augmented and virtual reality (AR/VR) technologies (such as Vuforia, Metaio, and Oculus Rift) and intuitive, innovative input technologies (such as Razer Hydra, STEM, Thalmic Myo, Leap Motion, and Emotive Insight).

Acknowledgments

This book would not have been possible if it hadn't been for the efforts and fine work of many people, all of whom were a pleasure to work with. There are simply too many people and I can't list them all here. But I feel special mention should go to: Michelle Lowman for helping to get this book started in the first place, Kevin Shea for keeping things on track, and Marc Schärer for ensuring technical correctness. In addition, I'd like to thank Douglas Pundick, Tim Moore, Kimberly Burton, and Dhaneesh Kumar for their editorial and production work; as well as everybody else at Apress. And finally, I'd like to thank you, the reader, for purchasing this book and taking the time to improve your C# skills. I hope the book proves highly useful for you.

—Alan Thorn

2014, London

Introduction

One thing I really love about the games industry today is its "openness" compared to many industries. To start out in the games industry you don't need a degree. All you need is a computer. And an Internet connection. If you log on online right now, you can immediately visit web sites such as Blender, GIMP, Inkscape, and (of course) Unity to get access to professional-grade game development software completely free of charge! The result is that almost anybody in any place on any budget, from any background and at any age, can sit at a computer and be a game developer *right now*.

Of course, none of that openness *guarantees* you'll automatically *know* how to use the tools, or that you'll even like the results you get from them. You need to bring a certain *something*, an understanding, to the tools to fully realize their power and potential in practice. To do that, you'll need to develop experience and to refine your knowledge, and to learn techniques and workflows using real-world examples, targeting your software of choice directly.

This book focuses on Unity development specifically. And when it comes to Unity development, there's one area where developers feel troubled or somewhat lacking in power. That area is in C# scripting. The general feel is that so much of the C# tutorials and guides out there today are so abstract and formal that it's difficult to see how all of it should come together and be applied properly in real-world cases to do what you need to do to give your games that professional edge. You already know about variables, functions, loops, enumerations, and the fundamentals. But what you need is something to take you further, to help you see how all these core features can be combined in creative ways to produce a real-world, working game. The kind of game you can not only play but study and see how it all comes together. This book aims to fill that need so you can become a more powerful game developer.

What Is This Book About?

This book will show you how to create a small but complete first-person shooter game in the Unity engine, step by step. In particular it'll focus strongly on C# scripting, and on a range of related ideas and techniques, for getting professional-grade results. We'll explore a lot of ground, including level design, vectors and mathematics, line-of-sight calculations, pathfinding and navigation, artificial intelligence, state machines, weapon creation, trajectories and paths, and load-and-save functionality, as well as a lot more! We'll see things not just from a more abstract and theoretical standpoint, but we'll see how theory is applied in real-world cases to get work done, gradually piecing together a complete game we can play and enjoy, and also extend upon and improve. The aim is to show you some real-world applications of C# scripting that you can take away to use on your own projects, achieving your creative vision more easily and effectively.

There are, of course, many things we won't cover here. Specifically, we'll be focusing only on C# scripting, and not on other languages such as JavaScript or Boo. That decision should not be taken as a negative judgment of those languages. Indeed, all of them are powerful and versatile in their own ways. But it simply reflects what most people are seeking (as I see it) when they approach Unity seeking to extend their scripting skills.

Additionally, we won't be covering C# basics, such as variables, functions, and loops. I'll assume you already know that stuff. Further, although we'll cover *some* level and game-design issues as we start out with our game project in Chapters 1 and 2, we won't be going too far in depth on that subject, as it's covered amply elsewhere and because the main focus here is on C# and scripting specifically.

And finally, we won't be covering every aspect of the C# language or every possible way it can be used. This is for the simple reason that no book could hope to do that, just as no English dictionary can tell you about every possible combination of words or every possible application of them. This book covers a specific set of C# features in a specific set of ways. The idea is that by showing you specific cases and specific applications, you can see how the general techniques apply to your own games.

Who Is This Book For?

Every technical book is written with a target audience in mind. That is, it's written for a specific "type" of reader. This means that when writing the book, I, the author, must make assumptions about you, the reader. The assumptions are about the book-relevant topics I think you'll already know, before even starting to read this book. Specifically, I'll assume you know the following:

- How to use the Unity Editor to import assets and build levels
- How to create script files and write some basic code in C#
- How to use fundamental programming concepts like variables, functions, loops, and conditional statements
- How to debug games using the Unity debugging tools

However, this book may not be for you if you're completely new to game development, or if this is your first time using Unity, or if you're completely new to programming specifically. In any of these cases, I strongly recommend your picking up an introductory title before continuing with this book, to ensure you get the most from it.

How Should This Book Be Read?

This book has been written to be a complete C# scripting course. For this reason, you'll probably get the most from it by reading it from start to end, chapter by chapter, consulting the source code and project files along the way. Further, it'd be really great if you could read this book while seated at the computer with Unity in front of you, along with the book files, to make comparisons, testing, and checking easier. You can read it on a train or plane or elsewhere and still benefit; but the greatest benefit will come if you can readily switch between the book and your computer, following the steps and instructions, and completing the exercises. There's a lot to do in this book; it's not intended to simply be read. It expects you to follow along and join in.

What Are the Companion Files?

As mentioned earlier, this book has a practical focus. That means it encourages you not just to read, but to do things. In each chapter, we'll be working in software, using the features of Unity and MonoDevelop, and other software, to create a working first-person shooter game. This book has been designed and configured for you to follow along with me, repeating the steps I take, while understanding them too, to build a first-person shooter in parallel. However, the book companion files feature all the assets I've used and the projects I've made for you to use should you wish to start at specific chapter or start from exactly the same place as me.

Each and every chapter features its own folder in the companion files, and features a start and end project. The chapter begins with the *start* project and move toward the *end* project. Each chapter features notes and comments directing you to the relevant companion files when appropriate; so please be on the lookout for those as we progress. The Apress companion files for this book can be found at www.apress.com/9781430267461.

Designing and Preparing

Welcome to Chapter 1, the beginning of a comprehensive and "professional" C# programming course for the Unity engine. The core objective of this book is to thoroughly explore the development of a first-person shooter (FPS) game from start to finish. Further, it aims to do so in a way that'll have strong practical relevance for you and your own projects. This book is intended to be read as a complete course; meaning you should read it on a chapter-by-chapter basis, in sequence from beginning to end, thinking of each chapter as an independent class or lesson. If you follow this book carefully in order, sitting at the computer and working along with me in Unity, then by the end, you should have completed a playable FPS game that runs on desktop platforms and has mobile potential. But much more than this: you'll have seen and explored many C# coding techniques that have wider relevance and importance than only to the specific game created here. As we progress, considering techniques and ideas, it's important to see them in their broader context, as tools you can use in your own ways and for your own games. Don't just think of them as ideas limited to *this* book and *this* project— because they're not.

A further and final quality of this book, which makes it unique among the tutorial literature available today, is its strong "professional" focus. The book title is *Pro Unity Game Development with C#,* and the word *Pro* has an important meaning worth clarifying before getting started with development. Pro (short for *professional*) and is especially vague in the games industry. This is because it means different things to different people, and there's little or no consensus about which definition is correct, if any. To some, being a professional simply means your main income stems from making video games. To others, you can also be a professional by making games part-time, or even as a hobby, so long as you sell them for money. For others, being a professional is about having a recognized degree or qualification from an established authority, like a university. And to others, professionalism has nothing to do with money or education, and is about making games of a specific quality and polish.

Now, it's not my intention to promote any of these definitions as correct exclusively. I want to capture at least something of them all in this book when I use the term *professional*. By "professional," *I mean* this book has a strong practical flavor and value, as opposed to a theoretical or academic flavor. Its aim is *not* to *introduce* you to Unity or C# development as though you were a complete newcomer, or to debate about the nuances or specifics of more advanced features. Rather, it assumes you're already familiar with the basics, and aims to show how you could *use* Unity and C# in a *practical context, making real-world games*—the kind you could seriously think about selling if you wanted. Consequently, reading this book should feel much like putting on a pair of magical glasses that allow you to see new possibilities in familiar surroundings. Its main benefit should be in allowing you to see new and creative ways to use the tools you already know.

> **Note**   It's important to be flexible and open-minded about solutions and approaches in game development. Just because the word *professional* is used in this book, don't think the techniques and methods I'll show you here will *always* be the best or optimal methods for your own projects in every case. Games are *highly* context sensitive. For any game there'll likely be many roads to the same destination, and choosing the right road often takes careful consideration. So be open to exploring and avoid rigidity. This book offers plenty of food and ideas to help you formulate alternative plans and to see things from new perspectives.

Designing

This is Chapter 1, so we'll be thinking here about how to get started making a C# Unity game. When most people begin making a game, there's typically a strong temptation, born from excitement and enthusiasm perhaps, to immediately fire up Unity and MonoDevelop, and to "jump in" and get started in a free-form style. The desire for instant, tangible results like this can be strong indeed. But resist it. Jumping into coding without any prior planning is almost always a recipe for disaster and drift; not to mention wasted time! If you want professional quality results, then invest time ahead simply to think, consider, and plan, and also to *write down* the results of your thinking, whether that's in words, pictures, or diagram form—whatever best helps you remember your own thoughts.

Maybe you think you know your own thoughts well and don't need to write them down. But resist this way of thinking, too. Get into the *habit* of making written plans. Over time, we typically forget, and our thoughts and ideas get fuzzy. But solid and dependable coding critically requires clarity of mind, and that's true no matter which programming language we use. Half the solution comes from understanding the problem. The famous philosopher John Searle echoed this when he said, "If you can't say it clearly, you don't understand it yourself." So make written plans and work on the basis of those. With that said, we'll begin by writing a summary and overview of the game we'll be making in this book.

Game Overview

The FPS game we'll make in this book will be titled *Crazy Mad Office Dude* (hereafter referred to as *CMOD*), as shown in Figure 1-1. You can also visit my YouTube Channel at www.youtube.com/user/alanthorngames to see the game in action. CMOD is an action-shooter in a deliberately comic and cartoon style, played in first-person perspective (from the eyes of the game character).

Figure 1-1. The game to be created—Crazy Mad Office Dude

In this game, the *Player* must struggle against its tyrannical employer (the *Corporation*), which, being incredibly evil, is holding back on paying the Player his due salary—many months' worth of money. So the Player, understandably enraged, must explore the Corporation's office environment (the *Level*), collecting *Cash Power-Ups*, which are scattered around. The aim is to reclaim the Player's salary in full, and maybe a bit more besides. The game is won and completed when the *Player* successfully collects all Cash Power-Ups in the level. To prevent the Player from achieving his goal, the Corporation has (of course!) dispatched evil minions (the *Enemies*) to attack and eliminate the Player once and for all.

Successful attacks on the Player reduce the Player's *Health*, and the Player is destroyed when his Health is reduced below 0. The Player may deal with these slippery enemies using two main strategies: he may cowardly avoid the Enemies altogether, hoping to evade all or most of their attacks. Or, he may resort to *Carpe Diem*, foolhardily attacking them in combat using up to two different weapons: fists or a pistol. Just as enemy attacks on the Player reduces the Player's health, Player attacks on the Enemy will reduce the Enemy's health—meaning that the Player and Enemies may attack and destroy each other. Of course, it goes without saying, the Enemies are quite smart. They don't just stand around doing nothing all day, twiddling their thumbs and waiting for the Player to appear. They patrol around the environment, intelligently hunting for the Player—making them appear and behave just like rational and sentient beings.

Note   The game developed here will feature only one level. Yes, creating the mechanics of just one level will fill the whole of this book! However, the game and concept could easily be expanded to include many more levels, as we'll see.

Game in Depth

We've now established a general overview of the game to be made, CMOD as whole. In writing and thinking about that, we have, however, relied on a range of smaller and dependent concepts. These are constituent ingredients of the game. These concepts include the Player, Enemies, Power-Ups, Weapons, Health, the Level, and more. In this section, we'll itemize and catalog these, offering an informative description of each. As we progress through the book, each concept will require its own specific implementation in C# and Unity.

- **The Player.** The Player in a first-person shooter usually has no substantial graphical representation in the game world, except for his or her hand holding a weapon at the bottom center of the screen. The Player is the character the gamer controls and moves around during gameplay. It's how the gamer interacts with the world: such as destroying enemies, opening doors, pressing buttons, and collecting power-ups. In addition, the Player also has a finite amount of *Health*, a numerical property measuring his well-being. The higher this value, the *better for the Player*. This value is reduced when Enemies successfully attack the Player. When this value is 0 or below, the Player dies and is removed from the game. Since CMOD will be a single-player game, as opposed to multiplayer, the removal of the Player from the game constitutes *Game Over* (the end of play).

- **The Enemies.** CMOD features three main Enemy types or species, whose shared aim is to kill the Player through attacks. These Enemies are as follows:

  - The *Drone* (see Figure 1-2), a genetically engineered bureaucrat with a penchant for long questionnaires and customer surveys. This Enemy is the weakest of the three. He attacks at close range using his bare fists.

Figure 1-2. Enemy Type 1: Drone. Contains three main frame-sets of animation: Standing Still (Neutral), Running, and Attacking

  - Next is the *Tough Guy* (see Figure 1-3), a professional hit man employed by the Corporation to eliminate those troublesome types who expect payment for their work, including the Player! A Tough Guy is the only Enemy to have a range attack: he'll fire a pistol whenever the player enters his line of sight.

Figure 1-3. *Enemy Type 2: Tough Guy. Contains three main frame-sets of animation: Standing Still (Neutral), Running, and Attacking...*

■ The final Enemy is *Mr. Big Cheese* (see Figure 1-4), the boss of the Corporation. Because he relies on protection from his Tough Guys, he doesn't have a range attack; but he's no lightweight either. When he strikes with his fists, the Player will suffer severe damage.

Figure 1-4. *Enemy Type 3: Mr. Big Cheese Contains three main frame-sets of animation: Standing Still (Neutral), Running, and Attacking...*

■ All three enemies also have a Health property, which can be reduced when the Player attacks them with a weapon. If an Enemy's health is reduced to 0 or below, it is destroyed and permanently removed from the game. In addition to health, all three enemies exhibit intelligence. Having been alerted to the Player's intrusion into their Corporation headquarters, they'll all be on patrol, searching for him or her. If they find the Player, they'll give chase until they enter attacking distance. When they do, they'll attack with all their mightiness.

■ **Power-Ups.** Scattered liberally around the Level are special collectible objects, called Power-Ups. These may be collected *only* by the Player (not by Enemies) and they're collected whenever the Player collides (or walks into them). Each and every Power-Up instance may be collected once only (it's destroyed on collection), and it'll have some immediate effect on the Player, depending on the Power-Up type. CMOD will feature four Power-Up types:

■ A *Cash Power-Up* (see Figure 1-5), which gives a specified amount of money to the Player.

Figure 1-5. *Power-Up 1: Cash*

- A *Weapon Power-Up* (see Figure 1-6), which upgrades the Player's default weapon (Fists) to a range attack (Pistol).

Figure 1-6. *Power-Up 2: Weapon Upgrade*

- An *Ammo Power-Up* (see Figure 1-7), which restores the ammo for the pistol weapon, if collected.

Figure 1-7. *Power-Up 3: Ammo Restore*

- A *Health Power-Up* (see Figure 1-8), which restores the Player's health to full.

Figure 1-8. *Power-Up 4: Health Restore*

■ **Weapons.** If the Player chooses to attack an Enemy, it must be done so with a Weapon. The Player can equip only one weapon at any one time, and there are a total of two weapons in the game, each behaving slightly differently and each dealing different amounts of *Damage*. At game-start, the Player begins equipped with the default weapon of Fists (see Figure 1-9). This weapon is permanently accessible and never runs out of ammunition because it's not the kind of weapon to require ammunition. This weapon, however, has the shortest attack range and deals the least damage to Enemies. There is also the Pistol weapon (see Figure 1-10), which offers ranged attack and deals more damage, but must be collected in the Level through a Power-Up. This weapon has limited ammo, which reduces each time the weapon is fired. The ammo can be restored by collecting an *Ammo Restore Power-Up*. When the ammo expires, the weapon becomes unusable. During game play, the Player will be able to cycle through all collected weapons, choosing which one to use.

Figure 1-9. *Weapon 1: Fists*

Figure 1-10. *Weapon 2: Pistol*

■   **Level.** The Level represents the complete game environment, plus everything else inside it. The level architecture, such as the walls and floors, will be composed into integrated wholes from separate and modular mesh pieces, which I've modeled beforehand using the free 3D software Blender. *Modular* means the environment was created in blocks, or modules, which match at the seams. So each module fits together with others and may be recombined, like Lego bricks, to form larger and more complete environments inside the Unity Editor. More on this later. See Figure 1-11 for the game environment, as seen inside the Unity Editor.

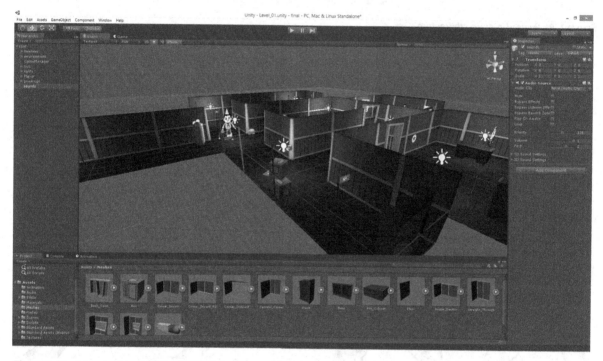

Figure 1-11.   Game environment for CMOD. Notice the modular mesh pieces inside the meshes folder of the Project panel. These are included in the associated project files (FBX Format), inside the AssetsToImport/Meshes folder

Note   Level design and modular techniques are considered briefly in the next chapter for the sake of completeness. However, the primary focus of this book is on using C# in Unity to code and customize game behavior specifically. Consequently, modular design and level building will not receive extensive coverage. But don't worry: this book provides a Unity project, already configured with a level assembled from meshes, from which we'll begin work together by adding C# code.

- **GUI.** In addition to all the core or game-critical objects discussed already, such as the Player and Enemies, CMOD will also feature a GUI (*graphical user interface*). This refers to all the 2D graphics or widgets overlaid on the screen to provide the user with access to game options or information. These elements are divided over two main parts or areas: the HUD (*Heads-Up Display*) and the main menu. The HUD (as shown in Figure 1-1) refers to all the small displays overlaid onto the screen while the game is being played (such as a cash counter and health information), to keep the player updated in real time on vital game statistics. In contrast, the main menu (as shown in Figure 1-12) is a separate screen or window that is shown to allow the Player access to game-wide features, such as restarting the game, exiting the game, and also loading and saving the game. While the main menu is visible onscreen, all other game events, such as the movement of Enemies and the actions of the Player, should be paused and frozen.

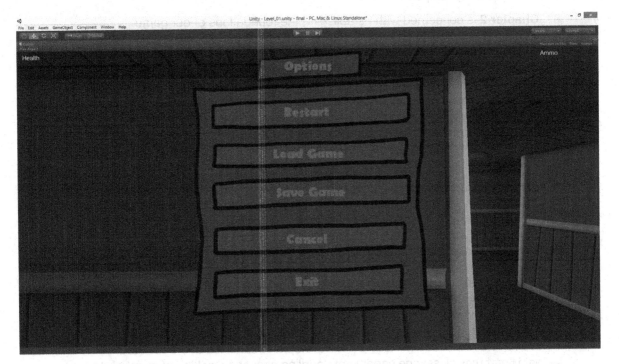

Figure 1-12. The Game menu allows access to game-wide features, such as Restart Game, Exit Game, Load Game, and Save Game. Later chapters in this book will implement all these features

Developing the Design: Looking Ahead

The previous sections, taken together in combination with the YouTube gameplay video (URL provided earlier), should offer a strong enough and clear enough vision of CMOD. These resources will constitute our game design document (GDD), a document clearly articulating the vision of the game to make. For most games, the GDD will typically be longer and more comprehensive than ours, but our GDD is sufficient and fit for purpose *in our case*. The design may initially seem "simple" (or maybe not!), but if it seems so to you, it's important not to confuse simple with simplicity. The game we've planned actually involves a lot of work, especially C# coding work. Each subsequent chapter is dedicated to a specific aspect or subset of development. In this section, we'll take a sneak glimpse of that future work: a general guided tour through some of the main issues and subjects we'll visit throughout this book. This work ranges from using the Unity Editor and tools, sometimes in new and creative ways, to heavy coding sessions in C# to create artificial intelligence and pathfinding. Let's see how these subjects, and our workload in general, are distributed across the book on a chapter-by-chapter roadmap.

- **Chapter 2** is concerned with establishing the foundations of our game. Game development is a specialization of software engineering, and like most engineering projects, it must begin by laying foundations. This involves lots of work in the Unity Editor—especially level design work—using both the scene and game views for assembling and building a level with modular environment pieces. It'll also involve lighting and lightmapping with the Beast lightmapper to get an appropriate mood and look for our environment. In addition, we'll also look at processes for automating asset importing to fix some mesh import issues we'll encounter. By the end of Chapter 2, we'll end up with a project that's ready to start customizing and defining through C# scripting.

- **Chapter 3** starts our coding adventure! It's where we *add* code to our project. It'll explore *event-driven programming* in depth, looking at what it is, how it works, and how to integrate it into our project to get efficient results. It'll also explore why we should start implementing this kind of system before anything else. Practically, every game needs to detect when things happen, such as when the Player dies or collects a power-up, among others (these will all be important events for us). In addition, other objects in the game need to know when those events occur, so they can respond in specific ways. The Enemies, for example, need to know when they're close enough to the player to launch an attack; otherwise, they'll never know when to *start* attacking. These issues concerning *events* and *responses* will lead us to develop a streamlined and dedicated Notifications class; one capable of handling almost every kind of event and response we could ever want in a game.

- **Chapter 4** will see us using concepts such as class *inheritance*, *Singletons*, and *vector arithmetic* for creating our four workable power-ups for the game: the Cash Power-Up, the Upgrade Weapon Power-Up, the Ammo Power-Up and the Health Restore Power-Up. Achieving this requires us to consider a range of ideas. We'll use the *Unity API* to work with *Physics Colliders*, *components*, and *2D sprites* (part of the 2D functionality added in Unity 4.3). We'll also develop a range of different and interacting classes, and build our own *Billboard* functionality to ensure sprites are always camera aligned. By the end of this chapter we'll have a clean, empty environment filled with solid and working power-ups we can collect.

- **Chapter 5** is about refining the Player character and the Player input to work consistently across multiple platforms, from desktop systems to mobile devices. Here we'll develop a customized First Person Controller based on the default Unity Controller, which works on Windows, Mac, Linux, Android, iOS, and Windows Phone. We'll also examine mathematical ideas, such as *sine waves* and *curves* to program a customizable *head-bob effect* to the first-person camera. That is, to simulate the natural effect of head movement, we'll make the camera bob up and down seamlessly as the Player moves around in the world. And we'll also work with Mecanim to create a death animation in which the camera falls to the ground.

- **Chapter 6** is where we give the player some fire power. Specifically, we'll code the ability to attack and inflict damage with Weapons, both the fists and pistol weapons. In this chapter, we'll look deeper at class inheritance and at concepts like *virtual functions* and *polymorphism*. In addition, we'll also see how to create animated sprites for creating weapon animations (such as gun fire) using *timing* functions and *coroutines*.

- **Chapter 7** throws our three evil enemies into the mix—namely Drones, Tough Guys, and Mr. Big Cheese. Building these guys will lead us into a veritable coding extravaganza. With these, we'll code enemies that can take and inflict damage, and behave with artificial intelligence that integrates well with the Unity Pathfinding and Navigation system. Here, we'll explore concepts such as *Finite State Machines* (FSMs), so enemies can make informed decisions and change their behavior, as well as how to program with *NavMeshes* and *NavMesh Agents*, allowing enemies to find their way intelligently about the level, while avoiding physical obstacles along the way.

- **Chapter 8** delivers us into the troublesome world of GUIs (graphical user interfaces), where we'll see the limitations of the Unity GUI system and the benefits of coding our own. Further, we'll consider concepts such as *resolution* and *aspect ratio*, as well as *anchoring* and *hierarchies*, to code fixed-sized interfaces that look good and act predictably at various screen sizes.

- **Chapter 9** explains how to code a load-and-save game system, allowing the user to save his or her gaming session to persistent storage, from where it can be restored without data loss at any later time. This chapter will explore XML files, the .NET Framework classes, and data serialization.

- **Chapter 10** completes our work, leaving us with a 100%-working FPS game. There will no doubt be room for improvement, of course. But in this chapter, we'll recap over all the concepts we've seen throughout the book, thinking about how we might apply them in other contexts and to other projects. In addition, this chapter will crystalize or condense many of those concepts into bite-size and easy-to-remember chunks, which will make the chapter especially useful as both a pseudo-appendix for this book, as well as a more general coding reference.

Game Development Workflows

Before jumping in and getting started with CMOD (reserved for the next chapter), I want to spend the rest of this chapter sharing with you some Unity tips, tricks, and techniques that I frequently find helpful when developing my own games. Making a game can be an intensive and heavy process, so it's important to develop a general workflow that you feel comfortable following. The advice presented here is not essential in the sense that you *need* to follow it to work along with this book. But rather, it's presented as a set of recommendations and suggestions that you may like to integrate into your own workflow, wherever you think it can be improved. Feel free to use it or ignore it until you find a workflow you like.

Tip #1: Interface Layout

The layout and arrangement of the Unity interface is *critically* important to the smoothness and speed of your working. So much so that even the slightest interface change, perhaps in the alignment of a panel or a dockable window, can have dramatic repercussions for your efficiency and speed in the long term. Consequently, when working in Unity, it's important to find a layout that supports your workflow and needs from the very beginning to avoid unnecessary setbacks and frustration. Typically, the "ideal" interface layout *for you* will not be general but will vary depending on the project you're developing. For games using little or no animation, it's likely you'll never need the animation editor or the Mecanim tools—and so you can hide those windows. Similarly, for games that never use Pathfinding or Navigation, you'll never need to see the NavMesh tools. For CMOD, however, we'll need all those things and more—but not necessarily throughout the whole of development. Figure 1-13 shows the layout I'm using for this project, which is based on the Default layout.

Figure 1-13. Unity interface layout configured for developing CMOD

Note   To create the CMOD interface layout, I began by selecting the Default layout to restore the UI defaults. To do that, select **Layout ➤ Default** from the top-right menu in the Unity Editor. Afterward, additional windows can be opened and docked into the interface as required, using the Window menu. For the CMOD layout specifically, open the following windows: **Window ➤ Animation**, **Window ➤ Animator**, **Window ➤ Sprite Editor**, **Window ➤ Lightmapping**, and **Window ➤ Navigation**. To save the completed layout for easy reference, select **Layout ➤ Save Layout…** from the Layout drop-down (see Figure 1-14).

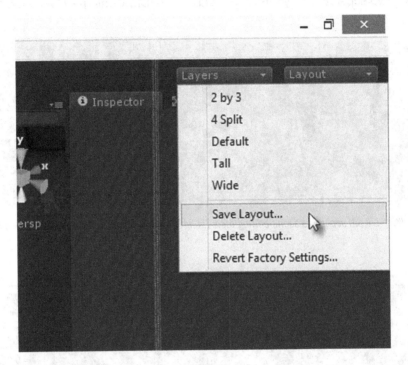

Figure 1-14. Saving a custom interface layout

The CMOD interface layout in Figure 1-13 consists of three notable panels or tabbed areas marked by the letters A, B, and C, with the exception of the left-aligned Hierarchy panel. The arrangement of these three areas is based on the principle of view-exclusivity. That is, the panels in A, B and C have been divided this way because of how we view and work with them. Area A features larger editors, such as the *Scene, Game, Animator (Mecanim),* and *Sprite Editor* windows. The reason for their tabular arrangement here is largely because these editors work *in combination* with the Object Inspector, as well as the Project panel and Hierarchy panels—and other editors in Groups B and C. We'll often want to open Group A editors *side by side* with the Object Inspector. So we don't want them tabbed with it. The same rationale applies to other editors in group B too. We'll often view these in combination with editors in Group A and C, but hardly ever with others in group B. Then finally there's Group C. These editors work much like those in B, because we'll often view them in combination with Group A. But unlike Group B editors, they are read and understood more intuitively when read horizontally (left-and-right) as opposed to vertically (up-and-down), such as the animation timeline window, or the Project panel.

Tip #2: Dual-Monitors

A Dual-Monitor (or Multi-Monitor) configuration is one where two or more displays are connected to the same PC or Mac, and together they show a wider desktop, which reaches across all monitors. This means you get to arrange your windows and panels conveniently over an even wider screen area than usual. If you're fortunate enough to be using such a setup already, then you can make especially good use of it in Unity. And if you don't have this setup but your budget allows it, I highly recommend investing in it. In Unity, Dual-Monitors are particularly useful in two contexts: scene editing (as shown in Figure 1-15) and scripting (as shown in Figure 1-16). To jump between these two configurations, it's sensible to create two separate UI layouts: (DM-Editing) and (DM-Coding) – *DM = Dual Monitor*.

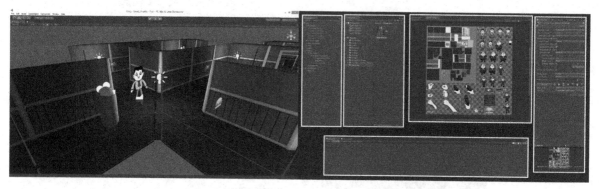

Figure 1-15. DM-Editing Layout separates scene editing tools (in left monitor) and property inspection tools and editors (in right monitor)

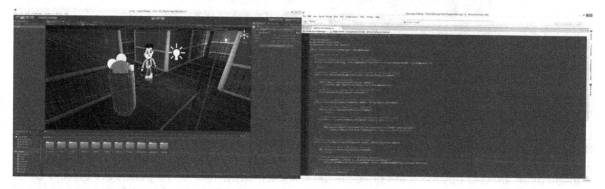

Figure 1-16. DM-Coding layout keeps a single monitor layout (in left monitor) for scene editing and inspector tools, and MonoDevelop for coding (in right monitor)

■ **DM-Editing.** This mode is tailored to scene building, property tweaking, and all other editor functionality that doesn't involve heavy coding. The greatest benefit of this layout is the large screen space dedicated to the Scene and Game viewports in the left monitor, giving us an unencumbered and easy view of our scene for level designing, testing, and debugging. By separating the scene and game views in the left monitor from the editors in the right, we achieve a useful kind of "decluttering" and spatial organization. This kind of functional separation between panels can be conducive to heightened focus and concentration, and its ability to enhance our workflow shouldn't be underestimated.

■ **DM-Coding.** This layout again achieves a functional separation between UI panels, as with the DM-Editing layout. But this time, the separation is between the Unity Editor Interface proper (in the left monitor) and the MonoDevelop IDE (in the right monitor)—or vice versa depending on your preference. With this layout, the left monitor is identical to the single-monitor layout for the Unity Editor (as shown in Figure 1-14), but here we also get separate and full-screen access to a coding window in the right-hand monitor. This makes debugging, visualization, and code reading somewhat easier because we get to read our code alongside Unity, especially when our game is running in Play mode.

Tip #3: Be Organized

Game development in Unity (and more widely) involves working with lots of related resources, including assets (such as meshes and textures) and code (such as C# source files). By "lots" of resources, I mean hundreds and thousands, and sometimes even more! For the sake of simplicity and sanity, therefore, it's important to be organized from the outset and *to remain* so throughout development. It's important to make organization a habit. However, saying that is one thing and achieving it is another. So to stay organized while project managing and coding, keep the following principles in mind:

■ **Name and group assets.** Every Unity project relies on assets. These include meshes, textures, audio files, animations, materials, scripts, scenes, and more. From the very beginning of your project, think seriously about how you'll organize and arrange these assets in terms of file names and the folders in which you'll put them. Don't just import assets of every kind into your project and then just leave them sitting together in the same folder. Doing that will lead to confusion in the long term. You'll grow weary of even looking at the Project panel. Instead, you'll need to group like items together, such as meshes inside a *Meshes* folder, and textures inside a *Textures* folder (see the Project panel in Figure 1-17 for asset organization in CMOD). For larger projects, you may even need to take organization further by creating *nested* folders (folders within folders), such as *Meshes/Enemies* and *Meshes/Props*. In addition, keep a constant watch on your assets over your project's lifetime to protect against "stragglers." Namely, assets that somehow wind up in the wrong folders, either by accident or because you put them somewhere temporarily and then forgot to put them back where they should be (it can easily happen!).

Figure 1-17. Asset organization in the Project panel for the CMOD project. Make asset organization a habit and development will become a lot simpler

- **Use meaningful object names.** Organization applies not just to assets in the Project panel, but to GameObjects in the scene, too. When building scenes with lots of objects, take a quick pause and scan through the Hierarchy panel and look at the names of your objects. Ask yourself: Are these names meaningful? One way to reach practical judgments about this is to see if you can guess what the object is, what it does, and where it is in the scene, purely from the object name alone, without looking in the Scene tab or Game tab at all. If you encounter names, such as *Cube01* or *Obj1*, and cannot reasonably determine what the objects do, then consider renaming your objects. If a cube mesh is supposed to be an ammo crate, for example, then think about changing its name from *Cube01* to *meshAmmoCrate_01*. Now, applying this kind of organization rigorously across your objects probably doesn't sound like much fun, especially if your scene has many objects. But it can ultimately save you hours of time when selecting objects.

> **Note**   Remember that *assets* are data files and resources used in a project, such as meshes and textures and audio files. *GameObjects* are specific instances of things, or entities, inside a scene—such as enemies, characters, weapons, and vehicles. GameObjects live in the game world. *Prefabs* are collections of game objects configured together into a standalone template, which is reusable as though they were one complete entity.

- **Use asset tags, object tags, and layers.** Don't think organization should stop at asset file names or folders, or GameObject names. Take it a step further and use *asset labeling*, *object tags*, and *layers*.

- **Asset labeling** lets you index assets in the Project panel by associating meaningful labels or "tags" with them, making it easier to search and find the assets you need according to their type and relevance for your project. For example, consider labeling environment meshes under *Architecture*, and character meshes under *Character*, and so on. Labeling an asset (or more than one) is simple. Select all assets to label in the Project panel, and from the preview pane (in the Object Inspector) click the blue Label button in the bottom-right corner (see Figure 1-18). Click a tag from the menu to apply an existing one, or else use the Edit Box to type in a completely new tag for the selected assets. Once labeled, your assets are then completely searchable from the Project panel, using the Search field (as shown in Figure 1-19). To search by Label, click the Label toolbar button and select the Labels to Search For. On selection, the Project panel is immediately filtered to show only matching results.

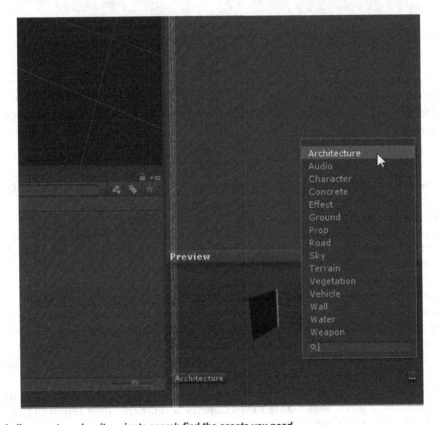

Figure 1-18. Labeling assets makes it easier to search find the assets you need

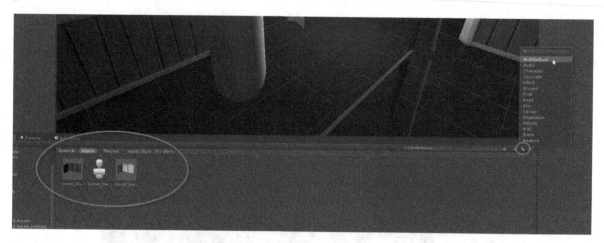

Figure 1-19. Searching for Assets by Label using the Project panel Search field

> **Note**   Labeling an asset *does not* affect its file name or the physical folder inside which it's stored in the Project. These remain unchanged regardless of labeling. Labels are Unity-specific metadata attached to the file for your convenience when searching through assets.

- **GameObject tagging.** In many respects, Tags are to GameObjects what Labels are to Assets. Tags are special identifiers that you may attach to objects in your scenes, to group them and search them, and to perform other kinds of operations to them directly in code. Unlike Labels however, *only one* tag may be assigned to an object—that is, an object can't have more than one tag assigned, although many objects can share the same tag. Tags will be used extensively in this book—and we'll see them at work in some form in almost every subsequent chapter. To create a new tag and assign it to an object, select any object in the scene and click the Tag drop-down list at the top-left corner of the Object Inspector. From the menu that appears, select **Add Tag** (see Figure 1-20). Doing this displays the Tag Editor, where you can create new and custom tags—as many as you need. Use the Size field to enter the number of tags to create, and then name each tag using the Element fields below (see Figure 1-21). Once created, the tags are added to the Tag list (see Figure 1-20). To assign a tag to one or more objects, select all relevant objects and choose their tag from the Tag list in the Object Inspector.

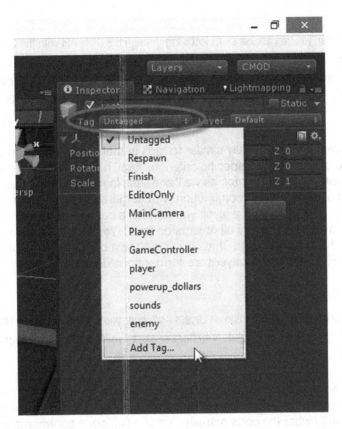

Figure 1-20. Adding new tags from the Tag menu

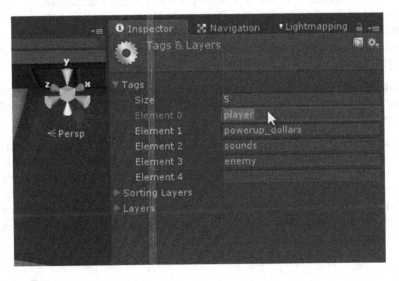

Figure 1-21. Naming new Tags

> **Note**   As we'll see later, you can access an Object's tag through the Unity API with the `GameObject.tag` property. You can also compare a tag with a String value using the `GameObject.CompareTag` function. See `http://docs.unity3d.com/Documentation/ScriptReference/GameObject-tag.html` and `http://docs.unity3d.com/Documentation/ScriptReference/GameObject.CompareTag.html`.

- **Layers.** Layers are functionally similar to tags in that they mark or group GameObjects together by a specific criterion. Tags, however, are typically used to select or identify objects *in script*, as we'll see later. In contrast, layers are typically (though not always) used in conjunction with cameras. By assigning a group of GameObjects onto a layer, you can tell a camera to selectively render or ignore a layer, and thereby all objects on that layer; so layers are especially convenient if you have objects that must be shown or hidden together—like GUI menus and HUD elements. Layers are further considered in Chapter 8.

> **Note**   If you're hungry for more information on Layers *right now*, you can check out the Unity Layer documentation at `http://docs.unity3d.com/Documentation/Components/Layers.html`.

- **Use concise code comments.** The final organization tip to mention concerns code comments: that is, human readable statements that accompany source code and clarify what the code actually does. In C#, code comments are written with the // or /* */ syntax. You can also use a XML commenting style with MonoDevelop (more information is at `http://unitypatterns.com/xml-comments/`). My advice is: use code comments. They make life much easier—when written concisely! It's common to hear criticism of code commenting, for various reasons. The following lists two of them, and I provide a reasoned response to illustrate the importance of commenting.

  - **Criticism 1:** I don't need to write code comments because *I know what I'm doing*. I know what this code does. And besides, nobody else is probably ever going to read my code anyway.

  - **Response:** The core assumption here is that code comments are exclusively for the benefit of *other* people. But this is not true. Code comments can help you write down and clarify your own ideas. They can help you remember what your own code is doing when you return to it weeks or months later. You may know what your own code is doing *right now*, but it'll not be so fresh in your mind after weeks and months pass without having seen it. So use code comments as an aid to memory.

■ **Criticism 2:** Code comments are pointless. I don't want to read a novel. They just get in the way and make things even more confusing. Far from being helpful, they can steer us in the wrong direction. Good code speaks for itself and doesn't need commenting!

■ **Response:** There's something true in this: code comments *should* be helpful. But, if they're poorly written and needlessly lengthy, they do stand to be more of an obstacle than a help. However, this danger needn't prevent us from using code comments altogether. It just reminds us to be careful and concise in our commenting, keeping them relevant and informative. So keep comments as short as possible and stick to the point.

Note   Code commenting need not be restricted to just standard, official comments. Commenting can be extended into your very coding style. By using meaningful function, variable, and class names, you can make your code a lot clearer and easier to work with.

Tip #4: Show Project Wizard on Start-up

At start-up, Unity will, by default, always open the most recently used project if there's one to open; otherwise, it'll display the Project Wizard to create a new project. Its decision to open the most recent project first is usually a convenient feature that you'll leave unchanged. But there are times when this behavior can be problematic. If you're working in a team and are using Unity in a networked environment, it's likely you've opened a project from a shared network drive. In itself, doing that will not generally cause any major issues. However, Unity expects to open projects on an exclusive basis—meaning that only one instance of the project may be open at a time. Consequently, if you restart Unity and it seeks to reopen the shared project but finds it's already open by another user on the network, it'll cancel the open operation altogether and will exit instead of showing the Project Wizard. The result is that you'll be permanently locked out of Unity until the other user on the network finally decides to close the project, allowing you exclusive access again.

Now, typically opening projects over networked drives is not something I'd recommend doing if it can be easily avoided. But even so, there's a way around this specific problem: specifically, by forcing Unity to always show the Project Wizard on start-up, as opposed to opening the most recent project. To achieve this, simply choose **Edit ➤ Preferences** from the Editor main menu. Then from the General tab, enable the feature Always Show Project Wizard (see Figure 1-22).

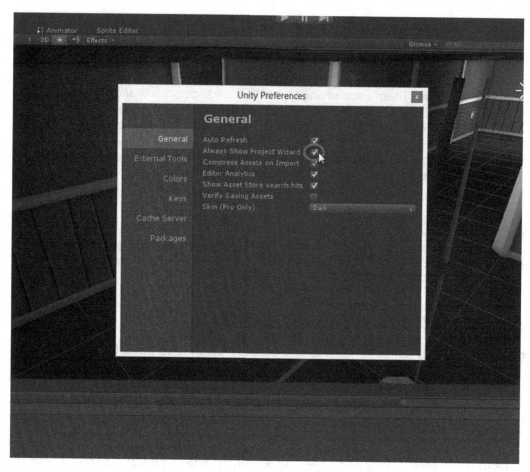

Figure 1-22. Force Unity to display the Project Wizard on start-up

> **Note**   Using Unity to access projects and assets across networked drives is not recommended. Many developers have experienced slow-downs and crashes in such circumstances.

Tip #5: Use FBX Meshes

Unity officially accepts meshes in an extensive variety of file formats, including *Blend*, *MA*, *MB*, *MAX*, *OBJ* and *FBX*, and others. These formats can be produced by a range of 3D applications, such as Maya, 3DS Max, Lightwave, Blender, Strata, Cinema4D, and more. Among all these file formats, however, two main types may be identified: *Proprietary* and *Exported*. Proprietary files are those saved directly from 3D modeling software, using the common **File ➤ Save** command. Exported formats are those saved using commands such as **File ➤ Export**. The ultimate purpose of both methods is to serialize or output meshes to a persistent file, which can be opened and read by many applications. However, despite the common aim, there are significant differences between the Proprietary and Exported files, which have implications when working with Unity. The upshot is generally this: *Always use meshes from exported formats—specifically FBX* (see Figure 1-23). Why should this advice be followed?

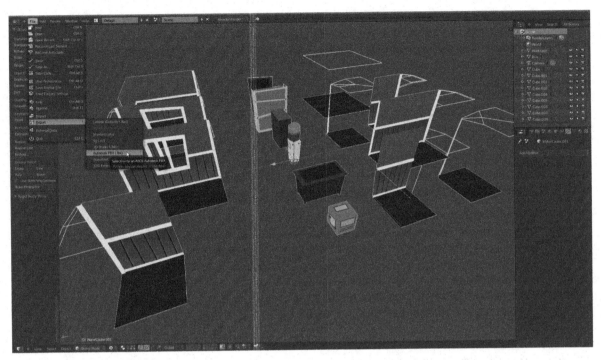

Figure 1-23. Manually exporting an FBX file from 3D modeling software (Blender). Blender is a free 3D modeling application that can be downloaded from www.blender.org/

■ **Proprietary meshes produce dependencies.** To import a Proprietary mesh into Unity (such as MA, MB, MAX, or Blend), you'll need to have the appropriate 3D software installed on your computer at the time of import. For MA and MB files, you'll need Maya installed; for MAX files, you'll need 3DS Max; and for Blend, you'll need Blender—and so on for other proprietary files. This is because the Unity Mesh Importer exports the Proprietary file to an FBX file behind the scenes. That is, during import, it loads the associated 3D modeling software, uses its internal FBX Exporter, and then accepts the outputted FBX version. Thus for Unity, Proprietary meshes create a dependency on their modeling software; Unity needs that software to import the mesh successfully. If the software isn't present during import, then the import will necessarily fail—although once imported, the software is not required (unless you need to import again!). Of course, this might not be a problem for you at all if you're sure that you'll be the only one using your meshes and you'll have access to your 3D software for as long as you need. But if you're sharing meshes between team members who may not have the same software, or if you're not sure you'll always be working at a computer with your modeling software installed, then proprietary formats will prove problematic.

- **Proprietary meshes create clutter.** As mentioned, when importing a Proprietary mesh, Unity calls upon the mesh's associated software and uses its FBX Exporter to create an exported version. In doing this, however, Unity asks you no questions and provides no options. It simply creates an FBX version with default settings applied. In contrast, if you export a mesh manually to FBX using the tools in your 3D software, then you'll get finer control and options over exactly how the FBX is exported and the kinds of meshes and objects in your scene that should be included in the file. The result is that manually exported FBX files are typically cleaner and more efficient, because they feature only the data you truly need. In contrast, the Unity-generated FBX files from proprietary files generally include plenty of data that you never wanted exported anyway, such as lights, dummy objects, meshes and faces you forgot to delete, and so on.

- **Proprietary meshes are unstable.** The term *unstable* is used here in a narrow but important sense. By "unstable" I mean that importing a proprietary file into Unity can lead to different results at different times, when different versions of the 3D modeling software are installed. This is due to possible changes or updates made to the FBX Exporter. In short, importing a Proprietary mesh with one version of the 3D software installed will not necessarily produce the same results when a *different* version is installed.

> **Note**   More information on Proprietary vs. Exported meshes for Unity can be found online at http://docs.unity3d.com/Documentation/Manual/3D-formats.html.

Tip #6: Disable Ambient Lighting

If you build a scene with some meshes but without any lighting, and then play-test it, you'll see that your scene doesn't appear completely black as you'd expect it to. In other words, your scene is not in total darkness—even though there are no lights! This base or default illumination is known as *Ambient Light*. It represents a non-shadow-casting light that is projected outward from the scene origin in all directions infinitely, and it affects every mesh surface with equal intensity. That is completely at odds with how "real world" lighting works, and so Ambient Light rarely produces believable results. But it's especially useful for lighting a scene during development and early play-testing. It lets you see "what's going on" before you've added any lights at all. But often (after creating your own lighting), you'll want to disable Ambient Light entirely.

To do disable Ambient Light, select **Edit ➤ Render Settings** from the Editor main menu to show the scene render settings in the Object Inspector. From the Inspector, use the Ambient Color swatch to specify Black RGB (0, 0, 0)—meaning *no intensity* (see Figure 1-24).

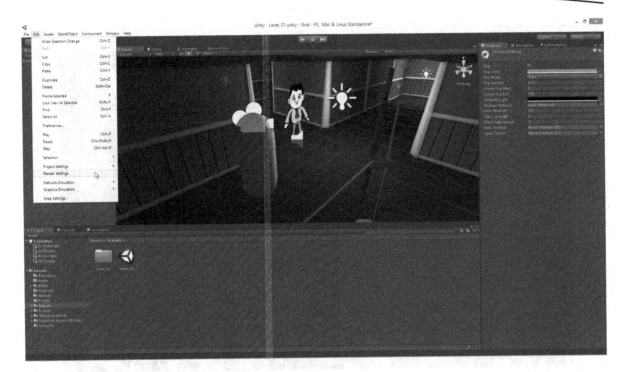

Figure 1-24. Disabling Ambient Light from the Render Settings menu

Tip #7: Use Root GameObjects

Every Unity scene is ultimately composed from a *hierarchy* of GameObjects. GameObjects exist within the scene in *relation* to each other, and this relationship (as defined by the hierarchy) is critically important to every object's transformation (*position*, *rotation* and *scale*). Specifically, child objects inherit the transformations of their parents. That is, the child adds its own transform to its parent's. This feature is useful for making objects move and interact together believably. This hierarchical relationship can be put to good use in many ways and not just at runtime; it can help at design time, too.

If you create an empty game object in your scene by choosing **GameObject ➤ Create Empty** from the Editor menu, and then make it the ultimate parent of all objects, you'll immediately have the ability to transform your entire scene, should you ever need to reposition everything in one step while building a level, or even at runtime (see Figure 1-25).

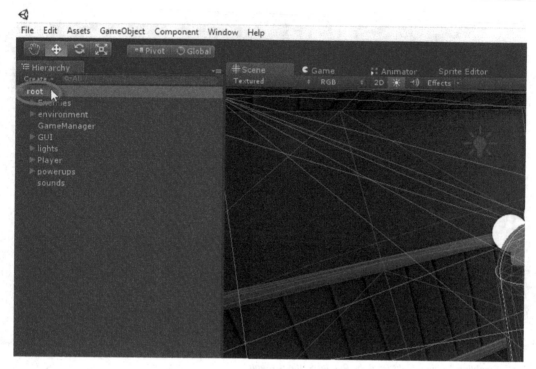

Figure 1-25. Creating Root GameObjects to control the scene hierarchy

In addition, as we'll see later, you can call GameObject.BroadcastMessage on the Root object to send an event or notification to every object in the scene, just by one line of code.

> **Note**   More information on BroadcastMessage can be found at the Unity documentation at
> http://docs.unity3d.com/Documentation/ScriptReference/Component.BroadcastMessage.html.

Tip #8: Incremental Backups

Making games takes time (sometimes a long time), and time is said to be a *wasting resource* because once it's spent and gone, there is no refund. You simply can't get back time that's passed. So put a value on your time, give it respect, and invest it wisely when developing. One way you respect your time and effort is by making *regular* backups of your data to prevent repeating work in the event of data loss. This is to protect you against unforeseen events, such as computer failures, data corruption, virus attacks, and other accidents. For Unity projects, making a backup is really as simple as making a copy of your project folder, and then archiving it onto a separate storage device, such as an external hard drive or cloud-based storage, or both. Don't make a backup on the same storage as the original, and keep the backup in a different physical location. For example, if the original files are at your office, then keep the backup at home. Be sure also to name your backups appropriately—use a numbering or date-based system—so that it's easy to quickly identify not just the latest backup, but also to understand the ordering of backups from the earliest to the latest.

> **Note**   One way to keep archives—and especially backups of source code—is to use version control systems. The Unity Team license includes a range of options, including Perforce, Plastic SCM, and the Asset Server. Other options include GIT, CVS, Mercurial, LibreSource, and others.

One question that commonly arises is "How often should I make backups?" The answer depends primarily on you and your circumstances. At the end of each work day or work session, ask yourself: "If I lost all my data now, and I had to resort to an earlier backup, how terrible and annoying would that be for me right now? How much work and time would I have to reinvest simply to catch up to where I was?" Think about these questions and be honest with yourself. If thinking about this makes you uncomfortable, and if the idea of losing your data is especially unpleasant, then it's time to make a backup.

> **Note**   The practice of making regular backups might seem to you so obviously important that it hardly requires mentioning at all. It surely goes without saying. If this is how you feel, then splendid! You don't need me to convince you to make backups. However, despite the lip service often given to the importance of backups, I often find people never making them and then later regretting that decision. So the importance of making regular backups cannot be overstated.

Tip #9: Batch Renaming

Sometimes you'll be working with lots of similar game objects in a Unity scene, such as a batch of enemies, or ammo crates, or power-ups, or trees, or rocks, and others. You'll typically want each object in the batch to have a similar but distinct name from all the others, such as *Tree_01*, and *Tree_02*, and *Tree_03*, and so forth. Now, it can tedious and time-consuming to name each of these objects individually. Unfortunately, Unity (at the time of writing) has no out-of-the-box functionality to automate this process. So often it's convenient to customize the Unity Editor and create our own Batch Renaming functionality. In this section, therefore, I want to introduce you to a custom-made Batch Rename tool, which is an editor extension that plugs into the Unity interface and offers simple renaming functionality for multiple objects. The source code for this tool is listed in Listing 1-1 for your viewing, and is also included in the Project Files (inside the Chapter01 folder).

Listing 1-1 BatchRename.cs

```
using UnityEngine;
using UnityEditor;
using System.Collections;

public class BatchRename : ScriptableWizard
{
        //Base name
        public string BaseName = "MyObject_";
```

```
        //Start Count
        public int StartNumber = 0;

        //Increment
        public int Increment = 1;

        [MenuItem("Edit/Batch Rename...")]
    static void CreateWizard()
    {
        ScriptableWizard.DisplayWizard("Batch Rename",typeof(BatchRename),"Rename");
    }

        //Called when the window first appears
        void OnEnable()
        {
            UpdateSelectionHelper();
        }

        //Function called when selection changes in scene
        void OnSelectionChange()
        {
            UpdateSelectionHelper();
        }

        //Update selection counter
        void UpdateSelectionHelper()
        {
            helpString = "";

            if (Selection.objects != null)
                helpString = "Number of objects selected: " + Selection.objects.Length;
        }

        //Rename
        void OnWizardCreate()
        {
            //If selection empty, then exit
            if (Selection.objects == null)
                return;

            //Current Increment
            int PostFix = StartNumber;

            //Cycle and rename
            foreach(Object O in Selection.objects)
            {
                O.name = BaseName + PostFix;
                PostFix += Increment;
            }
        }
    }
}
```

> **Note**   The specifics and details of this code are not explained here because it's not critical to developing CMOD. The Batch Rename tool is simply provided to help improve your general workflow. More details on the implementation of this tool, and others, are covered in the Apress Book Learn Unity for 2D Game Development, available at www.apress.com/9781430262299.

To install the Batch Rename tool into any project in Unity, first create a new folder named Editor in the Project panel (if there's not already a folder with this name). And then drag and drop the BacthRename.cs source file from Windows Explorer or Mac Finder into the Editor folder in the project. This imports the source file and stores inside the Editor folder (see Figure 1-26).

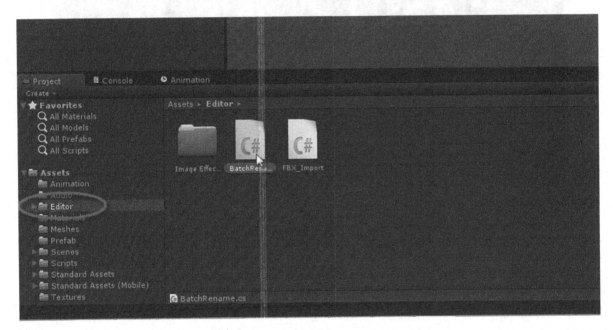

Figure 1-26. Importing the Batch Rename tool into the Editor folder

> **Note**   The Editor folder is a special folder in a Unity project. Source files inside this folder are recognized by the Editor as being Editor Extensions—as defining behavior, customizing how the editor works.

Once BacthRename.cs has been copied to the Editor folder, it's is ready to use! Let's give it a test run and rename some objects in the active scene. Create some empty objects using **GameObject ➤ Create Empty** (these are going to be renamed). Then select those objects in the Hierarchy panel. Once selected, access the Batch Rename tool by selecting **Edit ➤ Batch Rename** from the Editor menu (note that this option is only available if BacthRename.cs is inside the Editor folder). Clicking this displays the Batch Rename tool, as shown in Figure 1-27.

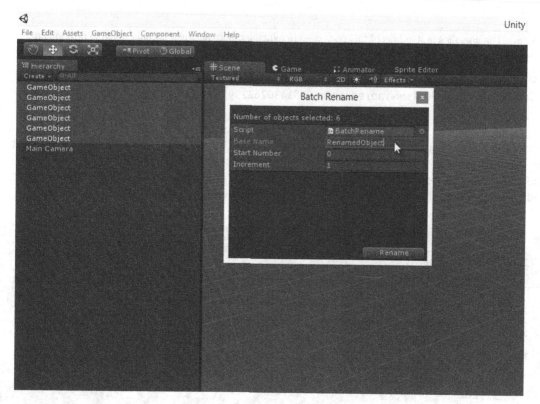

Figure 1-27. Accessing the Batch Rename tool

Enter a sample name into the BaseName field, which is the name that will be prefixed to any number, such as **Tree_01**. Leave the Start Number at 0 to begin numbering from, and leave the Increment at 1 so that numbering for the next object is increased by 1, for example Tree_01, Tree_02, and so forth (see Figure 1-28). Once specified, click the Rename button to complete the operation and rename the objects. Congratulations! You now have a Batch Rename tool.

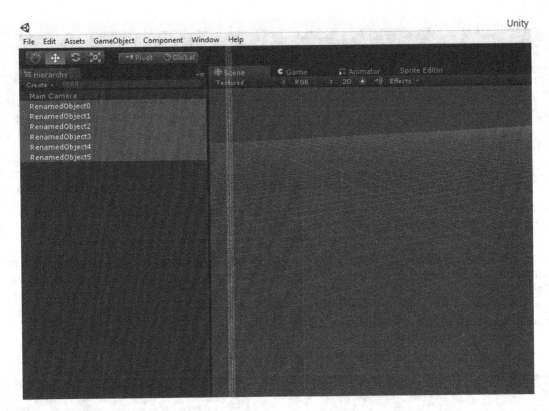

Figure 1-28. Completing the Rename operation

Tip #10: Showing Empty Objects in the Editor

Empty objects are very useful, as we'll see throughout later chapters. They serve a similar function to Dummies (or Dummy objects) in 3D software. An *Empty* is simply a GameObject that has no renderable components. There's nothing about an Empty that allows it to be seen, and so the player never knows that they're there. That's part of *why* they are useful. Their lack of visibility makes them great for marking respawn points in the scene, or for acting as pivot points (a point around which other objects revolve), or marking out regions in the level. However, despite their usefulness in-game, Empty objects come with a drawback for the developer when working with them in the Scene Editor. The problem is that Empty objects are only visible in the scene when they're selected. When selected, you can see the object's Transform gizmo (as shown in Figure 1-29). That helps you to know where the object is. But when deselected, you can't see the object anymore—you can't even select it again with your mouse because there's nothing visible to select. To reselect the Empty, you'll need to click its name in the Hierarchy panel. This can be a tedious workflow. But thankfully, there's a solution. That is, there's a way to show an Empty game object in the viewport without also making it visible to the gamer at runtime.

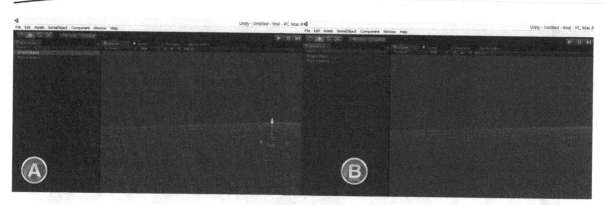

Figure 1-29. Empty objects are visible in the Scene viewport when selected, but not when deselected. A = selected (gizmo visible); B = deselected (gizmo hidden)

To show any Empty GameObject in the viewport (even when deselected), select the Empty, and from the Object Inspector, click the Icon button in the top-left corner (it can be difficult to recognize it as a clickable button). Once clicked, choose the icon to associate with the Empty (see Figure 1-30, where I've selected a diamond icon). And that's it! The Empty will now display as a diamond icon in the viewport—making it possible to see and select at all times.

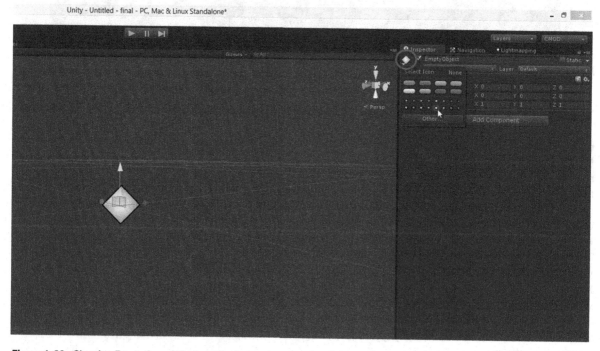

Figure 1-30. Showing Empty GameObjects in the Scene viewport

Tip #11: Use the Stats Panel

When play-testing and debugging your games inside the editor, be sure to make the *Stats panel* your friend; it is also known as the *Rendering Statistics window*. It features lots of helpful information, updated in real time while your game is playing. The Stats panel appears in the top-right corner of the Game tab and offers an overview of how your game is performing in terms of frame rate and resource usage, among others. It's important to note that the Stats panel is *system specific*, meaning that it can help you understand how well your game is performing on the current hardware you're using. For this reason, always be sure to test and benchmark game performance on your target hardware; that is, on the minimum specification for which your game is intended. To show the Stats panel, activate the Game tab and click the Stats button from the viewport toolbar (see Figure 1-31).

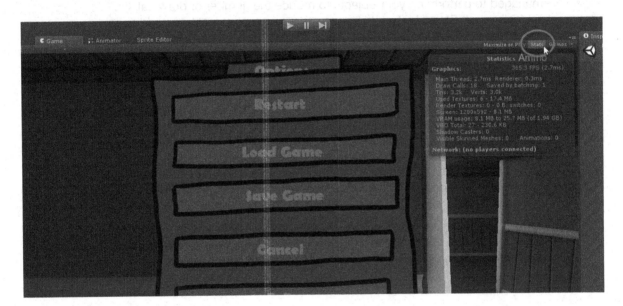

Figure 1-31. Accessing the Stats panel

There are many properties shown in this window. The following list details and explains some of them, including *FPS*, *Draw Calls*, *Saved by Batching*, *Tris*, and *VRAM Usage*.

FPS (frames per second). This shows the number of frames that your game is actually rendering to the screen each second. Generally, the higher and the more consistent this number, the better. There is no ultimate right or wrong definitive answer as to what this number should be; it will vary over time. The more important question is: Does your game look and perform as intended on your target hardware? If the answer is No, then there's a problem. And perhaps the Stats panel can help you diagnose what it is. That being said, the FPS should not usually be less than 15 frames per second. Below this rate, the human eye perceives stutter and lag, and that effect is exacerbated when the FPS is not consistent—when it fluctuates radically up and down.

- **Draw Calls.** This refers to the total number of times per frame that the Unity engine calls on the lower-level rendering functionality to display your scene to the screen. The higher this value, the more complex and expensive your scene is to render. For this reason, lower values are generally preferred. There are two easy ways to reduce draw calls. One is to use batching (we'll see this later) and the other is to reduce the number of different materials that your objects are using. Each unique material in your scene will cost an additional draw call. For this reason, if you merge textures together into larger atlas textures, and also share and reuse materials across multiple meshes, then you can significantly reduce draw calls and improve performance.

- **Saved by Batching.** This indicates the number of batching operations Unity managed to perform on your objects to reduce the number of draw calls. Typically, each Saved by Batching operation saves us at least one additional call. In most cases, the higher this value, the better.

- **Tris.** This is the total number of triangles being rendered *in the current frame*, after culling and clipping have been applied. (Thus, it doesn't refer to the total number of triangles in the scene). Most contemporary graphics hardware on desktop computers and consoles are adept at processing triangles quickly, meaning high tri-counts can, in principle, be achieved. The same cannot always be said of mobiles, however. Consequently, the lower this value, the better it'll be generally. Of course, don't be too ruthless in reducing triangles. Reduce only to a level that's *consistent with your artist vision*, and target hardware. If we always reduced triangle count to the *minimum number possible*, then every game we'd make would just be one triangle!

- **VRAM Usage.** Again, the lower this is, the better for performance—keeping within reasonable limits. It tells us how much video memory on the graphics hardware is being used for processing and texture storage.

> **Note**   More information on the Stats panel can be found in the online Unity documentation at
> `http://docs.unity3d.com/Documentation/Manual/RenderingStatistics.html`.

Tip #12: Testing Resolution and Aspect Ratio

If your game is intended for a specific resolution, such as 1920×1080 or 1024×768, or for a specific aspect ratio, such as 16:9, then it's useful to test your game in the Unity Editor at the appropriate size. Achieving this is easier now than it ever has been. Switch to the Game tab, and then click the Aspect drop-down box in the top-left corner. From here you can choose a range of preconfigured resolutions and aspect ratios, or you can click the Plus icon at the bottom of the list to input your own custom settings (see Figure 1-32).

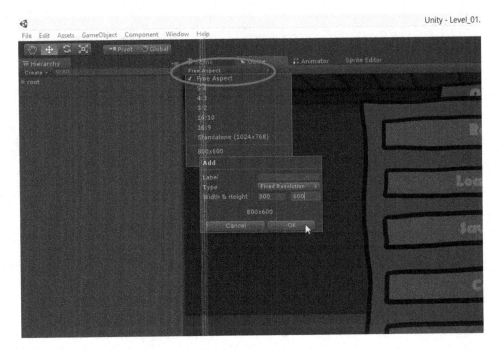

Figure 1-32. Testing the game's resolution and aspect ratio

Conclusion

This chapter achieved three main purposes. First, it detailed in overview the FPS game to be created throughout this book, *Crazy Mad Office Dude* (*CMOD*). Second, it outlined the structure this book will take to achieve that game—specifically, it detailed how the implementation work will be distributed across chapters. And finally, in preparation for that work, it listed a range of practical and relevant guidelines and workflows for using Unity in real-world projects. In short, by now you should be able to do the following:

- Understand the game to be created
- Understand the elements that compose the game, including enemies, weapons, guns, power-ups, and more
- Appreciate how the implementation work for the game will be structured
- Configure the Unity GUI for your comfort
- Understand organization principles when working with project assets—storing assets in folders, using tagging, and naming game objects
- Understand the reasons for using FBX meshes
- Read the Rendering Statistics window
- Be committed to making regular backups of work
- Use the Batch Rename tool
- Understand the benefits of Root GameObjects
- Configure the resolution and aspect ratio for in-editor testing

Chapter 2

Getting Started

In this chapter, we'll start developing the FPS game, *Crazy Mad Office Dude* (CMOD), from the very beginning. This involves a wide breadth of steps; specifically, creating a new Unity project, importing and configuring assets, building Prefabs and levels from modular environment pieces, building lighting and lightmapping, and configuring a NavMesh for pathfinding. By the end of this chapter, we'll end up with a complete Unity project that's entirely prepared and ready for C# scripting. This project is also included in the book companion files, in case you want to skip this chapter and concentrate just on C# coding, which begins in the next chapter. But I recommend working through this chapter, too—because it features plenty of helpful tips and advice for Unity projects in general. This chapter makes use of assets included in the book companion files, in `Chapter2/AssetsToImport`. So let's fire up Unity, get the project files ready, and get started!

Step 1: Create Folders

Once you've created a new and empty Unity project, start thinking about project organization. Make organization a priority—it can save you time. Create your project folders *first* so you can quickly arrange and categorize the assets you import right from the outset. For this project, the following folders will be required: `Animation`, `Audio`, `Editor`, `Materials`, `Meshes`, `Prefab`, `Scenes`, `Scripts`, and `Textures` (see Figure 2-1). Once created, be sure to save the autogenerated default scene (`Level_01`) inside the `Scenes` folder of the project, and from that point forward, save your work regularly using the keyboard shortcut *Ctrl+S* on Windows or *Cmd+S* on a Mac.

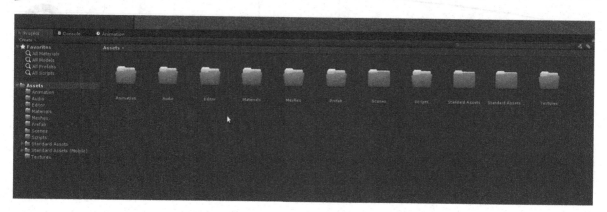

Figure 2-1. Organizing project assets into folders

> **Note**   This project will also make use of Standard Asset Packages that ship with Unity. Specifically, *Character Controllers* and *Standard Assets (Mobile)*. These can be imported from the main menu by selecting **Assets ➤ Import Package ➤ Character Controller and Assets ➤ Import Package ➤ Standard Assets (Mobile)**. These packages include a First Person Controller asset that we'll use later in the book.

Step 2: Importing Textures and Meshes

Importing meshes and textures is an interrelated process because meshes typically rely on textures. Consequently, you can make importing run smoother and easier if you import textures *before* meshes. By importing in this order, Unity detects which textures and materials to autoassign onto your meshes at import time. This means your meshes will automatically show their texture in the preview pane from the Object Inspector, and even on their thumbnails inside the Project panel. However, importing in the reverse order causes meshes to appear a textureless gray, in both the preview pane and Project panel, and usually this won't change automatically, even after you've imported the textures. So, working on this principle, import the texture first from the book project files AssetsToImport/Textures/mainTexture.png into the Textures folder inside the Project panel. For a single file like this, you can import using either the **Assets ➤ Import New Asset** menu option, or by directly dragging and dropping the files from Explorer or Finder into the Unity Editor. The latter method is preferable when importing multiple assets together. See Figure 2-2 to see the imported texture we'll be using.

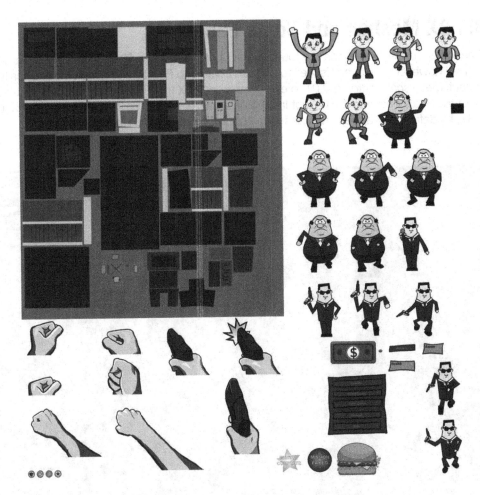

Figure 2-2. mainTexture.png is an atlas texture that'll be applied to all objects in CMOD

The file mainTexture.png is an *atlas texture* sized at 4096×4096 pixels, the maximum texture size supported by Unity. Atlas textures are essentially created by copying and pasting all your smaller and independent textures together inside a larger one—the larger one being known as the *atlas*. All meshes and objects inside the game will reference the appropriate texture areas inside the atlas, as opposed to referencing separate files. Doing this allows us to share a single material (or the fewest number of materials) across all objects, leading to improved rendering performance. Remember from Chapter 1, which discussed the Rendering Statistics window, that each unique material rendered to the display increases the draw calls.

Step 3: FBX Meshes and Scale Factor

Next, it's time to import meshes, which are found in the book companion files at AssetsToImport/Meshes. Before doing so, however, there's an "issue" to discuss relating to FBX files in general. Specifically, Unity applies a default mesh *scale factor* of *0.01* to every imported FBX file. To see that, import a single FBX file and check out the Scale Factor in the Object Inspector, as shown in Figure 2-3. The result is that every imported FBX, by default, will appear in your scene 100 times smaller than its original size.

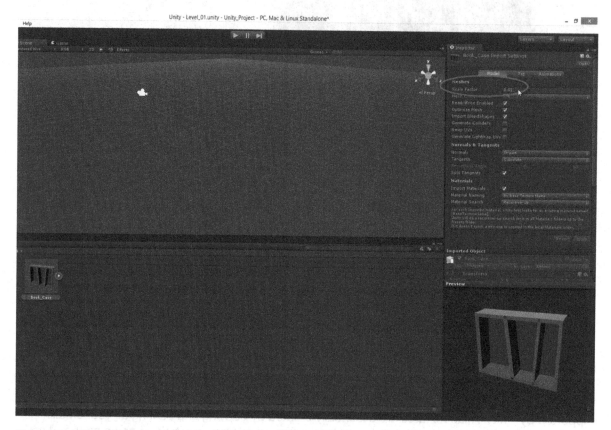

Figure 2-3. FBX meshes are imported into Unity with a default scale factor of 0.01. This may not be what you want...

The scale factor of 0.01 may, in fact, turn out to be suitable for your imported mesh, depending on how it was modeled. But if it is, then presumably it's only by accident. Typically, you'll want the scale factor to be *1.0* and not 0.01. The value 1.0 means the mesh will appear at its original size, unless it's also being scaled in the scene. In any case, you can easily change the scale factor for a mesh from the Object Inspector. But typing this in manually can be tedious. Instead, we can code an editor extension to automate the process, forcing Unity to apply a scale factor of 1.0 to every imported mesh. Let's create this now, before importing our meshes.

> **Note** Try to keep your meshes sized at nice, round numbers; keeping in mind that 1 Unity unit generally corresponds to 1 meter. Due to floating-point inaccuracy that can result from arithmetical operations, avoid having your meshes very small or very large.

To create an editor extension, you'll need to follow a Unity-established convention. Create a new C# source file inside the Editor folder of the project. It's really important for the file to be stored here, in the Editor folder (or a subfolder). Nowhere else is acceptable. Once created, name the file FBX_Import.cs and paste the C# code listed in Listing 2-1 into the file using MonoDevelop or your code editor of choice. Important lines are highlighted in bold.

Listing 2-1. FBX_Import.cs

```
using UnityEngine;
using UnityEditor;
using System;

//Sets FBX Mesh Scale Factor to 1
public class FBX_Import : AssetPostprocessor
{
        public const float importScale= 1.0f;

        void OnPreprocessModel()
        {
                ModelImporter importer = assetImporter as ModelImporter;
                importer.globalScale  = importScale;
        }
}
```

> **Note** In summary, the FBX_Import.InPreprocessModel method will be called once automatically by the Unity Editor for each imported mesh. On each execution, the mesh scale factor (represented by the globalScale property) will be set to 1.0.

After this code has been saved and compiled, it's time to import all the FBX meshes into the Meshes folder of the Project panel. Once imported, notice first that every mesh has a Scale Factor of 1 (due to the FBX_Import class), and second, note that all meshes have textured previews in the Object Inspector and textured thumbnails in the Project panel, because we imported our texture beforehand (see Figure 2-4).

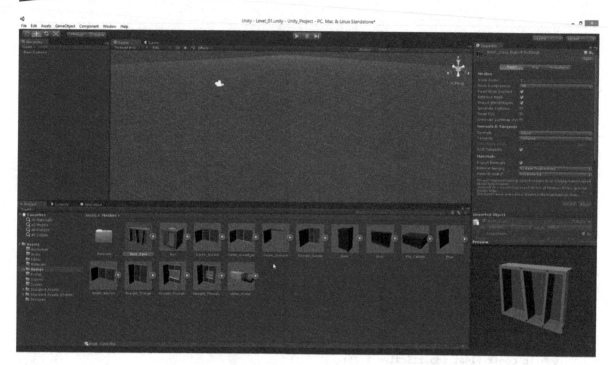

Figure 2-4. Imported meshes with Scale Factors of 1.0 and textured previews. Some meshes may appear rotated by 90 degrees in the preview pane, but this is not a problem. They will appear at their correct orientation when added to the scene

Step 4: Configuring Meshes

After importing meshes into the project, there's usually further configuring to do. First, when importing meshes, Unity autocreates a new material inside a `Materials` folder, which is further nested inside the `Meshes` folder—or wherever the meshes were stored. This material is assigned automatically onto all imported meshes. Although we want to keep the material itself, the folder organization is not neatly compatible with our own system and folder structure. So let's move the material into our original `Materials` folder at the root of the project, and delete the empty autogenerated `Material` folder inside the `Meshes` folder. This leads to a cleaner folder arrangement (see Figure 2-5).

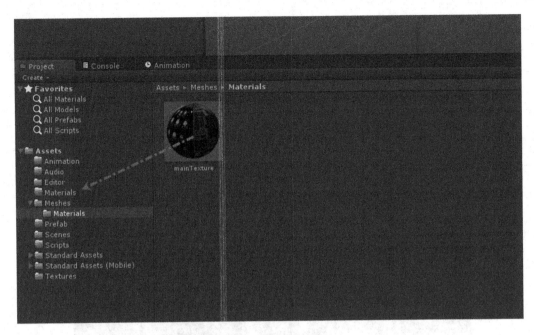

Figure 2-5. Moving the autocreated material to the Materials folder

Caution   Items deleted from a Unity project are sent directly to the Recycle Bin on Windows, or the Trash on Mac. So if you accidentally delete something from your project, you can easily restore it again. Unless you empty the Recycle Bin or Trash!

Secondly, imported meshes lack collision information by default. This means that Charatcer Controllers, such as the Third and First Person Controllers, will simply walk through the meshes in the scene, rather than collide with them, as you'll often want them to do. There are several solutions for fixing this. One way is to *generate mesh colliders*, and the other is to manually surround the meshes (when added to a scene) with basic collision primitives, like box and sphere colliders, which can be added to any game object from the main menu under **Component ➤ Physics**. For the first method, select all meshes in the Project panel and then enable *Generate Colliders* from the Object Inspector, being sure to click the Apply button afterward to confirm the setting change (see Figure 2-6). Doing this autogenerates a mesh collider component (with appropriate collision data based on mesh geometry) and attaches it to the mesh. This collision data typically produces accurate results, leading to high-quality collisions. But for complex meshes (with lots of vertices) it can turn out computationally expensive, leading to performance issues—especially on mobile devices. Consequently, the second method is often a preferred alternative. But our game (with its low-poly meshes) may safely use the first method.

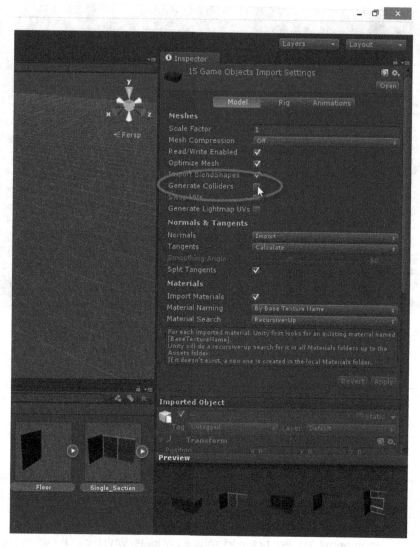

Figure 2-6.   Enabling Generate Colliders to add collision data to imported meshes

Note   For more information on approximating environment collision data using basic collision primitives, I recommend viewing my 3DMotive three-part video course, "Creating Blender Modular Environments for the Unity Engine," at https://www.3dmotive.com.

Tip   In Unity 3.5 and above, you can generate colliders for all your meshes simultaneously—you don't need to generate them individually. Just select all meshes in the Project panel and click Generate Colliders from the Object Inspector.

Every mesh in Unity features lightmap UVs in some form, regardless of whether they're really used in-game. Like regular UVs, lightmapping UVs are a set of mapping coordinates for meshes. Standard UVs define how regular textures, like Diffuse and Bump textures are projected onto the mesh surface in three-dimension. In contrast, lightmap UVs help Unity and the *Beast lightmapper* understand how to project baked lighting (such as indirect illumination) from *lightmap textures* onto the mesh surface. If your mesh has only one UV channel (UV1), then Unity, by default, will use that channel also for lightmapping UVs. There are occasions when this choice may not be troublesome: such as when a mesh has no overlapping or tightly packed UVs.

But usually, it's a good idea to avoid using UV1 for lightmap UVs. It's usually better practice to leave UV1 reserved for standard mapping, and have UV2 (a second and separate UV channel) for lightmap UVs. To achieve this, however, a mesh needs a second UV channel, and there are two main options available for creating this channel. One method is to create the channel manually in your 3D modeling software—the steps for doing this are software specific. And the second method is to have Unity generate a second lightmap UV channel. This latter approach is achieved by selecting all appropriate meshes in the Project panel, and then by enabling the Generate Lightmap UVs check box from the Object Inspector. For CMOD, lightmap UVs should be generated for all meshes (see Figure 2-7).

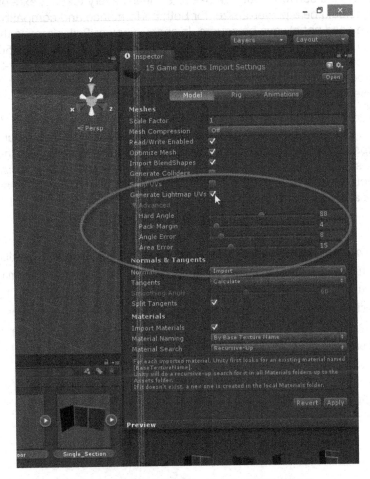

Figure 2-7. Unity can generate lightmap UVs for imported meshes with only one UV channel

As seen in Figure 2-7, when the Generate Lightmap UVs check box is enabled, additional options are revealed in the inspector, which influence the generation process. Typically, if your meshes are hard-angled environment meshes—with sharper 90 degree turns and corners—then the default settings will likely prove sufficient. If your meshes are organic, curved, spherical, and smooth, then better lightmap UVs can usually be generated with higher values for the Hard Angle setting. For CMOD, the default settings will be suitable.

> **Note**   More details on generating lightmap UVs can be found at the Unity online documentation at http://docs.unity3d.com/Documentation/Manual/LightmappingUV.html.

Step 5: Planning and Configuring Textures

CMOD features only one texture, namely a 4096×4096 atlas. Its dimensions have been chosen for two reasons. First, it's a conventional power-2 size. Nearly every texture, except a GUI texture or dedicated sprite, should be a power-2 size, for both performance and compatibility reasons. However, the texture need not always be square. In short, a power-2 size means the texture's width and height (in pixels) may be any of the following sizes: 2, 4, 8, 16, 32, 64, 128, 256, 512, 1024, 2048, and 4096. Second, 4096 has been chosen, as opposed to any other power-2 size, because it's the *largest* size supported by Unity and our target resolution is not clearly defined or known (I want to support many screen sizes, resolutions and platforms).

By making textures to the largest size possible therefore we can always downsize, if required, through all the possible sizes that Unity supports. This is always preferable to making textures smaller than needed, because *upsizing* always incurs quality loss and blur, due to resampling. In general, make textures exactly the size you need, and no smaller or larger. This is because *all* resizing involves resampling. But if you're not sure about the sizes required, or if you need different sizes, then always create your textures at the largest size, since downsizing incurs less degradation than upsizing.

> **Note**   Through the Texture Properties dialog in the Object Inspector, Unity offers built-in features for resizing textures "nondestructively." That is, for resizing textures up or down, always based on the original. You can simply select a texture in the Project panel and then pick a new size for it (see Figure 2-8). Of course, this still involves implicit resampling and quality loss as described earlier, but the resized versions are always generated from the original imported texture and not from any other resized versions we may have generated previously. This means any quality loss incurred through resizing is not accumulative, even if you resize multiple times in succession.

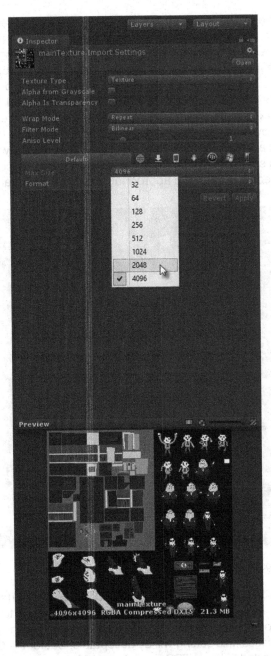

Figure 2-8. Texture Properties are accessible through the Object Inspector when a texture asset is selected. Using these settings, you can up- and down-size textures as required for your platform and build

When importing the CMOD atlas texture into Unity, several default properties are applied—and these can be viewed using the Texture Properties dialog, as shown in Figure 2-8. Sometimes the default settings will be just what you need, in which case no further tweaking is necessary. In our case, however, the default settings are probably very different from what we need. How so? And what should be changed? The following points answer our two questions.

■ **Maximum texture size.** As mentioned, the CMOD atlas texture is sized at
4096×4096 pixels. By default, however, Unity imports this and resizes it to
1024×1024. This size might be suitable for legacy hardware and some mobile
builds. But for desktop PCs and Macs, the size should be 4096×4096. To
solve this, use the *Max Size* field in the Object Inspector to "upsize" the
texture back to its original size. "Upsize" here is not true upsizing: Unity is not
stretching a 1024×1024 texture to 4096×4096. Rather, it restores the original
texture without downsizing it. Notice the Per-Platform settings for textures,
as shown in Figure 2-9. Switching between these tabs means we can specify
different textures sizes on a *per-build* basis, allowing Unity at compile time to
automatically select and build the appropriate texture for our target platform.

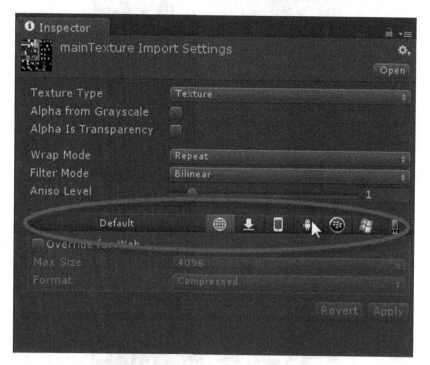

Figure 2-9. Tweaking texture settings on a per-platform basis

■ **Changing the Texture Type.** By default, the CMOD atlas is imported with the default
Texture Type set at *Texture* (as shown in Figure 2-9). Texture refers to general textures
applied to most types of 3D meshes, including environment meshes and animated
meshes. In many cases, this setting will be acceptable. But for the CMOD atlas it
isn't. CMOD is intended to be an FPS game in a comic/humor style. We'll need the
atlas not just for environment meshes, but also for the *interface* and for *sprites*. As we'll
see, both the enemies and power-ups will be implemented as old-school billboard
sprites. That is, as 2D images constantly aligned upright and facing the camera.
This means the atlas will be multipurpose. It'll be used for meshes, for the GUI, and
for sprites (which are 2D GameObjects introduced in Unity 4.3). To configure the
texture for our *specific* needs, we'll change the Texture Type setting from Texture to
Advanced. When Advanced is selected, additional properties appear in the Object
Inspector, allowing even further customization (see Figure 2-10).

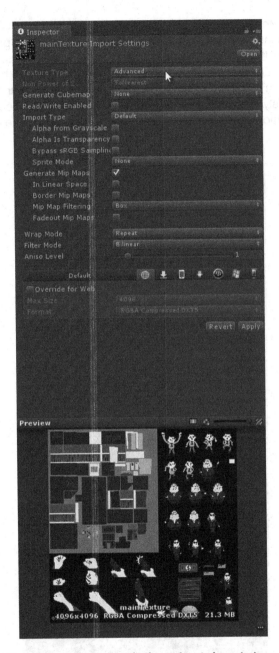

Figure 2-10. Advanced Texture settings offers greater customization and control over textures

■ **Specifying advanced settings.** For our atlas to act as intended, we'll
need to specify some advanced settings. The settings required are shown in
Figure 2-11. Go ahead and copy over those settings on your system. But I also
want to explain in brief why they've been chosen. First, *Alpha is Transparency* is
enabled. Transparency is important for sprites. Since we're using a transparent
PNG file, texture transparency should be based on the PNG file transparency.

Second, *Sprite Mode* has been set to *Multiple*, because the texture contains multiple sprite characters and animations. We'll later use the Sprite Editor to select and define these. Third, *Pixels to Units* is set to *200*. This will be an ideal ratio between pixels to units (*in our case*) that'll allow sprites to be seen at an appropriate size in relation to the environment meshes. For your own projects, this value will likely require tweaking. Fourth, *Wrap Mode* has been set to *Clamp* to prevent distortion or tiling artifacts from appearing around the edges of sprites.

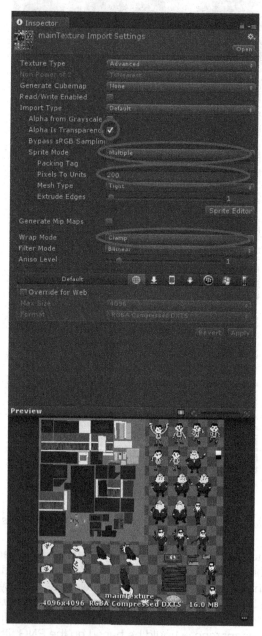

Figure 2-11. Specifying advanced settings for the CMOD atlas texture

> **Note**   More details on texture properties can be found at the online Unity documentation at
> `http://docs.unity3d.com/Documentation/Manual/Textures.html`.

Step 6: Building Sprites

Unity 4.3 introduced a range of features tailored for creating 2D games. These features primarily include *Sprites*, the *Sprite Editor*, and the *Sprite Packer*. As mentioned, CMOD will make use of some of these features for creating billboard sprites in the level. These sprites will represent enemies, power-ups, weapons, and other GUI elements, as shown in Figure 2-12.

Figure 2-12.   Sprites will be used to create enemies, power-ups, weapons, and more

To add Sprite instances to a scene, we'll need to generate Sprite assets. These are produced using the Sprite Editor. In short, the Sprite Editor allows us to mark rectangular regions (UV rectangles) inside an existing atlas texture to use as a sprite. Marking these regions manually with the mouse can be a long and tedious process, but right now, there's no quicker method. In addition, to make the sprites accurately, you'll probably need to work alongside your image editor application (such as Photoshop or GIMP) to read and measure pixel coordinates and positions. Remember, I've already created the sprites for you in the sample project, featured in the book project files, in the `Chapter2` folder. The Sprite Editor can be accessed from the Texture Properties page by clicking the Sprite Editor button (see Figure 2-13).

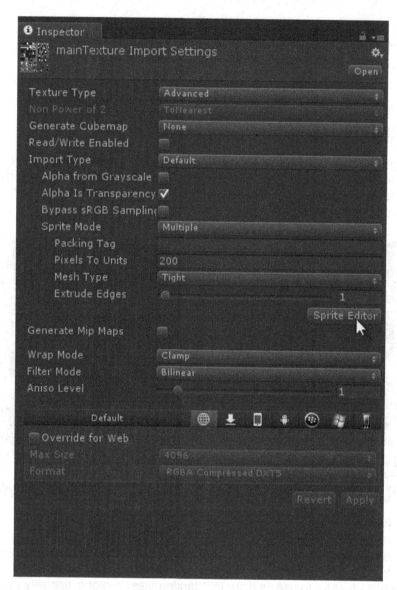

Figure 2-13. Using the Sprite Editor to mark out the sprites for CMOD

For CMOD, each separate character, each frame of animation, and each power-up and GUI element will count as a separate sprite. All of them must be marked by clicking and dragging a Sprite Selection rectangle around them. See Figure 2-14 to see how I've marked the sprites. When you've finished creating sprites, don't forget to click the Apply button at the top-right corner of the editor to confirm the changes and generate the Sprite assets.

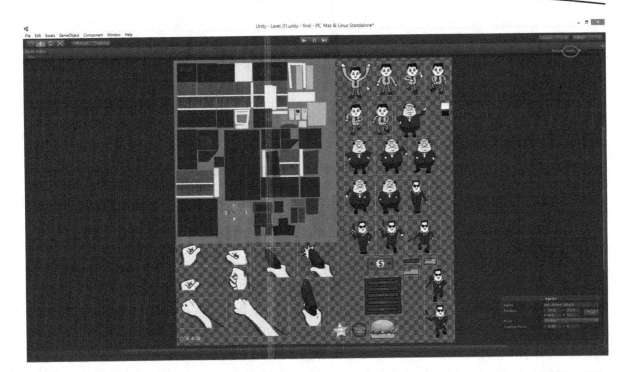

Figure 2-14. Sprite sheet for CMOD using the Sprite Editor

Once you've defined all sprites in the Sprite Editor, Unity will automatically generate Sprite assets from them. These are grouped together under the atlas texture asset in the Project panel. You can expand the texture asset to reveal all sprites contained within (see Figure 2-15). In doing this, CMOD now has all required sprites. You can even drag and drop sprites from the Project panel and into the scene, via the Hierarchy panel, to instantiate a sprite in the scene.

Figure 2-15. Generate Sprite Assets are grouped under their associated atlas texture in the Project panel

> **Note** More information on the Sprite Editor can be found in the online Unity documentation at
> http://docs.unity3d.com/Documentation/Manual/SpriteEditor.html.

Step 7: Importing Audio

Next, it's time to import audio assets into the project. The book companion files for CMOD feature only a few audio sound effects, created using the sound generator tool *SFXR*, which can be downloaded for free from www.drpetter.se/project_sfxr.html. SFXR is software for procedurally generating the kinds of sound effects commonly used in old-school video games, such as the original *Super Mario Bros.* and *Sonic the Hedgehog*. For CMOD, there are a total of four sound effects, all in WAV format, stored in the Chapter2/AssetsToImport/Audio folder. These include Explosion.wav, played whenever enemies are destroyed; Powerup_Collect.wav, played whenever the player collects a power-up object, such as cash or a weapon; Weapon_Gun.wav, played whenever the player fires the gun weapon; and finally, Weapon_Punch.wav, played whenever the player uses the default punch weapon. Go ahead and import all these sound effects into the Unity project, using the conventional drag-and-drop method. Make sure the sounds are added to the Audio folder in the Project panel (see Figure 2-16).

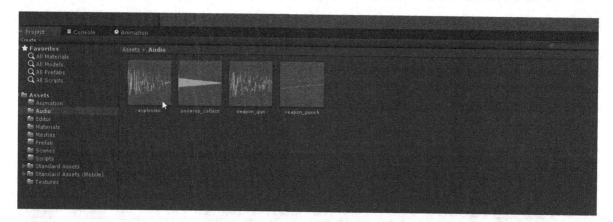

Figure 2-16. Importing retro-style audio assets into the project. The audio assets for this book were generated using the free program SFXR

Every audio file for this project shares an important characteristic that requires us to adjust the default import settings applied to them. Specifically, every audio file will be *2D* and not *3D*. That is, none of our sounds are located at any specific 3D position in the scene. We don't want or need their volume to raise or lower based on the nearness or farness of the Player from others in the world. Rather, the sounds should simply play in all speakers at a single and constant volume. Their purpose is primarily that of feedback for the Player's actions in-game, such as collecting a power-up or firing a weapon. To adjust the default import settings to reflect this, select all imported audio assets, and disable the 3D Sound check box from the Object Inspector (see Figure 2-17). Once completed, all audio assets are now successfully imported and configured ready-for-use in the scene.

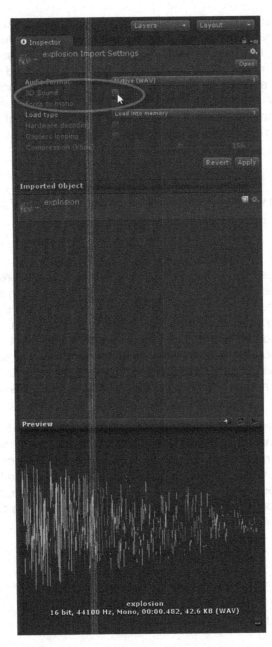

Figure 2-17. Configuring the imported audio as 2D sounds, and not 3D sounds

Step 8: Create Prefabs

Importing assets is primarily about collating together and preparing the raw materials on which our game will be founded and assembled. It's essentially the lowermost layer or root stage of development, on top of which all subsequent layers are made. Once importing is completed, the next stage of development is to create abstracted assets. That is, to use the raw and imported assets (the asset files) to create any further or more complex assets inside the Unity Editor. One such asset is the *Prefab*. In short, the Prefab allows us to drop a collection of assets, like meshes and scripts, into the scene to compose a more complex entity or thing. Based on that, we may create an asset, which can thereafter be treated as a complete and separate whole. Prefabs are especially useful for building modular environments, which is how they'll be used here for CMOD. But they're not limited to simply environment assets: any time we have a collection of objects that work together as a complete entity, we can use a Prefab. They save us from building and rebuilding similar objects across different scenes, and even within the same scene.

> **Note**   More information on working with Prefabs can be found in the online Unity documentation at http://docs.unity3d.com/Documentation/Manual/Prefabs.html.

The meshes imported into the Project at steps 3 and 4 consist almost entirely of *environment pieces*, and not *complete environments* (see Figure 2-4). Specifically, these pieces include individual items of furniture, such as file cabinets and desks, and architecture and props like corner sections, crossroad sections, T-junctions, and door sections. These pieces are designed to be instantiated in the scene, where they may be combined and recombined into unique arrangements to form more complete and seamless environments. To form an analogy, we'll build our game environment from mesh pieces directly in the Unity Editor, just as physical statues and models are made from Lego bricks—or other kinds of interlocking blocks that are fitted together. This building-block method of level creation is often called the *modular method* because each environment piece is seen as a *module* in a larger set.

Of course, you *can* alternatively build a single and huge environment inside your modeling software of choice, and then import that into Unity as a final and unchangeable mesh. There's nothing "wrong" or "incorrect" in doing that per se—it can work. But doing that comes at the cost of flexibility and versatility, as well as performance. By importing separate and reusable environment pieces instead, you can recombine them together into a potentially infinite number of environment combinations. This allows you to assemble many different levels from the same, basic mesh ingredients. Plus, it works better with Occlusion Culling.

> **Tip**   If you need to make large and complex levels (and maybe many of them), then be sure to make the modular building method your friend. It can save you lots of time. Plus, it's a really fun and easy way to build levels, assuming you enjoyed playing with building blocks!

> **Note**   More comprehensive information on the modular method of level design can be found in my book *Practical Game Development with Unity and Blender* (Cengage Learning, 2014), and also in my 3DMotive online video course, "Creating Unity-Ready Modular Environments with Blender."

Importing environment pieces for the modular building method typically leads us into using Prefabs. Why is this? Take a look at Figure 2-18. There I've assembled several pieces together to form a larger corridor section with an inward corner turn. From the Hierarchy panel, as well as the Project panel, you can see that this larger arrangement is formed from a total of eight smaller mesh instances, using four different mesh assets. These meshes are included in the book project files, and are `Corner_Inward`, `Corner_Outward`, `Straight_Through`, and `Single_Section`. Together these form a complete corner section for a corridor.

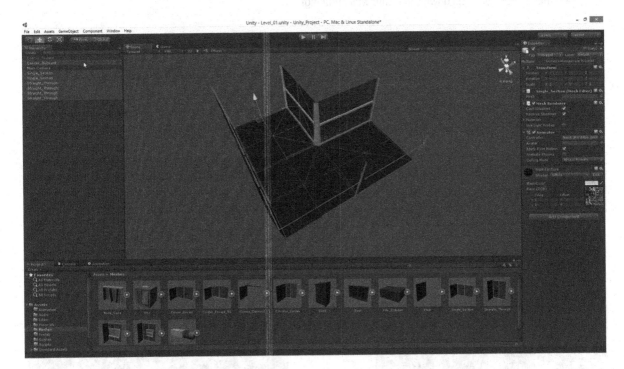

Figure 2-18. Building common environment modules from meshes

Now, assembling these smaller pieces together into larger areas like this works well enough, at least for *one* corner section or *one* T-section, but overall it takes time and patience to build. However, a scene will typically have many corridors with turns and corners and T-sections, as well as other similar architectural configurations that repeat themselves over and over again. Without using Prefabs, we'd have to duplicate (copy/paste) the different arrangements where required, selecting all pieces that compose a section, and then duplicate it for reuse elsewhere in the environment. By using Prefabs, we can dramatically reduce our workload in this context. In the case of a corner section, we can build just *one* corner section, make it a Prefab asset, and then reuse that asset for every repetition, as though it were a separate mesh—just like a rubber stamp can be reused to print many instances of the same pattern. This can make Prefabs an invaluable tool for making modular environments.

Tip   While level building, don't forget to use Vertex, Grid and Rotation snapping in combination with the Transform tools (Translate, Rotate, and Scale). Vertex snapping lets you align meshes together, exactly at the seams. To access Vertex Snapping, activate the Translate tool (W key) and then hold down the V key (Vertex Snapping) to align two meshes together at the vertices. To access Grid Snapping, to move along the grid in discrete increments, hold down the Ctrl (Cmd) key while translating objects. You can also rotate in discrete increments too—just hold down Ctrl (Cmd) while rotating!

To make a new Prefab for the corner-section meshes, as shown in Figure 2-18, right-click the mouse inside the `Prefab` folder in the Project panel. From the context menu, select **Create ➤ Prefab** to produce a new Prefab asset, which begins as an empty container. You can also create the same Prefab object by choosing **Asset ➤ Create ➤ Prefab** from the application main menu (see Figure 2-19). I've named the Prefab `prefab_Corner_Section`.

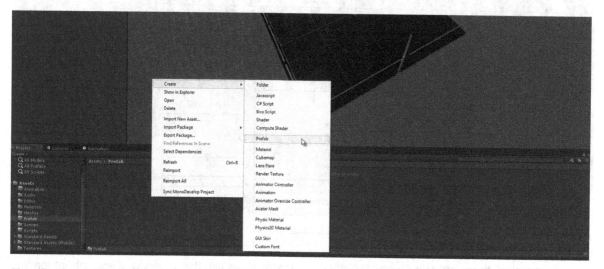

Figure 2-19. Generating a Prefab asset in preparing for mesh reuse. Prefabs are especially useful tools when creating modular environments

By default, a Prefab is created as an empty container object, and has no association with any other assets. To build this association, a parent-child relationship should first be established between all meshes that you want to include in the Prefab. For the corner section, simply use the Hierarchy panel to choose any mesh instance in the scene, and then parent all the *other* meshes to it as child GameObjects (see Figure 2-20).

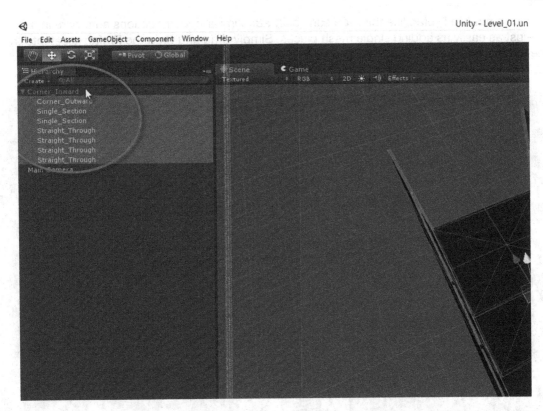

Figure 2-20. Creating a Parent object for a group of GameObjects, in preparation for creating a Prefab asset

Once a parent-child hierarchy is established, simply drag and drop the parent GameObject from the Hierarchy panel to the Prefab asset in the Project panel. Doing this establishes the essential connection between the meshes in the scene and the Prefab asset. In one operation, we will have generated a Prefab asset featuring all corner-section meshes, *and* will have replaced the original and independent meshes in the scene with the Prefab asset (see Figure 2-21).

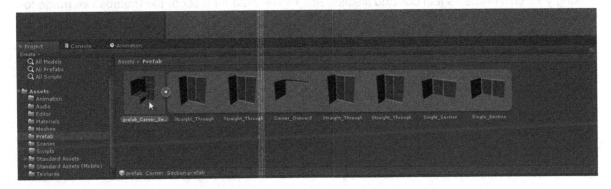

Figure 2-21. Building a Prefab for the modular building method

After you've made a Prefab like this, you can easily add similar corner sections anywhere in the level—just as easily as adding single mesh pieces. Simply drag and drop the Prefab asset into the scene to create new instances (see Figure 2-22).

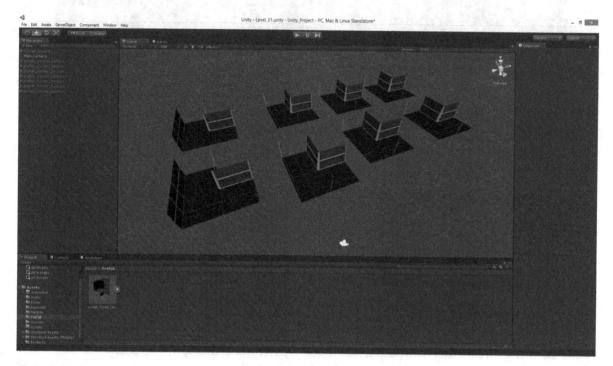

Figure 2-22. Instantiating multiple corner sections from the same Prefab

Don't stop here, however! Use this technique to identify all other relevant architectural configurations that could be abstracted into reusable Prefab objects. The earlier you do this in your workflow, the easier your level-building experience will be in the long term. However, exercise caution when reusing only a few Prefabs, because it's easy for the repetition to become noticeable to the gamer, making your environments feel dull and lifeless. See Figure 2-23 for a list of the Prefabs I've made for CMOD.

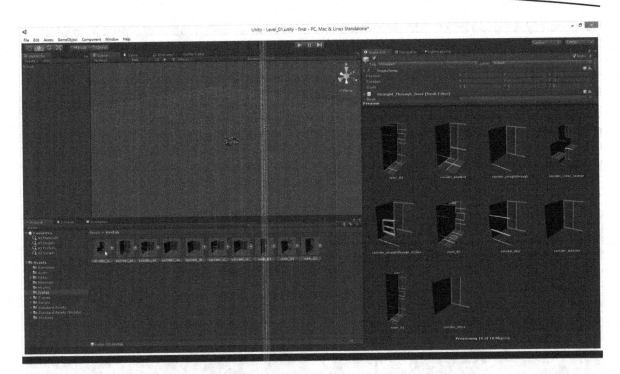

Figure 2-23. Breaking down environment pieces into Prefabs

Step 9: Scene Building

When you've imported all relevant assets and established all Prefabs, it's usually a good time to start building your scene. Both Mesh assets and Prefabs will inevitably form the raw materials and ingredients from which scene geometry is made. When inserting the first environment piece (whether a mesh or a Prefab), I typically use the Transform properties in the Object Inspector to position it exactly at the world origin, unless there's a strong overriding reason not to do so. Doing this is not essential, of course, as you can effectively position your meshes anywhere. But starting at the world origin and building outward adds a certain degree of neatness and cleanliness to your mesh positions and scene limits. This might at first seem a trivial preoccupation, but investing time upfront for good organization and a desire for tidiness like this helps make development smoother. Ideally, development *should* smoothly flow along from beginning to end, each step logically and reasonably following the previous.

> **Note**   By level building from the origin and working outward, you can even improve performance on some platforms, such as mobile devices.

Once you've established a first piece in the scene, you can simply add your other pieces onto it, repeating this procedure until your level is fully constructed as desired. For CMOD, I constructed the scene in an ad-lib way: just adding different pieces together until I arrived at a design that felt right.

But generally, it's good practice to plan ahead and even draw a scene map or blueprint from which you can work. Doing this allows you to foresee and correct for structural or logistical problems that could arise from specific scene arrangements, such as: Won't this level be too large and tedious for the player to navigate back and forth? Will that enemy be able to fit through that walkway? Wouldn't a longer hallway add some dramatic tension as the player approaches the final room? And so on.

Once you've completed your scene arrangement (as shown in Figure 2-24), consider grouping all environment pieces under a single GameObject, even if that object is an Empty. This allows you to move the entire scene by transforming one object, should you want or need to. In addition, it allows you to apply static batching to the environment in one operation, as we'll see. Before doing so, let's consider batching in more detail as it pertains to level design.

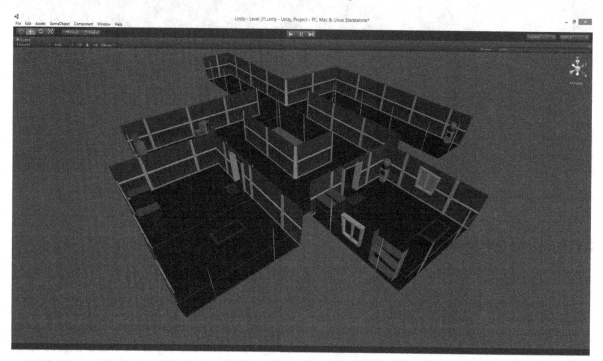

Figure 2-24. My completed CMOD scene, ready for lighting and NavMeshes

Unity, and most game engines, draw a sharp technical distinction between objects that have the *potential* to move during gameplay (*dynamic objects*) and those which *will* never move or change at all (*static objects*). Dynamic objects include those such as the player character, enemies, weapons, vehicles, doors, particle systems, and many more. Static objects include walls, floors, ceilings, tables, chairs, stairs, windows, mountains, hills, rocks, and more. Typically static objects account for the majority of scene objects and dynamic objects for the minority (this is not true of *every* game, but probably true for *most* games, and certainly most FPS games). This distinction is an important one for games and for performance. It influences processes as diverse as lightmapping and navigation meshes. In short, if an object is static and never moves, then we can mark it as such directly from the Unity Editor by using the Static check box available for meshes in the Object Inspector. Enabling this for static objects achieves a range of performance benefits. For example, only static objects can be lightmapped and only static objects can be baked into navigation meshes. So make sure you enable this for all static objects; just select the static object and tick the box (see Figure 2-25)!

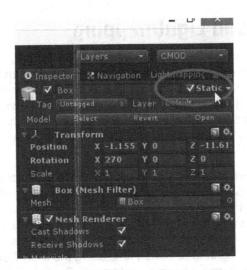

Figure 2-25. *Be sure to enable the Static check box for static scene elements*

If you've grouped all your environment pieces as children under a single parent object, then you can enable static batching for them all in operating, simply by enabling static batching on the parent. When you enable static batching for the parent, you can cascade the operation downward to all children, too (see Figure 2-26).

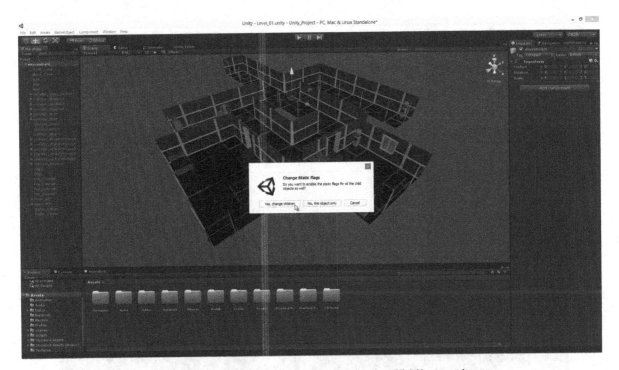

Figure 2-26. *Enabling static batching for all environment pieces in one operation. Click Yes to apply*

Step 10: Lighting and Lightmapping

Now it's time to consider lighting and lightmapping for CMOD. For me, lightmapping is one of the most fascinating ideas in game development. It was introduced as a limited solution to an intractable problem; one which even today has no all-encompassing solution. The problem is that calculating the effects of real-world lighting in a 3D environment—such as shadows, reflections, and indirect illumination—is such a computationally expensive process that even the best consumer hardware cannot approximate the effects with strong believability in *real time*. Lightmapping is one of the solutions to this problem. But it has important limitations, as we'll see.

Lightmapping is achieved in Unity via the Beast lightmapper, which is accessible from the main menu via **Window ➤ Lightmapping** (see Figure 2-27). This is a tool that casts rays of light into the scene, outward from all light sources, and then traces how those rays bounce and react to scene geometry. The purpose of this is to assess how bright or dark (and which color) the impacted surfaces should be. This process can be time-consuming (in terms of hours or even days), but it lets developers *precalculate* the effects of scene lighting at design time using the Unity Editor, and to bake the results of that process into dedicated textures, known as *lightmaps*. The lightmaps contain information about shadows, color bleeding, indirect illumination, and more. Unity then automatically blends the lightmaps onto the scene geometry at run-time, on top of the regular textures and materials, to make the geometry *appear* illuminated by the lights. Lightmapping is an intricate "trick," but it can produce powerful results. The famous author Arthur C. Clarke once said, "Any sufficiently advanced technology is indistinguishable from magic," and indeed, lightmapping has a certain kind of "magic" about it.

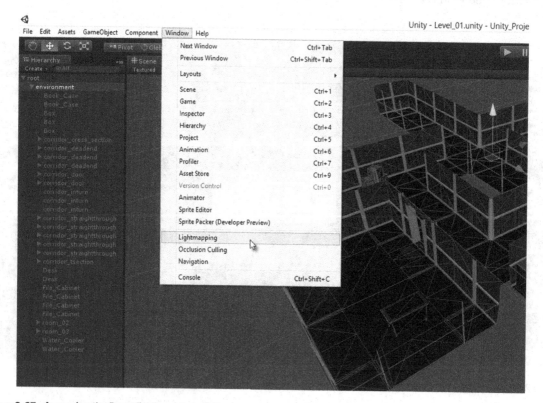

Figure 2-27. Accessing the Beast lightmapper in Unity

However, lightmapping has its limitations. Since its effects are all *precalculated*, lightmapping cannot account for shadows and illumination cast by dynamic objects—objects that move and change *while the game is running*. The solutions to this problem take various forms, and Unity offers *Dynamic Lighting* and *Light Probes* (a special kind of semidynamic lighting). For CMOD and its low-contrast 'toon style, we'll use lightmapping for static objects and full dynamic lighting for moveable objects. Light probes will not be considered further in this book. Dynamic lighting is simply the process of calculating lighting for moving objects in real time. For performance reasons, this kind of lighting doesn't consider indirect illumination and other more realistic effects. This means moving objects will be rendered less realistically than static ones. But for a cartoon-style game, this shouldn't prove problematic.

> **Note**   When lightmapping, take care over performance to use the LightMap Resolution field to size your lightmap textures appropriately for your levels and target hardware.
>
> For those interested in light probes, more information can be found at the Unity official documentation at `http://docs.unity3d.com/Documentation/Manual/LightProbes.html`.

Before you can illuminate any scene with lightmapping in Unity, you'll need two things: a scene with lights and at least one mesh instance marked as *Static*. If you've followed along from the previous section, then all your scene architecture should be marked as Static, making it eligible for lightmapping. Lights can be added to the scene using the main menu: **GameObject ➤ Create** Other (see Figure 2-28). From here, Unity offers a range of light types—namely, the *Directional Light*, *Point Light*, *Spotlight*, and *Area Light*.

Figure 2-28. Adding lights to your scene

The light types differ radically in their performance implications. But one general rule to follow when lighting is *less is more*. That is, don't add more lights than are truly necessary. Cut back on excess and get the best results possible from the fewest number of lights. For CMOD, both the Directional Light and Area Light can be excluded as viable options. Directional Lights can be excluded because they're designed primarily for outdoor environments, which are illuminated by either the sun or moon. Directional Lights simulate bright light sources at a distant location, casting infinite rays of light in a single direction. And Area Lights can be excluded generally because we must illuminate both static and dynamic objects, and they pertain only to lightmapped objects. This leaves us with a realistic choice between two light types to use (we can use a mixture, too); specifically the *Point Light* and the *Spotlight*. In terms of performance, points are "better" than spots. That is, Spotlights are typically more expensive than Point Lights. For CMOD then, I will use only Point Lights for the scene (see Figure 2-29 to see my configuration of Point Lights).

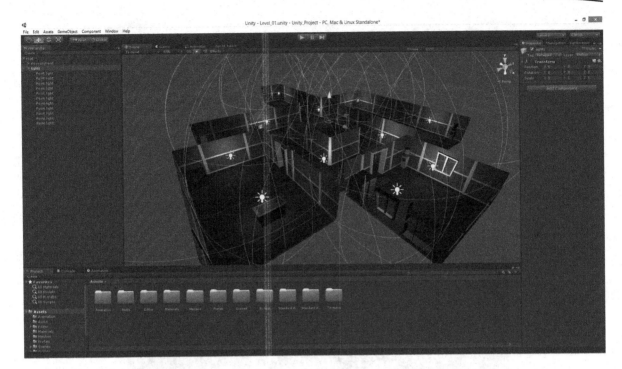

Figure 2-29. Adding lights to your scene

Note   See from Figure 2-29 that I've applied the GameObject parenting principle I recommended for environment meshes. All scene lights are grouped as children beneath a single, parent GameObject.

Once you've created a lighting setup you're happy with, it's time to lightmap. As mentioned in the previous chapter, I've docked the Lightmapping window as a tab alongside the Object Inspector so I can view it easily beside the Scene and Game tabs. You may like this arrangement, too. From the Lightmapping window, open the Bake dialog. Here is where you'll control how the lightmaps are generated (see Figure 2-30 to see the settings I've used). The points that follow explain some of the options available and the reasons behind my decisions.

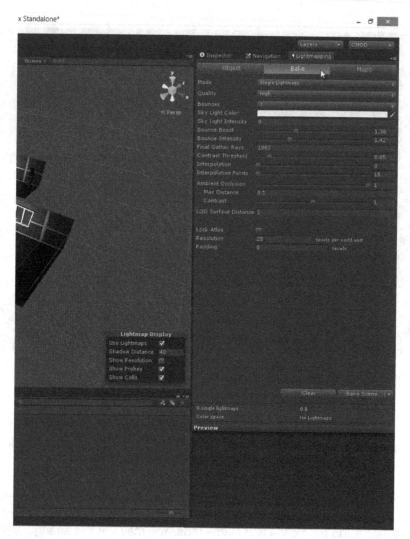

Figure 2-30. Lightmapping CMOD

■ **Mode.** In Unity 4.3 there are three lightmapping modes available: *Single Lightmaps*, *Dual Lightmaps*, and *Directional Lightmaps*. Both dual and directional lightmapping produce two set of lightmaps. Dual lightmapping produces a *Near* map and a *Far* map, and directional lightmapping produces a *Color* map and a *Scale* map. The usage of these maps varies. The point of both of these modes is to increase realism, giving you a balance between prebaked lightmaps and per-pixel dynamic lighting, with effects such as specularity and normal maps. However, for the *implied realism* of CMOD, we can resort to the "simpler" Single Lightmaps. This mode produces only one lightmap set, as opposed to multiple. This map (or set of maps) features *all* the direct and indirect illumination for the scene. No matter where your camera is in the scene during gameplay, Unity will *always* be applying the lightmap to static objects. Static objects will not receive Dynamic Illumination.

- **Quality.** The default Quality is *High*—though this setting can be toggled between High (for production use) and Low (for testing). The value to use here depends on how you like to work and how long it takes to produce lightmaps and to make adjustments. But, when building the final lightmaps for your game, be sure to use the High quality setting.

- **Bounce Boost and Bounce Intensity (Pro Only feature).** Together these values control the influence and power of indirect illumination in the lightmaps. During the lightmap generation process, the lightmapper emits rays from all light sources in the scene, and these travel in a straight line until they strike and bounce away from any surfaces they contact. The bounced light loses some of its intensity and inherits some of the color from the surface it previously hit. This is why (for example) a white floor near a red wall will be "splashed" with a tint of red, as light from the wall bounces and strikes the floor. In the "real world" there is no known limit to the number of light bounces allowed. But for computers, this kind of potentially infinite regression is not permitted, and so a concrete limit must be set on the number of bounces. This limit is controlled by *Bounce Boost*. Higher values theoretically produce more accurate and believable results at the cost of calculation time. In practice, however, you don't usually need to go very high for results that are "believable enough." The *Bounce Intensity* value is a multiplier (brightness increase) for each bounced ray. For the CMOD level in Figure 2-29, I think the values of 1.38 and 1.42 work for Bounce Boost and Intensity, respectively. I did not calculate these numbers in anyway. I simply played around and made multiple lightmap bakes, tweaking the settings and trying again several times, before finally settling on these values. Through successive builds and refinement you can arrive at values that work best for you.

- **Ambient Occlusion (Pro Only feature).** Ambient Occlusion (AO) simulates one symptom of indirect illumination known as *Contact Shadows*. This refers to the darkening that occurs inside and near the crevices that form when two solid surfaces meet, such as where the floor meets a wall, or a coffee mug base meets the table. In and around those regions there's a thin border of shadow or darkening that results because light rays are more occluded or blocked from those regions. By using Ambient Occlusion, you can enhance the general volume of your environments and the embeddedness of your objects—making them feel much more of an integrated part of the world. By default, Ambient Occlusion is disabled. You can enable it (on the Pro version of Unity) by switching the Ambient Occlusion slider to a value above 0. A value of 1 means AO will take full effect, and lower values between 0 and 1 act as an opacity control. The Ambient Occlusion slider works in combination with the *Max Distance* and *Contrast* sliders to control the size and darkness of the AO shadows generated in crevices. For CMOD, the values of 0.1 and 1 work well for Max Distance and Contrast, respectively.

- **Resolution.** This works in combination with the total surface area of your meshes in the scene to determine the final size of the generated lightmaps in pixels. When the Lightmapping window is active, you'll see an accompanying Lightmap Display dialog in the Scene viewport (see Figure 2-31). By enabling the Show Resolution check box, a checker-pattern texture map will be projected over all static scene geometry, indicating how the pixels in the lightmap will be distributed. Each box in the checker-pattern stands in for a single pixel in the lightmap. In short, the "ideal" value for resolution should be the lowest possible while still retaining the lighting quality suitable for your game and while making best use of the texture space in the lightmap. Like most other values in the Lightmapping window, a certain degree of tweaking and retesting is required. For my CMOD level, a value of 25 looks good.

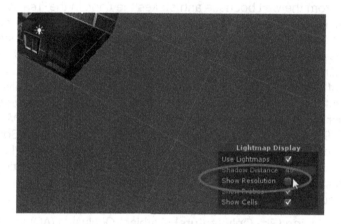

Figure 2-31. Previewing lightmap resolution using the Lightmap Display dialog

Once you're happy with the settings you've specified, the lightmap textures can be produced by pressing the Bake Scene button from the Lightmap Bake panel (see Figure 2-30). You may have to wait a while (the progress status is viewable in the lower-right corner of the Editor window). Once generated, the Lightmapping window indicates how many lightmap textures were generated and their size in pixels, which is based on the total mesh surface area in the scene and the Resolution setting (see Figure 2-32). The lightmaps themselves are added as texture assets in the Project panel (see Figure 2-33).

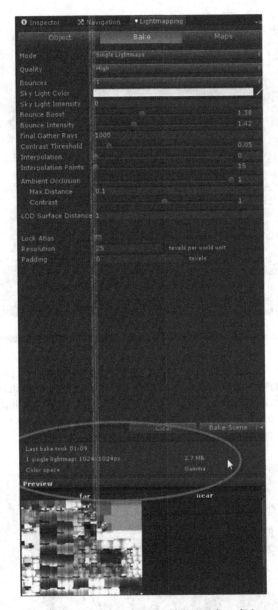

Figure 2-32. Information on the generated lightmaps displayed in the Lightmapping window

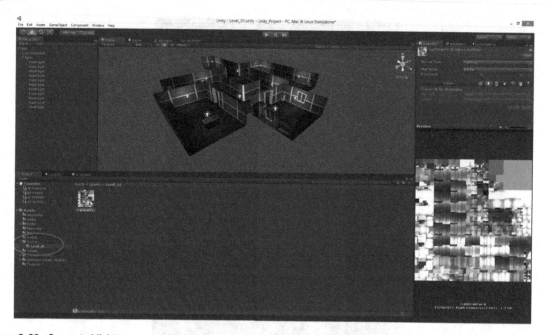

Figure 2-33. Generated lightmaps are added to the project like a regular texture and are accessible via the Project panel

Figure 2-34 shows you how the CMOD level looks after lightmapping. To prove the level is really lightmapped, you could delete all lights in the scene. If you did that, the illumination wouldn't change because the lighting is now being taken from the maps and not from the lights. However, be sure to undo any such deletion once you're done testing, as we'll need the lights for dynamic objects and if we ever need to rebake the lightmaps.

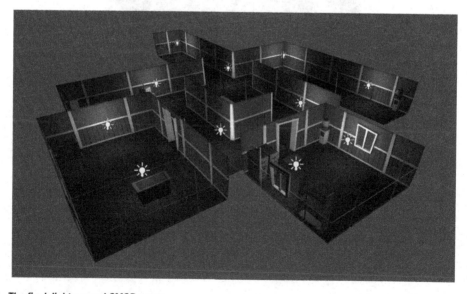

Figure 2-34. The final, lightmapped CMOD scene

> **Note**   More information on lightmapping in Unity can be found at the Unity online documentation at `http://docs.unity3d.com/Documentation/Manual/LightmappingInDepth.html`.

Step 11: Building a Navigation Mesh

Later in this book, we'll be creating three distinct Enemy characters to which we've been introduced already. These are the *Drone*, the *Tough Guy*, and *Mr. Big Cheese* To see these characters, check out Figures 1-2, 1-3, and 1-4 in Chapter 1. As mentioned, these enemies will be "intelligent." I use the word *intelligent* here in a narrow and precise sense. I mean the characters will not simply stand around the scene motionlessly doing "nothing," like props or inanimate objects. Instead, they'll move around and actively search for the Player. This process of "moving around" and "searching" for the Player involves intelligence.

The scene I've created for CMOD—assembled from environment pieces—consists of larger rooms connected by narrow and winding corridors, as shown in Figure 2-29. These corridors have twists and turns, and they also connect with one another to form junctions, points at which it's possible to travel in more than one direction. This kind of scene layout means that anytime an Enemy needs to move, it must make *reasoned decisions* about where it should go and how it should get there. The enemy shouldn't simply walk through walls and material objects. It's supposed to avoid these. This kind of obstacle avoidance is known as *navigation*. Further, the enemy should move in a determined and concerted way, travelling from one point to a clear destination elsewhere, as opposed to moving erratically backward and forward with no sense of direction at all. This kind of route planning is known as *pathfinding*. Both of these concepts are achieved in different ways in Unity, but perhaps the most common is through *navigation meshes*. The details of implementing navigation and pathfinding are considered in Chapter 7. However, in getting started with this project, and in generally building the scene, some preliminary steps must be taken here for pathfinding. Specifically, we'll build or *bake* a navigation mesh, much like we baked lighting through lightmaps. The navigation mesh will be used later in Chapter 7, when creating enemies.

> **Note**   Most navigation mesh features are included in the Unity free version, as of Unity 4.3. However, off-mesh links (for connecting multiple NavMeshes), are a Pro Only feature.

In Unity terminology, an enemy is an agent (or more fully a *NavMesh Agent*). A NavMesh Agent is simply any GameObject that must intelligently move around the scene when required. Whenever an agent is told to move toward a destination (any Vector3 location within the scene), it first needs to plan the most sensible route based on its current position, and then to follow that route while avoiding all tangible obstacles. To calculate this route and to follow it optimally, Unity relies on an internal and special asset, known as a *navigation mesh*. The navigation mesh is a special kind of mesh asset that Unity generates automatically. It's composed like a regular mesh, from vertices, edges, and faces, but it's not renderable, unlike most other meshes. The purpose of the navigation mesh is to approximate, in low-poly form, the *walkable* topology of the scene. Put simply: it represents the scene floor on which agents can walk. By isolating just the walkable regions of the scene in mesh form, Unity can quickly and more easily calculate valid routes to destinations and have agents navigate there with as little error as possible. In this section, we'll generate the navigation mesh for the scene. Chapter 7 will then make use of this mesh, as we build intelligent enemies.

To access the Navigation Mesh tools, select the main menu option **Window ➤ Navigation** (see Figure 2-35). For convenience, this dialog can be docked as a tab alongside the Object Inspector, allowing you to see the Scene and Game views alongside the Navigation tools.

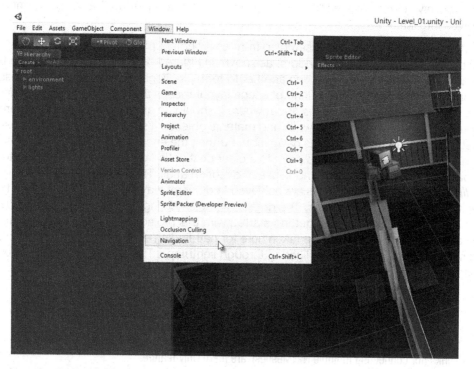

Figure 2-35. Accessing the Navigation tools

Before we can bake a navigation mesh, ensure all the environment pieces are marked as *Static*, and specifically as *Navigation Static* (see Figure 2-36). This marks the environment meshes as a nonmoveable and walkable region. Unity detects the walkable region as horizontally-aligned faces whose normals point upward in the Y direction, as opposed to vertically-aligned faces, such as walls and other obstacles.

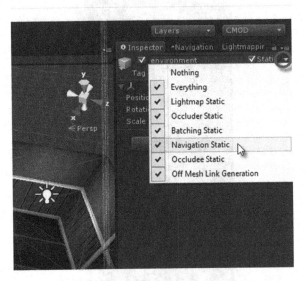

Figure 2-36. Only meshes marked as Navigation Static are factored into the navigation mesh

After all static architectural meshes are marked at least as Navigation Static, we can proceed to generate the Navigation Mesh asset. To do this, switch to the Navigation window (as shown in Figure 2-37, docked alongside the Object Inspector), and accept the default settings (for now), and then click the Bake button. For smaller scenes, like our CMOD scene, the Bake process should be fast—maybe even a second or less!

Figure 2-37. Navigation meshes are generated from scene geometry

Once generated, the navigation mesh (*NavMesh*) appears as a planar blue mesh in the viewport, on top of the scene floor. The NavMesh asset itself can also be found in the Project panel, alongside any generated lightmaps. Using the default settings from the Navigation window, the NavMesh will differ from scene to scene, depending on its layout and meshes. Consequently, if your scene arrangement is not exactly like mine or if your meshes are at a different scale, then your navigation mesh may differ considerably. Mine is shown in Figure 2-38. If you don't see a navigation mesh in the viewport, then be sure to enable the *Show NavMesh* option in the *NavMesh Display* dialog (also shown in Figure 2-38), which appears in the bottom-right corner of the Scene viewport whenever the Navigation window is active.

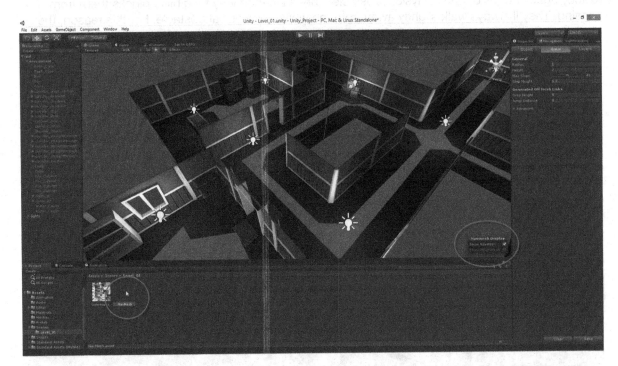

Figure 2-38. Previewing a navigation mesh in the viewport. These are the default Bake settings I'm using for CMOD. They'll be edited and tweaked further as the chapter progresses

The blue NavMesh on the floor represents the area inside which NavMesh Agents may walk and move whenever they travel using Pathfinding. NavMesh Agents generally don't walk outside the boundaries of a NavMesh; and thus the NavMesh marks the limits of where an agent may exist in the scene at any one time. Like my default NavMesh in Figure 2-38, your NavMesh may also exhibit a number of anomalies. These can be corrected by tweaking the Bake settings, as we'll see here. The following lists these anomalies along with their solutions.

- **NavMesh is too skinny and is cut apart!** The NavMesh generated in Figure 2-38 is highlighted in blue. From this, it's clear the mesh doesn't extend over all the walkable regions of the scene. For example, there are stretches of space on the floor between the walls and the NavMesh edges. The NavMesh appears as just a thin sliver of a mesh, snaking its way along the center of the floor without ever expanding outward to meet the walls. Furthermore, the mesh is not continuous but is broken apart inside the doorways, leaving gaps or holes in the mesh that cannot be bridged. NavMesh agents typically expect a single and continuous NavMesh inside which they may walk. There are exceptions to this rule, but these are not considered in this book.

This problem occurs because of the Radius setting in the Navigation window. *Radius* defines an imaginary circle that would entirely encompass a hypothetical agent, expected to walk on the mesh. Since agents are usually characters, they have both width and depth. Therefore, agents can't walk exactly against walls or other physical obstacles, because their very tangibility blocks them from passing. They'll always walk slightly away from the wall or a physical obstacle. For this reason, the Radius setting adds an extra unwalkable buffer of space between the NavMesh edge and a physical obstacle, such as the wall, to prevent clipping and errant collisions.

This also explains why there's breakage or disconnection in the NavMesh at doorways. This is because there's simply not enough room on the floor between either sides of the door to allow an agent to pass. This hints at the solution: to reduce the Radius setting. If your NavMesh seems too thin for your floor or is broken apart inside doorways, then try reducing the radius. For my scene, I've lowered the radius from 1 to 0.4. This still leaves appropriate space between the NavMesh and walls, but also allows travel through doorways. Take a look at Figure 2-39. Later in Chapter 7, when adding enemy agents, this value may need further revision.

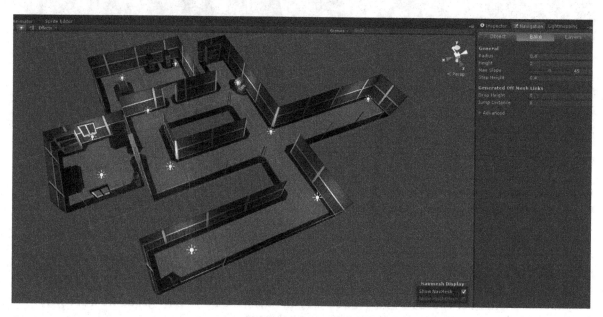

Figure 2-39. Decreasing NavMesh Radius to increase the walkable regions in the scene

- **NavMesh is offset upward above the floor.** The NavMesh is an approximation of the environment geometry in general, meaning there's room for inaccuracy. Sometimes your NavMesh will seem to hover above the true scene floor, rather than rest on it or close to it, as you might expect it to do (see Figure 2-40).

Figure 2-40. Generated NavMesh sometimes hovers above the true scene floor

In some cases, such as with terrains, this problem can be fixed by enabling the Height Mesh check box and then rebaking the NavMesh. But more often, it's solved by reducing the Height Inaccuracy setting, under the Advanced group in the Navigation window. Be sure to rebake the NavMesh on editing each setting. For my CMOD level, I reduced Height Inaccuracy from 15 to 1 (see Figure 2-41).

Figure 2-41. Adjusting height inaccuracy to position NavMesh onto the floor

Note   More information on navigation meshes can be found at the online Unity documentation at http://docs.unity3d.com/Documentation/Manual/NavmeshandPathfinding.html.

Conclusion

This chapter charted the beginning of *Crazy Mad Office Dude* in terms of project creation, asset importing and configuration, as well as scene building and general project management. The completed project so far can be found in the book companion files, inside the `Chapter2` folder. The scope of this chapter is vast, covering a range of powerful Unity features; features that together would occupy many chapters in an introductory book. In doing this, many subjects were necessarily discussed only briefly or parochially—that is, in ways specific to *this* project. The reason is because the *main* focus of this book is on *C# development* in Unity, as opposed to wider tasks such as lightmapping and navigation meshes.

Taken as a totality, this chapter documents everything you need to do and know for CMOD to take the project from an empty state to one that's prepped and ready for customization through C#. Of course, this general preparation process and workflow applies more widely and to potentially many more projects than CMOD. The principles put into practice here, such as the *modular building method* and *lightmapping*, can be abstracted from their particular context for CMOD and seen generally. But, the main point of this chapter is to show you a practical case study in Unity; one that begins from an empty project and moves toward a state where we're ready to start programming. At this point, we've now reached that state, and before moving onward, let's recap what we've learned here. By now, you should be able to do the following:

- Create Unity projects and import and configure assets, as well as understand the rationale behind specific importing and organization techniques

- Apply a C# FBX ScaleFix to imported meshes, automatically customizing their scale to 1

- Appreciate import considerations around mesh colliders and lightmap UVs

- Understand Texture Import settings and their relationship to Sprite assets

- Know how to use the Sprite Editor to create sprites from atlas textures

- Import and configure 2D audio files

- Understand the modular building method and the importance of Prefabs

- Generate usable lightmaps and work with Lightmap assets

- Understand the importance of Lightmap settings

- Generate navigation meshes

- Understand how to edit Generation settings to produce appropriate navigation meshes for your scenes

Chapter 3

Event Handling

Now we're ready to begin game coding in C#, and there's a lot to do. At this stage, you should have a prepped Unity project available, either a project you've created manually by following along with previous chapters or the ready-made project provided in the book companion files in the Chapter2 folder (as shown in Figure 3-1). This project represents CMOD so far and includes one scene file with a complete level, including meshes, prefabs, textures, lighting, and navigation. From this project, we'll begin in this chapter to add new behavior and functionality through C# scripting.

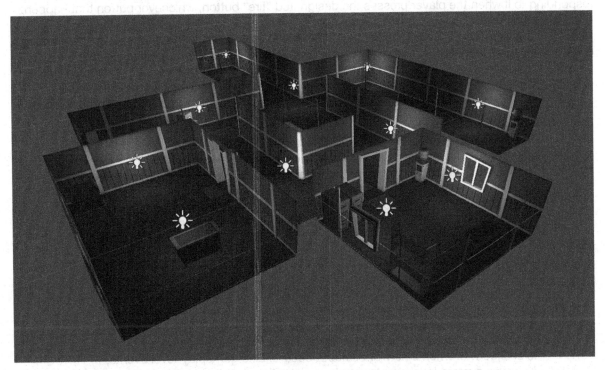

Figure 3-1. The completed project so far, which can be found in the book companion files in the Chapter2 folder. In this chapter, we'll start add C# script by coding an event-handling system

There are many ways to begin game coding and implementation. Some developers start by creating a GameManager class to handle the central game logic and rules, such as the win and loss conditions. Some instead focus on building critical game entities, such as the Player character and enemies. And others take alternative approaches. None of these approaches are *right* or *wrong* in any objective sense per se. They simply represent different and pragmatic approaches, which may be more or less suited to your specific needs or to your particular style. But regardless of which approach you take, it's certain that development has to begin somewhere. For my part, I typically begin by creating an event-handling system and I think that approach is serviceable here, for reasons I'll state shortly. First, let's consider events and event handling, and specifically how it more generally relates to a game.

Events and Responses

For game developers, game worlds are ultimately *deterministic* systems. This means that, once the game begins (the beginning of game time), everything else that follows does so *because* of a sequential flow of events. That is, everything that happens is a calculated *response* to a related and previous cause, which we may call an *event*. For example, enemies attack the player *when* he or she comes into their line of sight *because* there exists artificial intelligence (AI) functionality telling the enemies to act that way under those very conditions. Similarly, the Player character fires its weapons when it does, only because there exists an underlying mechanism watching for human input and for responding to it when the player presses the designated "fire" button, whichever button that happens to be. Seen in this way, a video game can be conceived as an integrated system of events and responses. Specifically, an event happens and something else happens in response. And this process goes on each and every frame, until the game is terminated in some way—hopefully by the player pressing Quit as opposed to the game's crashing from a bug! Among these events, two main kinds can be identified: *gameplay-level events* and *system-level events*. These two terms are not part of an industry standard vocabulary so much as terms I'm inventing here for convenience and description.

- **Gameplay-level events.** These describe all events, which even a reflective and thoughtful gamer might identify themselves during gameplay, as being events in the game world. These include events such as *when the player presses a lever on the wall*—perhaps to unlock a door or open a secret passageway, or *when an enemy is killed*, or *when the player enters a room or region in the level*, or *when all power-ups have been collected*. The total number of possible events belonging to this group is potentially infinite, but all of them happen *in the game world*. They are an integral part of the "fiction."

- **System-level events.** These events are in a fundamental sense hidden from the gamer and exist outside the game world. These are the events that only the game developer knows about and include all core events, which are part of the underlying game mechanics. They pertain to the foundational wheels and cogs of the game. Such events include *when the player saves and loads her game*, *when an error occurs*, *when the game is paused*, *when the system resolution is changed*, or *when a network timeout occurs*. Like gameplay-level events, however, system-level events may be a potentially infinite in number. They may not, of course, be infinite in practice because computers have a maximum capacity. But they are potentially infinite in that there's no obvious limit to the number of events you could invent or think about.

The core ingredient uniting all events, however, whether gameplay or system level, is that they *may* invoke a response, although sometimes no response need actually occur. In other words, *when an event happens* (and they usually happen very often) the game may *need to do something else* (which is usually very often, too). That "something else" could be small and relatively inconsequential, or it could be mammoth and potentially game-changing. In principle, there's really no limit to the number of responses that follow from an event, or to the significance of those responses. In fact, when you think about it further, there really are only events, because every response or reaction to an event could potentially be an event itself for further action, and so on. But essentially, the important point to take away from all of this is that events and responses are all-pervasive in games. They're everywhere and there's no avoiding them. There are only different ways of handling and working with them. Those methods and ways can indeed differ quite significantly, but all of them rest on the same core concepts.

Event Handling

Games, as we've seen, can be conceived as a chain of events and responses. Event handling is the practice of *working* with and *managing* those events and responses in-game. Thus, event handling is something we must engineer and build into a game. It's not something that exists ready-made for us, even with Unity. In this chapter, we'll be using C# to engineer such a system. However, the question arises as to why we should begin game development here, as opposed to elsewhere. After all, if there are different ways to begin development, and none of them necessarily right or wrong, then it surely cannot be wrong to begin elsewhere. And this is true. But nonetheless there are *compelling* reasons to begin here. These are as follows:

- **Events are foundational.** Events are everywhere in games. Whenever an underlying action or function in code has the potential to effect something else in-game, then in practice an event is happening, even if you don't always see it that way at the time. And every time you think it'd be useful for some process to detect and respond to a situation happening elsewhere, you've just thought about an event-and-response scenario. Events are thus so foundational to games that it's almost impossible to create any functionality or classes or behavior without referring to them or using them. Consequently, since the practice of making games is essentially an exercise in engineering and building, it's good practice to begin with foundations. It's good practice to make those foundations strong so they may sustain the complexities of the structure above.

- **Events are abstract.** This means that events are relevant to almost every kind of game. And something important and powerful comes from this; namely, events are *not* design-restrictive. That is, being so general and widely applicable, events themselves never place constraints or limitations on how you should implement or make the rest of your game. Events, for example, never say that enemies cannot have range or magical attacks. They never require you to keep the vehicles in your game to only ground-based ones, as opposed to airborne or seaborne ones. Events as a concept really don't care about these specifics or particular instances. They have a more general and abstract nature that frees them from specifics. And so in practice this frequently means that if you create events from the outset, you don't put any technical or logistical restrictions on the kinds of things you may have elsewhere in the game. Thus, coding events empower you and never limit you. There's no good reason to narrow your horizons before it's necessary to do so.

Planning Event Handling

Before jumping into coding an event-handling system, or any functionality for that matter, it's a good idea to plan and think ahead. This *reduces* our chances of making mistakes and wasting time. Of course, it doesn't eradicate our chances entirely! In this chapter, we'll code a *dedicated* event-handling class, and there are strong reasons for doing this. Rather than list them, let's see what they are *in practice*. Specifically, let's consider some "simpler" and alternative ways of handling events, and examine the attendant problems or limitations associated with them.

Perhaps the simplest method to event handling is to forget about creating a dedicated class altogether, and to code event-handler functionality directly into all the classes that need it. For example, let's imagine we need to detect an event, such as when Player health falls to 0 or below, so we can kill the Player and display a "Game Over" message. The event is *when Player health falls to 0 or below*, and the response is *die and show "Game Over"*. This kind of functionality could be coded into the Player class, as shown in Listing 3-1.

Listing 3-1. Player Class Detecting Death Events

```
using UnityEngine;
using System;

//Player class
public class Player: MonoBehaviour
{
        //[...] Other stuff declared here

        //Health variable
        public int Health = 100;

        //[...] Other functions would be included here

        //Update function called on each frame
        void Update()
        {
                //Check player health
                If(Health <= 0)
                        Die(); //Is <= 0, then run death functionality
        }
}
```

> **Note**   The class coded in Listing 3-1, and in subsequent parts of this section, is hypothetical only. That is, it's an imaginary class used merely to demonstrate a point. It's not necessary to code this class yourself or to include it in the final CMOD project.

This code will *work* in the sense that it'll always detect when the Player's health falls to 0 or below, and then initiates the appropriate death behavior as a response. However, the code is really not efficient because it executes many more times than necessary. Specifically, on *each and every frame* (which could be over 100 times *per second*) the code *always* checks Player health, even if the health has never changed since the last frame. The solution to this problem initially is simply to arrange our code more effectively. On closer inspection, we see that the only time it's truly necessary to evaluate Player health is when it changes, either when it increases or decreases; a *health change event*. At no other time would it be necessary to check Player health, because we'd know that, without any changes, it'd always be the same as when we last evaluated it.

So how could we recode this hypothetical Player class to support the proposed repair? One way is to use *accessor methods* or *C# properties*. These are special kinds of functions that provide controlled, public access to private variables or members of the class. It is a specific kind of variable-function pairing in which the only way to set or read the variable is through its property function, or accessor method. This means that every time the property function is called to set the value for a private variable, we get the opportunity to execute behavior, including event functionality and data validation. This is shown in action in Listing 3-2.

Listing 3-2. Using C# Properties to Detect Health Change Events

```csharp
using UnityEngine;
using System.Collections;

public class Player : MonoBehaviour
{
        //Properties to access and validate variable
        public int Health
        {
                //If reading variable then return health
                get{return iHealth;}

                //Chang health value, now validate
                set
                {
                        //Update health
                        iHealth = value;

                        //Check if player should die
                        if(iHealth <= 0)
                                Die();
                }
        }

        //Private health variable
        private int iHealth = 100;

        public void Die()
        {
                //Handle Die Code Here
        }
}
```

> **Note** The disadvantage to using C# properties in Unity, as opposed to using directly accessible public variables, is their lack of visibility in the Object Inspector. In short, C# properties are always hidden to the Object Inspector and so cannot be changed from the Editor. You can only access them from code.

This code is much better. It lacks an Update function and no longer wastes precious time executing health validation code unnecessarily on every frame. Health validation has instead been shifted from Update to the Set aspect of the Health property, which is executed *only* when the Health value is changed. The Set function will be executed for every assignment to the Health variable (see Listing 3-3).

Listing 3-3. Setting Player Health: This Code Will Execute the Set Function for the C# Health Property

```
PlayerInstance.Health = 0;
```

This refined Player class is fine and functional insofar as it goes, but perhaps it doesn't go quite far enough. Though this code is better at detecting and responding to health change events than its previous incarnation, there's still a logistical problem we simply can't get around if we just go on restricting our refinements to the Player class alone. Specifically, what should we do if a different class (not the Player) needs to detect and respond to Player health changes? For example, a hypothetical GameManager class might need to know that when Player health reaches close to 0, it needs to play a warning and alert sound. We could, of course, fix this in a specific and ad hoc way by adding some extra code to the Player Health(Set) function, which notifies a separate GameManager class about the health change event. This update might look like Listing 3-4.

Listing 3-4. Adapting the Player Class Health Change Event to Notify a Game Manager Class

```
using UnityEngine;
using System.Collections;

public class Player : MonoBehaviour
{
        //Properties to access and validate variable
        public int Health
        {
                //If reading variable then return health
                get{return iHealth;}

                //Chang health value, now validate
                set
                {
                        //Update health
                        iHealth = value;

                        //Check if player should die
                        if(iHealth <= 0)
                                Die();
```

```
                //Update Game Manager about health change event
                GameManager.OnPlayerHealthChange();
        }
    }

    //Private health variable
    private int iHealth = 100;

    public void Die()
    {
            //Handle Die Code Here
    }
}
```

This solution, however, is not robust. After all, if even more classes (beyond the GameManager) needed to know about and respond to Player health change events, then we'd have to return to the Player source code (as we did earlier) and edit the Health(Set) function to call even more functions, propagating the health change event on an *individual, per-class* basis. Unfortunately, this problem is part of a larger and more general one that's in no way restricted to player health change events. The problem of broadcasting events to objects applies to *all* kinds of objects and *all* kinds of events. For every kind of event, there could be potentially many objects in need of notification, not just the object that triggered the event or that was first notified. It is, of course, possible to solve the problem for each event in a very specific and ad hoc way, as we've done here with the hypothetical GameManager class. But in games that handle many events, this would needlessly increase the complexity of our source code to unmanageable extents. It's easy for event handling to "get out of hand" unless we take a more disciplined and streamlined approach. This is exactly what we'll do next.

Planning a Dedicated Event-Handling System

The previous section justified the general desirability for taking a more focused and streamlined approach toward events and event handling in games. In this section, we'll establish the beginnings of a dedicated and centralized C# event-handling class, which I'll name the *NotificationsManager*. I'll create the code for this class inside the script file NotificationsManager.cs. In general, a game or scene should have only *one* active instance of this class in memory, and *no more* than one. This kind of object is known as a Singleton object, a concept considered further in the next chapter. In short, the NotificationsManager will be singularly responsible for broadcasting *all* events to *all* other objects that *must* know about those events. In other words, its duty will be to *notify* every object in the game about every event it must handle, as and when the event happens. In essence, the NotificationsManager will work as follows (also see Figure 3-2).

Figure 3-2. NotificationsManager workflow

1. An event happens during gameplay and is detected immediately by a class, such as when the Player class adjusts player health through a C# property. The object that *causes* or *detects* an event is known as the *Poster*. Once the event occurs, the Poster proceeds to *post a notification* about it to the NotificationsManager object. The notification sent to the Manager by the Poster is essentially a data structure containing event-specific information, such as the *event type*. Event types may include OnPlayerHealthChange, OnLevelCompleted, OnEnemyDestroyed, and others. The types themselves will vary from game to game, depending on the events you need.

2. Any objects that must be notified about the occurrence of specific event types, such as OnPlayerHealthChange, should register themselves as Listeners with the NotificationsManager class. By registering itself as a Listener for a specific event type, the class is effectively asking the NotificationsManager to tell it about all matching event occurrences, as and when they happen.

3. Based on this, the NotificationsManager can perform its work effectively. Specifically, on receiving an event notification from a Poster, the NotificationsManager immediately notifies all registered Listeners for that event. In this way, every Listener is always immediately notified about every relevant event, and can respond as appropriate.

> **Note** The NotificationsManager developed will be based loosely on the well-known, third-party class `NotificationsCenter`, available online for free from the Unity Community web site at `http://wiki.unity3d.com/index.php?title=CSharpNotificationCenter`.
>
> However, although NotificationsManager will be based on `NotificationsCenter`, it will take a slightly different approach, as well as implement additional functionality. It's worth mentioning, too, that you *don't* need to be familiar with the `NotificationsCenter` to implement the NotificationsManager here. We'll explore NotificationsManager creation from the very beginning.

There are two significant and distinct advantages to this event-handling system:

- **It is centralized.** There should be one and just one instance of NoticationsManager in memory at any time, and this instance carries the entire responsibility for event handling between objects. Its dedicated purpose is to broadcast all event notifications to all appropriate objects. Thus, through centralization—by assigning the workload of event handling to a single class in this way—we achieve two important benefits. First, we improve debugging simplicity because, if there's ever a problem with event-handling, we immediately know where in our code to start our bug search: specifically inside the NoticationsManager class. And second, we simplify all other classes and objects because none of them need concern themselves with event handling anymore, now that we have a NoticationsManager to do that work for us.

- **It is abstract and recyclable.** The NotificationsManager distills the concepts of events and event handling into a single class in both a general and abstract way that makes no specific demands or requirements upon other classes. In short, it doesn't tell other classes how they should be implemented—their implementation is separate and independent from the NotificationsManager. This means the NotificationsManager can be used *not just* for event-handling in CMOD specifically, but more widely in practically any kind of game. It means, in theory, we can import `NotificationsManager.cs` into any other Unity project and use it straightaway to manage events, without making any code changes. That, in itself, saves us lots of work and time!

Getting Started with NotificationsManager

Let's now put our NotificationsManager plan into practice inside Unity. To create this class, we'll need to start by creating a new C# source file. I'll explain how to do that here in case you need a refresher, but for subsequent classes created throughout the rest of the book, I'll assume you already know how to do it. To create a new C# source file, right-click the `Scripts` folder of the Project panel, and select **Create ➤ C# Script** from the context menu (as shown in Figure 3-3). Alternatively, you can select **Assets ➤ Create ➤ C# Script** from the application menu. Be sure to name the file `NotificationsManager.cs`.

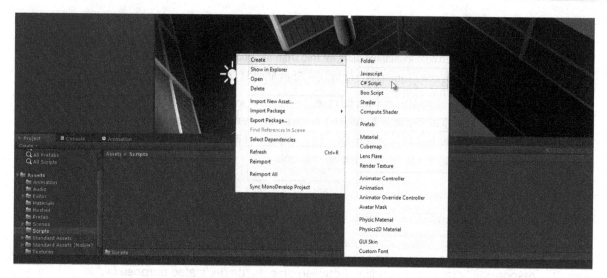

Figure 3-3. Creating a new C# script file for the NotificationsManager class

Double-click the NotificationsManager.cs file inside the Project panel to open it for editing in MonoDevelop (as shown in Figure 3-4), a separate and third-party IDE that ships with Unity. You may also use your own code editors if you'd prefer, such as Visual Studio, Notepad++ (http://notepad-plus-plus.org/), or any other text editor. To compile the code, you only need to save the file in the editor, and then return to the Unity Editor window. Unity detects the code changes in the file and compiles the code automatically. While the code is compiling, Unity displays a spinning Busy icon in the lower-right section of the application toolbar.

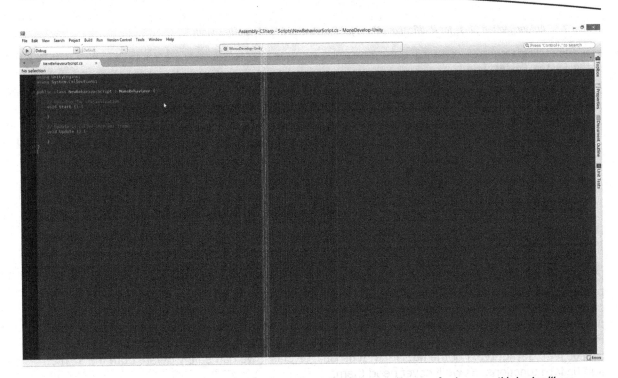

Figure 3-4. *Editing code inside MonoDevelop. You can use other code editors, too, if you prefer; however, this book will use MonoDevelop*

If any compile-time errors are encountered, these are listed in the Editor Console window, which can be shown by selecting **Window ➤ Console** from the application main menu, as shown in Figure 3-5.

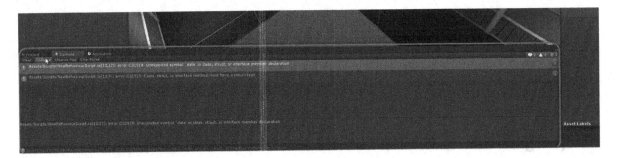

Figure 3-5. *Compile-time errors are printed inside the Console window*

By default, all newly created C# classes in Unity are descended from class MonoBehaviour, which is part of the Unity API. See Listing 3-5 to see the autogenerated code. In essence, MonoBehaviour represents the base class from which all components are ultimately derived. For the NotificationsManager, and indeed for many classes, MonoBehaviour is an entirely suitable default class from which to derive, and so can be left as-is. In some cases, however, as we'll see later, we'll need to change the super-class to a different type.

Listing 3-5. Autogenerated Class for NotificationsManager, Descended from MonoBehaviour

```
using UnityEngine;
using System.Collections;

public class NotificationsManager : MonoBehaviour
{
        // Use this for initialization
        void Start () {

        }

        // Update is called once per frame
        void Update () {

        }
}
```

In addition to being descended from MonoBehaviour, all newly generated classes come with predeclared Start and Update functions. The Start function is called automatically once at object creation (after the Awake function), and the Update function is called automatically once per frame, *provided* the GameObject is active—that is, provided the object has its *active* member set to true. By default, all GameObjects are active unless they are explicitly deactivated with a call to GameObject.SetActive. For the NotificationsManager class, we can safely delete both the Start and Update functions, as we'll never need them.

> **Tip**   If your class never needs or uses a function, such as Start and Update, then remove them from the class. This makes your code neater generally, and there are even marginal performance improvements to be gained.

> **Note**   More information on MonoBehaviour can be found at the online Unity documentation at http://docs.unity3d.com/Documentation/ScriptReference/MonoBehaviour.html.

Keeping Track of Notifications with .NET Dictionaries

Thinking carefully about the NotificationsManager class we know that (a) Posters must tell the NotificationsManager when an event occurs, and (b) when told about an event, the NotificationsManager should notify all registered Listeners *for that event*. This entails that the Notifications Manager must internally maintain a list of all listeners that should be notified for an event when it happens. These listeners should be organized into lists by *event type*. That is, for any event type (such as OnPlayerHealthChange) *there could be none, one, or more listeners*. Regardless, however many or however few objects are listening for an event, it's the responsibility of the NotificationsManager to notify them all whenever that event happens. And so ultimately our class has two main technical requirements: we must maintain a list of *events*, and for each type we must maintain a list of associated *listeners*.

There are several ways such a configuration could be implemented into a C# class. One way would be to use a two-dimensional array: one dimension for the events and another for the listeners. Listing 3-6 shows you how this could work in practice by using a two-dimensional array of strings.

Listing 3-6. Using a Two-Dimensional Array to Manage Events and Listeners

```
using UnityEngine;
using System.Collections;

public class NotificationsManager : MonoBehaviour
{
        //Creates an array for 2 Event Types, each allowed a total of 2 listeners (Identified by
GameObject Name)
        string[,] Listeners = new string[2,2];

        //Function to notify listeners for a matching event (specified by integer ID)
        void NotifyListeners(int EventThatHappened)
        {
                //Loop through listeners
                for(int i=0; i<2; i++)
                {
                        //Get listener GameObject in scene based on name
                        GameObject Listener = GameObject.Find(Listeners[EventThatHappened,i]);

                        //Notify listener here. Call function.
                }
        }
}
```

The chief problem with this approach is its "static" and inflexible nature, which can be found in the declaration line for the two-dimensional array. There, the maximum array size was specified and *fixed at declaration time* to a size of (2, 2), which allows for a total of two events and two listeners. Now, this wouldn't be troublesome if we knew in advance that we only needed exactly two events and two listeners for each type; but typically, we don't have such foreknowledge. Typically, we need flexibility. We need to keep track of any number of events and any number of listeners for each type. If we stick with fixed-size arrays, we'll usually end up with either more elements than we need, or fewer.

Instead, we'll want an array that sizes itself at runtime to exactly what we need, no more and no less. Plus, we'll want that array to dynamically change its size, too—to shrink if we remove events and listeners, and to grow if we add them. This kind of array in which we can add and remove items at runtime is called a *dynamic array*, because its size can change to accommodate exactly the number of items being held at any one time. The disadvantage of dynamic arrays compared to the "conventional" static arrays pertains to performance. Specifically, dynamic arrays are more computationally expensive than static ones, as they typically have "more to do" at runtime, such as changing size. For this reason, it's recommend to always use *static* arrays when dealing with array-like data whose size and quantity *are known in advance*. But often, we'll need to use dynamic arrays just as we do here, because we can't avoid them effectively.

Dynamic arrays take various forms and implementations, being optimized for different purposes. One famous implementation is called a *linked list*, which is simply a linear list of items that grows and shrinks as and when items are added and removed, respectively. For the NotificationsManager, and for keeping track of events and notifications, we'll use a linked list, plus a hash table–like list, known as a *Dictionary*. The Dictionary is a special dynamic-array class and is not part of the Unity API specifically, but a part of the Microsoft .NET Framework. Unity allows us to make use of these .NET classes through a cross-platform implementation known as Mono (www.mono-project.com/Main_Page). This framework is used by Unity "under the hood." The Dictionary class works like a *key-value* database. Take a look at Figure 3-6 to see how it relates to the NotificationsManager class.

KEY (Event Type)	VALUE (Listeners)
OnHealthChange	[...] = {Obj1, Obj2...}
OnLevelStart	[...] = {Obj3, Obj5...}
OnEnemyDestroyed	[...] = {Obj1, Obj4...}
OnLevelEnd	[...] = {Obj1, Obj4...}
OnNetworkTimeOut	[...] = {Obj3, Obj5...}
OnAmmoCollected	[...] = {Obj1, Obj4...}
OnHealthRestore	[...] = {Obj1, Obj2...}
OnRespawn	[...] = {Obj3, Obj5...}
OnGameSaved	[...] = {Obj3, Obj5...}
OnGameLoaded	[...] = {Obj1, Obj2...}
OnCriticalError	[...] = {Obj3, Obj5...}
OnSettingsChanged	[...] = {Obj1, Obj4...}

Figure 3-6. Example structure of a Dictionary for the NotificationsManager class. Lists of Listeners are organized and searchable by Event Type

A great feature of the Dictionary is its searchable nature. Not only can you keep complete lists of listeners organized by event type, but you can throw an event type at the Dictionary and have it give you back the complete list of associated listeners, as we'll see. Let's start by declaring a Dictionary for storing events and listeners (see Listing 3-7).

Listing 3-7. Adding a Dictionary of Listeners to the NotificationsManager

```
01 using UnityEngine;
02 using System.Collections;
03 using System.Collections.Generic;
04
05 public class NotificationsManager: MonoBehaviour
06 {
07        //Internal reference to all listeners for notifications
08        private Dictionary<string, List<Component>> Listeners = new Dictionary<string,
          List<Component>>();
09 }
```

> **Note**   To use the `Dictionary` class, as well as the `List` class, we must include the `System.Collections.Generic` namespace (see line 03).
>
> More information on the `Dictionary` class can be found online at `http://msdn.microsoft.com/en-us/library/xfhwa508%28v=vs.110%29.aspx`.
>
> Information on the `List` class can be found at `http://msdn.microsoft.com/en-us/library/6sh2ey19%28v=vs.110%29.aspx`.

The declaration itself occurs at *line 08* and makes use of `Generic` (or `Template`) classes (further considered in the next section). In essence, this line creates a Dictionary of events and listeners. The key values (*event types*) are specified as string elements—representing human-readable names of events we'll use (such as `OnHealthChange`), and the listeners themselves are specified as a *list* of *components*, using the .NET `List` class. All components associated with an event will be notified when the event happens through function calls.

Generic Classes and C#

In the previous section, we added a two-dimensional dynamic array member to the NotificationsManager to act as an organized and searchable collection of `Event` and `Listener` objects. This was implemented on line 08 of Listing 3-7, using the `Dictionary` and `List` classes from the .NET Framework. In declaring both these classes in just one line, we relied on the concept of `Generic` (or `Template`) classes. Let's discuss these further here for clarity.

If you go online and examine the Microsoft documentation for the `List` class at `http://msdn.microsoft.com/en-us/library/6sh2ey19%28v=vs.110%29.aspx`, you'll see from the title section that List is written as `List<T>`. Notice the `<T>` post-fix in that title. What does that mean?

In short, the post-fix `<T>`, when applied to a class, means the class is *not* strictly typed, and instead uses *Generics,* which are a loose, stand-in data type that mean whatever you want them to mean. It means the `List` class is not restricted to being a list of *integers*, or a list of *strings*, or a list of *chars*, or a list of *components*. It can be *any* of these if you want it to be, as well as any other data type you may want it to be. Consequently, a list of integers can be made with

```
List<int> MyIntegers = new List<int>();
```

And a list of strings with

```
List<string> MyStrings = new List<string>();
```

And a list of components with

```
List<Component> MyStrings = new List< Component>();
```

This means that the first element in the list, at List[0], will be an integer for integer lists, a string for string lists, and so on. This powerful data-type versatility that comes from using Generics is not just restricted to the .NET List class or to the .NET Framework itself. It is a C# language feature. The Dictionary class also uses Generics. Let's look at line 08 from Listing 3-7 again.

```
private Dictionary<string, List<Component>> Listeners = new Dictionary<string, List<Component>>();
```

The Dictionary has two "dimensions," based on key-value pairs: `Dictionary<TKey, TValue>`. For the NotificationsManager, I've set the first dimension to be a list of *strings* (for Event Type names), and the second as `List<Component>` (for Listener objects). MonoBehaviour derived components ultimately descend from type `Component`. I could, of course, have chosen different data types if I'd wanted, since the `Dictionary` class uses Generics. However, these two types, `strings` and `List<Component>`, will suit our needs, as later sections will show. By using these two types, we can access *all* listeners as a list for any event of name *N*, with the following code:

```
//N is an event name: such as "OnHealthChange" or "OnLevelComplete"
List MyListenersList = Listeners[N];
```

Registering As a Listener

So the NotificationsManager now has a private Dictionary member, which makes use of *Generic types*, and this allows us to maintain a searchable list of potential listeners for events, and the size of the list can grow and shrink over time. Each listener in the list is specified as being of type `Component`, but thanks to class inheritance and polymorphism, it can really be of *any* type *descended from* `Component`, including MonoBehaviour. For more information on polymorphism, see Chapter 10. In essence, this means our list of listeners can be a wide mix of different types. In this section, we'll add functionality to the NotificationsManager that lets us *add* a new Listener to the list. If an object expects to be notified about any event, then it must previously have registered itself as a Listener with the NotificationsManager. When an object registers itself as a Listener, it's effectively saying, "Hey, NotificationsManager. I want you to tell me about every occurrence of event X, as and when it happens!" To achieve this functionality, a new public method `AddListener` can be added to the NotificationsManager (see Listing 3-8).

Listing 3-8. Adding Listeners to the NotificationsManager

```
01 //Function to add a listener for an notification to the listeners list
02 public void AddListener(Component Listener string NotificationName)
03 {
04       //Add listener to dictionary
05       if(!Listeners.ContainsKey(NotificationName))
06             Listeners.Add (NotificationName, new List<Component>());
07
08       //Add object to listener list for this notification
09       Listeners[NotificationName].Add(Listener);
10 }
```

The `AddListener` method accepts two arguments: namely, `Sender` and `NotificationName`. The `Sender` is a `Component` reference to the object that should become the registered listener. This is the object that must be notified by the NotificationsManager, if and when the event occurs. `NotificationName` is a string indicating the custom event type for which the `Sender` is listening. This is a user-defined string naming the events for our game.

This method is short but powerful. It can be broken into two main stages.

1. **Lines 04–06.** First, the function searches through all key values (event types) in the Dictionary, if there are any. The argument NotificationName specifies the specific event for which to listen for this Listener, and line 05 calls the method Dictionary.ContainsKey to see if this event type already has an entry in the Dictionary. It *will* have an entry *if* there's been a previous call to NotificationsManager.AddListener, listening for the *same* event. Otherwise, an entry for the event will not be present. *If there's no existing entry* (no matching key) for the event in the Dictionary (line 06), then a new entry is created using the Listeners.Add method, and a new Listener list is instantiated (the value), which will hold *all* listeners for this event.

2. **Line 09.** If *there is* an existing entry (a matching key) in the Dictionary for the event, then there will also be a valid and associated Value object. That is, a List<Component> object, representing the complete list of listeners for this event. If such a list exists, we don't need to create a new one—we simply need to *add* the argument Sender to the end of the existing list, as it becomes an additional listener for the event.

> **Note** Lines 05 and 06 of Listing 3-8 check the Dictionary for a valid entry, and then retrieves the value of that entry. However, you can also achieve this same process in just one call using the TryGetValue method (see http://msdn.microsoft.com/en-us/library/bb347013%28v=vs.110%29.aspx).

So, how would a potential Listener object use the AddListener function in practice to register itself as a Listener for an event with the NotificationsManager? In essence, any script derived from Component or MonoBehaviour would register itself, as shown in Listing 3-9. Later code samples in this chapter, and in the book, will demonstrate in more depth how to work with the NotificationsManager. We'll be seeing this class in action a lot!

Listing 3-9. Sample Class Registering Itself As a Listener for Event Notifications

```
01 using UnityEngine;
02 using System.Collections;
03
04 public class MyCustomClass : MonoBehaviour
05 {
06          //Assign this object an instance of the NotificationsManager
07          public NotificationsManager NM = null;
08
09          void Start()
10          {
11                  //Add me as a listener for a Custom Event
12                  NM.AddListener(this, "EventToListenFor");
13          }
14
```

```
15        //Function name should match event name
16        //Function will be called by the NotificationsManager for every event occurence
17        void EventToListenFor()
18        {
19              //Enters here when event happens
20        }
21 }
```

The hypothetical class MyCustomClass *demonstrates* how a GameObject might interact with an instance of the NotificationsManager. It uses the Start function to register with the NotificationsManager as a Listener for a custom event (note: a class only needs to register for an event once). And it also implements an additional method whose name matches the event to listen for. This event will be called automatically by the NotificationsManager every time the event occurs—this calling behavior is still added to NotificationsManager. See the next section!

Posting Notifications

The *reason* an object registers itself as a listener for an event in the first place is to *receive* notifications when the event actually happens. So far, however, the NotificationsManager only implements the AddListener function, which just builds a list of listeners. The class doesn't (yet) notify those listeners when events happen. This posting behavior should be implemented now, through the NotificationsManager.PostNotification method. This method should be called by any and all classes that *cause* or *detect* events. Effectively, these classes say "Ah ha! An event has happened. I detected it. So now, I'll tell the NotificationsManager. He'll know what to do. He'll pass on this notification to all registered listeners for this event." Take a look at Listing 3-10.

Listing 3-10. Posting Notifications to the NotificationsManager

```
01 //Function to post a notification to a listener
02 public void PostNotification(ComponentListener, string NotificationName)
03 {
04      //If no key in dictionary exists, then exit
05      if(!Listeners.ContainsKey(NotificationName))
06                  return;
07
08      //Else post notification to all matching listeners
09      foreach(Component Listener in Listeners[NotificationName])
10              Listener.SendMessage(NotificationName, Listener,
                    SendMessageOptions.DontRequireReceiver);
11 }
```

This is where the "magic" really happens for this class. The following points break it down.

1. **Line 02.** The PostNotification function accepts two arguments: Sender and NotificationName. The Sender argument refers to the component or object that first detected or caused the event, and that notifies the NotificationsManager. In other words, this argument will be a reference to the object that invokes or calls the NotificationsManager.PosNotification method. The NotificationsName argument is a user-defined string indicating the event that occurred.

2. **Lines 05 and 06.** Here, `PostNotification` searches the Listener Dictionary keys for a matching event to see whether there are *any* listeners registered for this event. If there's no matching key (event) in the dictionary, then this event has no registered listeners. Therefore, `PostNotification` can exit immediately, as there's nothing further to do.

3. **Lines 08–10.** `PostNotification` uses a C# ForEach loop to iterate through all registered listeners for this event. Notice that the event element in the Dictionary is accessed using the standard C# array syntax: `Listeners[NotificationName]`. For each registered listener, the `SendMessage` function is called to notify the object of the event occurrence. This is the crucial line, notifying an object of an event. The `SendMessage` function is inherited from the `Component` object and is a part of the Unity API. It's an important method because it allows you to call any function on an active object through its Component interface, simply by referring to the function name as a string argument. You don't need to know about the function's return type or even its argument list. You just need to know the function's name, and Unity does the rest to make the function call possible. The next section considers `SendMessage` in more detail.

SendMessage and BroadcastMessage

When working in Unity, and with the *component-based paradigm*, (or with *entity-based programming*, as it's sometimes called), the chances are high that'll you be creating a lot of C# script files and adding them to your game objects as components. The components you create, which are classes, will be your own custom types, typically derived from `MonoBehaviour`, or from other descendent classes. As such, your classes will support a range of different variables and functions to define their own behavior, making each class specific and unique. This is to be expected. However, this raises a problem in C#, which is a strictly typed language. Specifically, there are often times when you'll want to work with many game objects together, invoking functions and behavior on their components without having to know or worry about their specific data type and interface. For example, due to a destructive explosion event in your game, you may want to destroy a batch of different but nearby objects clustered together in the scene, such as enemies, power-ups, props, and maybe even scenery parts.

Before destroying the objects, however, it'd be useful to call a function or event on them all, notifying them about their impending doom, so each has the opportunity to respond appropriately. Maybe some objects play a destruction sound, while others flash red. In these cases, you'll want to call a function on *all* the objects, but *without* having to know anything specific about their component classes or data types. You simply want to invoke a function in all components across multiple objects, whatever their data type and interface may be. The `SendMessage` and `BroadcastMessage` functions both allow you to do this in different ways.

> **Note**   Both the SendMessage and the BroadcastMessage functions are useful, but can cause performance overhead when used extensively in frame-based functions, such as Update. For this reason, use them judiciously and in a way that works well with your game. If you find their use to be generally too costly for your game, then consider implementing an event system using C# interfaces. This subject will be explored in brief in the final chapter.

- **SendMessage.** When you want to run a function of a specified name on *all* components of a *single* GameObject, then you'll need the SendMessage function. The declaration for this function is given as follows (also see the Unity online documentation at http://docs.unity3d.com/Documentation/ScriptReference/ Component.SendMessage.html):

  ```
  void SendMessage(string methodName, SendMessageOptions options);
  ```

- An example of its use is as follows:

  ```
  MyGameObject.SendMessage("Myfunction", SendMessageOptions. DontRequireReceiver);
  ```

- This function accepts two arguments: MethodName and Options. MethodName refers to the function name to execute on *all* components of the specified game object. The Options argument simply specifies what should happen if a component is encountered that has no function with a matching name to execute. Options can be either DontRequireReceiver or RequireReceiver. DontRequireReceiver means that if a component is found with no matching function to execute, then that component is simply ignored. RequireReceiver means that if no function is found, an exception or error will be invoked automatically by Unity and will be printed to the console.

- **BroadcastMessage.** Usually, SendMessage is all you need to invoke generic behavior on a GameObject without knowing the implementation specifics and interfaces of its components. But sometimes, you'll need more than this. Specifically, you'll occasionally want to invoke functions and behavior on all components across *multiple* GameObjects, and not just one object. If you need multiple objects to simultaneously hide, show, die, move, explode, change color, or do something else, then BroadcastMessage is your friend. With BroadcastMessage, you simply send a message (invoke) a function on the components of a single GameObject (as with SendMessage), but BroadcastMessage will proceed to cascade that invocation downward to all child GameObjects automatically in the scene hierarchy (see Figure 3-7).

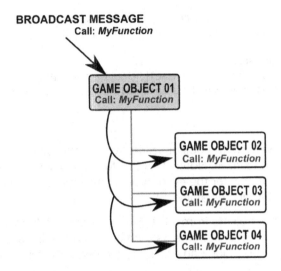

Figure 3-7. BroadcastMessage works like SendMessage, except it cascades function calls downward through the GameObject hierarchy, rather than applying to only one GameObject

Note   If, after reading this section, you still don't feel comfortable or familiar using SendMessage and BroadcastMessage, then don't worry: both SendMessage and BroadcastMessage will be used extensively in this book. We'll get plenty of practice using them!

SendMessage and BroadcastMessage work for both the Component and GameObject classes. When called on GameObjects, SendMessage invokes a named function on *all* attached Components. For single Components, SendMessage invokes a named function on only the specified Component.

Removing Listeners

The NotificationsManager, with the help of AddListener and PostNotification, can now build a list of registered listeners for events, and further notify those listeners when their events happen. But should we do if a Listener no longer wants to be notified about an event? What if the Listener wants to unregister itself as a listener, removing itself from the Dictionary entirely? Right now the Notifications Manager doesn't support this behavior. But we can easily add support for it. Consider Listing 3-11.

Listing 3-11. Removing a Listener from the Dictionary

```
01 //Function to remove a listener for a notification
02 public void RemoveListener(Component Sender, string NotificationName)
03 {
04        //If no key in dictionary exists, then exit
05        if(!Listeners.ContainsKey(NotificationName))
06                return;
07
```

```
08          //Cycle through listeners and identify component, and then remove
09          for(int i = Listeners[NotificationName].Count-1; i>=0; i--)
10          {
11                  //Check instance ID
12                  if(Listeners[NotificationName][i].GetInstanceID() == Sender.GetInstanceID())
13                          Listeners[NotificationName].RemoveAt(i); //Matched. Remove from list
14          }
15 }
```

The RemoveListener function allows the object Sender to remove itself from the Listener list for the registered event NotificationName. Notice that this function will *not* unregister the object as a Listener for *all* event types, but only for the event type it specifies. The removal process begins in line 09, with a For loop, and terminates at line 14.

Take care about the deletion of objects from a list during a loop. The loop in line 09 decrements backward through the list rather than increments forward, because as items are deleted, the list length or size reduces each time, which can invalidate the iterator *I*, if it increments.

Removing Redundancies

The RemoveListener method is useful in cases where an object explicitly removes itself as a Listener from the Dictionary. This is a respectful and tidy way to work, whenever an object no longer wants event notifications. But the possibility remains that a valid Listener object could be deleted from the scene without ever calling RemoveListener to remove itself from the Listener Dictionary. If that were to happen, the associated entries in the Dictionary for that object would remain intact but become null references and thus be redundant. This could later cause exceptions and errors when methods, such as PostNotification, iterate through all associated listeners, calling SendMessage. It would be problematic because we cannot legitimately call SendMessage on null references, since no object exists to support the function call. For this reason, we'll need to add a new method, which can be called to cycle through all listeners for all events, and to remove any redundancies if they are found (see Listing 3-12).

Listing 3-12. Removing All Redundancies from a Dictionary

```
01 //-------------------------------------------------
02 //Function to remove redundant listeners - deleted and removed listeners
03 public void RemoveRedundancies()
04 {
05          //Create new dictionary
06          Dictionary<string, List<Component>> TmpListeners = new Dictionary<string,
            List<Component>>();

08          //Cycle through all dictionary entries
09          foreach(KeyValuePair<string, List<Component>> Item in Listeners)
10          {
11                  //Cycle through all listener objects in list, remove null objects
12                  for(int i = Item.Value.Count-1; i>=0; i--)
13                  {
14                          //If null, then remove item
```

```
15                    if(Item.Value[i] == null)
16                        Item.Value.RemoveAt(i);
17                }
18
19                //If items remain in list for this notification, then add this to tmp dictionary
20                if(Item.Value.Count > 0)
21                    TmpListeners.Add (Item.Key, Item.Value);
22            }
23
24        //Replace listeners object with new, optimized dictionary
25        Listeners = TmpListeners;
26 }
```

In essence, the RemoveRedundancies method cycles through every listener for every event type, and removes any null references where found. Then it regenerates a new Dictionary containing only the valid entries.

Completing NotificationsManager

We've now seen the core parts of the NotificationsManager—the things that make it work and be what it is. Critically, this includes the AddListener, PostNotification, RemoveListener, and RemoveRedundancies methods. Together, these constitute the backbone or infrastructure of the event-handling system. With just these methods, we can receive and send event notifications to practically any kind of GameObject and Component in a Unity scene. Let's see the NotificationsManager class in full, leaving out no code, as shown in Listing 3-13. This class can also be found in the book companion files, inside the Chapter03 folder.

Listing 3-13. The Completed NotificationsManager Class (NotificationsManager.cs)

```
01 //EVENTS MANAGER CLASS - for receiving notifications and notifying listeners
02 //-------------------------------------------------
03 using UnityEngine;
04 using System.Collections;
05 using System.Collections.Generic;
06 //-------------------------------------------------
07 public class NotificationsManager : MonoBehaviour
08 {
09        //Private variables
10        //-------------------------------------------------
11        //Internal reference to all listeners for notifications
12        private Dictionary<string, List<Component>> Listeners = new Dictionary<string,
           List<Component>>();
13
14        //Methods
15        //-------------------------------------------------
16        //Function to add a listener for an notification to the listeners list
17        public void AddListener(Component Sender, string NotificationName)
18        {
19                //Add listener to dictionary
```

```
20              if(!Listeners.ContainsKey(NotificationName))
21                      Listeners.Add (NotificationName, new List<Component>());
22
23              //Add object to listener list for this notification
24              Listeners[NotificationName].Add(Sender);
25      }
26      //------------------------------------------------
27      //Function to remove a listener for a notification
28      public void RemoveListener(Component Sender, string NotificationName)
29      {
30              //If no key in dictionary exists, then exit
31              if(!Listeners.ContainsKey(NotificationName))
32                      return;
33
34              //Cycle through listeners and identify component, and then remove
35              for(int i = Listeners[NotificationName].Count-1; i>=0; i--)
36              {
37                      //Check instance ID
38                      if(Listeners[NotificationName][i].GetInstanceID() == Sender.
                        GetInstanceID())
39                              Listeners[NotificationName].RemoveAt(i); //Matched. Remove from
                                list
40              }
41      }
42      //------------------------------------------------
43      //Function to post a notification to a listener
44      public void PostNotification(Component Sender, string NotificationName)
45      {
46              //If no key in dictionary exists, then exit
47              if(!Listeners.ContainsKey(NotificationName))
48                      return;
49
50              //Else post notification to all matching listeners
51              foreach(Component Listener in Listeners[NotificationName])
52                      Listener.SendMessage(NotificationName, Sender, SendMessageOptions.
                        DontRequireReceiver);
53      }
54      //------------------------------------------------
55      //Function to clear all listeners
56      public void ClearListeners()
57      {
58              //Removes all listeners
59              Listeners.Clear();
60      }
61      //------------------------------------------------
62      //Function to remove redundant listeners - deleted and removed listeners
63      public void RemoveRedundancies()
64      {
65              //Create new dictionary
66              Dictionary<string, List<Component>> TmpListeners = new Dictionary<string,
                List<Component>>();
67
```

```
68                //Cycle through all dictionary entries
69                foreach(KeyValuePair<string, List<Component>> Item in Listeners)
70                {
71                    //Cycle through all listener objects in list, remove null objects
72                    for(int i = Item.Value.Count-1; i>=0; i--)
73                    {
74                        //If null, then remove item
75                        if(Item.Value[i] == null)
76                            Item.Value.RemoveAt(i);
77                    }
78
79                    //If items remain in list for this notification, then add this to tmp
                     dictionary
80                    if(Item.Value.Count > 0)
81                        TmpListeners.Add (Item.Key, Item.Value);
82                }
83
84                //Replace listeners object with new, optimized dictionary
85                Listeners = TmpListeners;
86        }
87        //-------------------------------------------------
88        //Called when a new level is loaded; remove redundant entries from dictionary; in case
           left-over from previous scene
89        void OnLevelWasLoaded()
90        {
91            //Clear redundancies
92            RemoveRedundancies();
93        }
94        //-------------------------------------------------
95 }
```

Working with the NotificationsManager

So how does the NotificationsManager work in practice? Practically every subsequent chapter in this book will use it, so we'll see plenty of examples of the class at work. However, to distill the basics into a simple project and to put things into perspective, let's create a sample application here that uses the NotificationsManager directly. The steps for creating this project follow.

First, create a new Unity project, if you've not already done so. The project name and import packages are not critical in themselves—since we're simply building a test-project to try out the NotificationsManager class. Be sure to the save the default autogenerated scene (I've named mine TestingNotifications.scene), and then import the NotificationsManager.cs C# file from Windows Explorer or Mac Finder into an appropriately named folder inside the Unity Project panel, such as Scripts (see Figure 3-8).

Figure 3-8. Importing NotificationsManager.cs into the Unity project. Remember: get into the habit of using meaningful folder names, to bring organization to your assets

As mentioned in earlier sections, the NotificationsManager should be a *Singleton object*, meaning there should be only one instance of it in memory at any one time. That instance should last throughout the duration of the scene and beyond, if there are multiple scenes. The details of creating and accessing Singleton objects globally are considered in depth in the next chapter. Here we'll simply use a more informal, make-shift Singleton object. Just drag and drop the NotificationsManager onto the Camera object in the scene (or onto an empty game object) to instantiate the class as a Component. Since *we know* that NotificationsManager should be a Singleton, then we'll simply *remember* that our scene already has an instance of this class and that we need to create no more instances (see Figure 3-9).

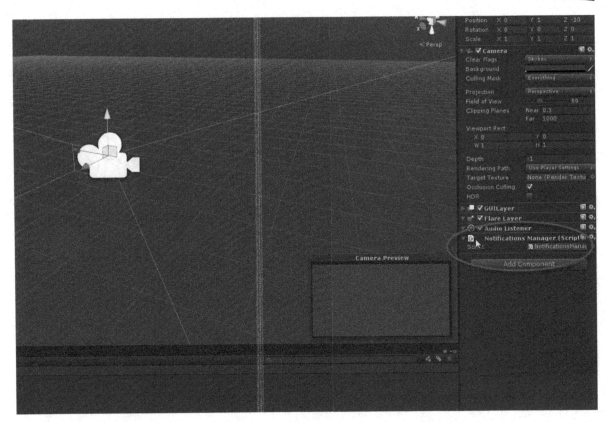

Figure 3-9. *The NotificationsManager should be a Singleton object; there should be one instance of it in the scene*

For this sample application, we'll set up a trivial scenario. Specifically, we'll create two additional GameObjects in the scene. One object will be responsible for detecting user input, such as keyboard button presses, and for notifying the NotificationsManager when such presses happen. The other object will print a console message, *whenever* it receives a notification about keyboard input from the NotificationsManager. Let's start by creating two additional GameObjects: namely, obj_Poster and obj_Listener (see Figure 3-10).

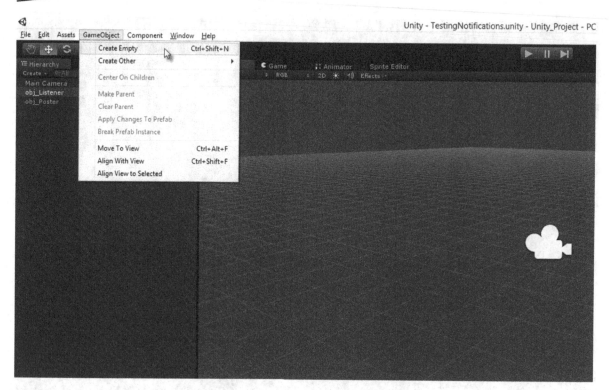

Figure 3-10. Creating two additional objects in the scene to test the NotificationsManager

To detect live keyboard input and to post appropriate notifications at the NotificationsManager, we'll need to create a new script file in the project. This will be attached to obj_Poster. See Listing 3-14 for the code I'm using. Drag and drop this script file into the obj_Poster to add it as a component.

Listing 3-14. Detecting Keyboard Input and Posting Notifications (Poster.cs)

```
01 using UnityEngine;
02 using System.Collections;
03
04 public class Poster : MonoBehaviour
05 {
06        //Reference to gloabl Notifications Manager
07        public NotificationsManager Notifications = null;
08
09        // Update is called once per frame
10        void Update ()
11        {
12                //Check for keyboard input
13                if(Input.anyKeyDown && Notifications != null)
14                        Notifications.PostNotification(this, "OnKeyboardInput");
15        }
16 }
```

The Poster class features a public member variable Notifications, which keeps a reference to the NotificationsManager object in memory. By default, this variable is assigned and null. We should assign this variable a value directly from the Unity Object Inspector. To do this, simply drag and drop the Camera object (or Empty object), with the NotificationsManager component attached, from the Hierarchy panel and into the Notifications slot in the Object Inspector, when the obj_Poster object is selected. This completes the assignment (see Figure 3-11). Notice that Unity is smart enough to detect which component on the source GameObject should be assigned to the Notifications variable in the Object Inspector.

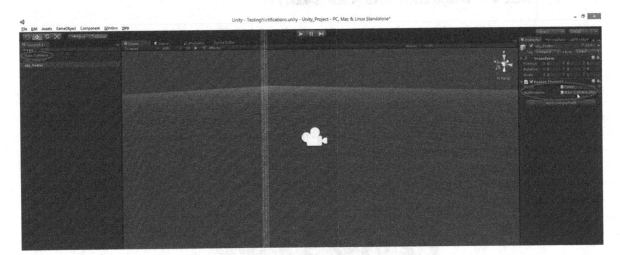

Figure 3-11. Assigning the NotificationsManager instance to the Notifications variable of class Poster, using the Object Inspector

Note   For more information on the Unity Input class, see the online documentation at http://docs.unity3d.com/Documentation/ScriptReference/Input.html.

We'll also need to create an additional script for the Listener object, which should register with the NotificationsManager for keyboard events, and then respond to them when they occur. The Listener script can be seen in Listing 3-15.

Listing 3-15. Responding to Keyboard Events with a Listener (Listener.cs)

```
01 using UnityEngine;
02 using System.Collections;
03
04 public class Listener : MonoBehaviour
05 {
06         //Reference to gloabl Notifications Manager
07         public NotificationsManager Notifications = null;
08
```

```
09        // Use this for initialization
10        void Start ()
11        {
12              //Register this object as a listener for keyboard notifications
13              if(Notifications!=null)
14                    Notifications.AddListener(this, "OnKeyboardInput");
15        }
16
17        //This function will be called by the NotificationsManager when keyboard events occur
18        public void OnKeyboardInput(Component Sender)
19        {
20              //Print to console
21              Debug.Log("Keyboard Event Occurred");
22        }
23 }
```

Be sure to drag and drop the Listener.cs file onto the Listener object in the scene, and then assign the public Notifications member in the Object Inspector to the NotificationsManager component, as we did for the Poster object. Notice in Listing 3-15 that a correspondence exists between the two classes, Poster and Listener, regarding the event name as a string. The Poster posts notifications for event OnKeyboardInput, and the Listener registers for the same event, as well as implements a function of that name, which will be invoked by the NotificationsManager using the SendMessage API function (see Figure 3-12).

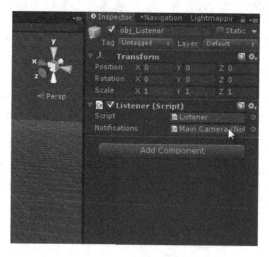

Figure 3-12. Remember to assign the Notifications member of the Listener to the single instance of NotificationsManager in the scene

Once the two minor classes, Poster and Listener, are configured in the project, the NotificationsManager can be used as intended. Simply play the scene and press any key on the keyboard. When this happens, the Poster object notifies the NotificationsManager, which in turns notifies the one and only listener for this event (see Figure 3-13). You could, of course, add more listener instances to the scene, and the NotificationsManager would update those objects, too! Sure, it's a simple setup in this isolated case, but it represents a powerful mechanic that works for any event we can imagine, and it'll become indispensable to us as we progress further with CMOD.

Figure 3-13. The NotificationsManager at work, using the Listener and Poster sample classes

Conclusion

In this chapter, we established an abstract but highly important starting point for CMOD in the form of a NotificationsManager class. This class is general in the ultimate sense that it stands apart from any particular game project, and has wider relevance to practically every game project imaginable, including CMOD. Its purpose is to centrally receive a single notification from any object in a Unity scene that detects and causes events. And then, having received that notification, it should immediately go on to dispatch it to any and all objects that have registered an interest in the event—these objects being referred to as Listeners. Don't be fooled by the simplicity and "shortness" of this class. As we'll see, it is powerful! At this point, you should be able to do the following:

- Create C# script files and define custom behavior

- Understand the problems of events and event handling, as well as the need for streamlining and managing events

- Understand how the NotificationsManager works, and its relationship to Notifications and Listeners

- Know what a Singleton object is and why it is important
- Use the Mono implementation of .NET classes, such as List and Dictionary
- Understand the advantages and disadvantages of dynamic arrays
- Understand the purpose of Generic classes in C#
- Invoke specified functions on GameObjects and Components using SendMessage and BroadcastMessage
- Implement a NotificationsManager, complete with Listener and Poster functionality
- Understand redundancies and null references
- Use the NotificationsManager in your own projects

Chapter 4

Power-Ups and Singletons

CMOD will feature a total of four different power-up types, scattered around the level for collection. First, the game-critical power-up of *Cash* (see Figure 4-1). Each level features multiple Cash Power-Ups, and when all of these are collected without the Player dying, the level is classified as complete. Second, a weapon-upgrade power-up that equips the Player with the gun weapon. Third, an ammo-restore power-up to replenish the gun ammo back to maximum. And fourth, a health-restore power-up to restore Player health back to maximum. All four of these power-ups will be collected and applied when the Player collides with (or walks into) them. To implement this behavior efficiently and to integrate it with the NotificationsManager (coded in the previous chapter), we'll make use of a very powerful type of C# object, known as a *Singleton*. This object was discussed briefly in the previous chapter, but here we'll examine it in more detail. So let's get started at creating power-up objects for CMOD!

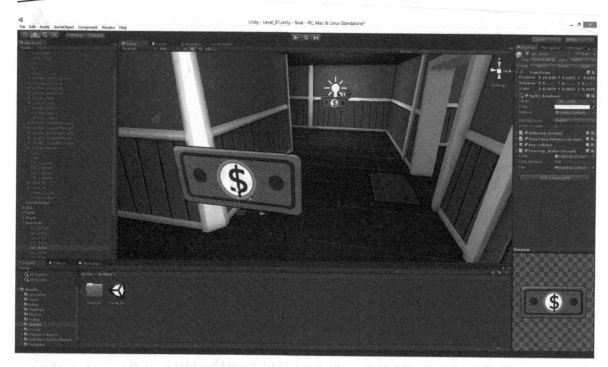

Figure 4-1. Cash Power-Ups (with a scale of 0.3039) prepared and added to the level in the Unity Editor. The power-ups will be created as a Prefab objects, with scripts attached, for easy reuse

Creating the Cash Power-Up

The first power-up to address is perhaps the most significant in terms of general game-mechanics, namely the Cash Power-Up. The Cash Power-Up is the most significant because without this power-up, the player can't complete the game. The aim of the player in any level of CMOD is to explore the environment, collecting all Cash Power-Ups. When all Cash Power-Ups are collected, the level is completed. Like all power-ups in CMOD, the Cash Power-Up will be sprite based. That is, its appearance and form in the level will be based on a sprite from the main atlas texture, as opposed to a "true" 3D mesh. As with the environment pieces configured in Chapter 2, we *could* make the power-up by simply dragging and dropping sprite instances into the scene, one sprite for each power-up instance, and then customize each one with scripted components, one at a time. But an easier way is simply to create *one* power-up instance, and then package it as a Prefab that we'll reuse as many times as we need. That's the approach we'll take here. So to start creating the Cash Power-Up, open the main atlas texture for the game in the Project panel, and drag and drop the Cash Power-Up sprite from the texture into the scene hierarchy. This instantiates one cash sprite in the scene—ready for scripting. Notice in Figure 4-2 that I've applied some scaling to the sprite, to better fit it into the level.

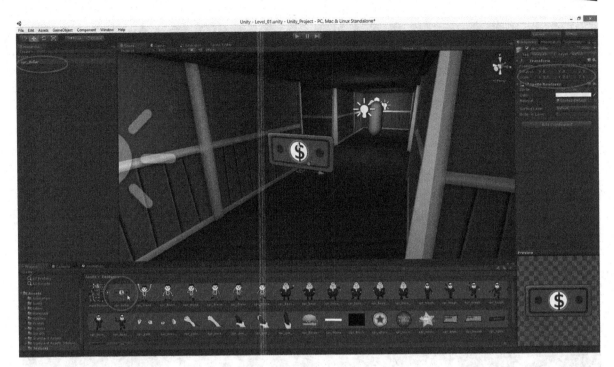

Figure 4-2. Instantiating the cash sprite in the scene using the atlas texture. Scaling has been applied to better fit the sprite in the scene

Note   Working with sprite objects from the atlas texture, such as the Cash Power-Up sprite, requires us to use the Sprite Editor 2D feature, added in Unity 4.3. This tool was explored in Chapter 2, for creating sprite objects. You can create the required sprites manually, but if you're working along with each chapter, the book companion files for this chapter feature a ready-made Unity project (Chapter4/Unity/Project_Start), complete with all necessary sprites already configured for use.

Power-Ups and Billboards

If you add the Cash Power-Up sprite to the scene and then take a look at it in-game with a First Person Controller, looking at the sprite from many possible angles, you'll notice a problem, as seen in Figure 4-3. Specifically, the Cash Power-Up looks like a cardboard cutout, completely flat. In fact, it's even possible to walk around the side of the power-up, catching it at an angle where it's almost lost from view entirely, because it has no thickness or depth. This is not a flaw or fault of the sprite per se so much as it's a *consequence* of the sprite's 2D-ness. A sprite is supposed to be 2D. This is usually not a problem for 2D games that have fixed orthographic cameras always focused on one side or aspect of the sprite, but when you mix 2D and 3D together, as in CMOD, the flatness of sprites can become troublesome in this way.

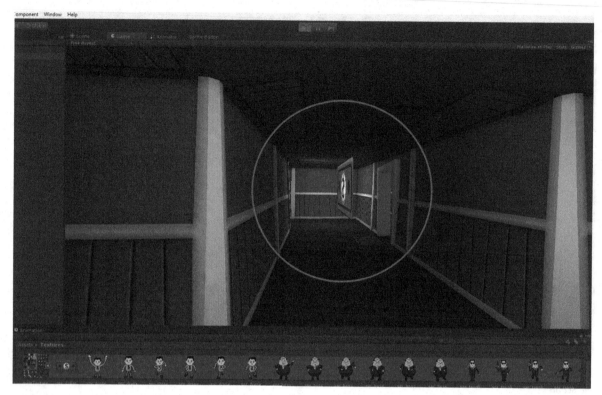

Figure 4-3. Sprite objects are 2D and have no thickness. Consequently, they look like cardboard cutouts

One way to fix this is to code a *Billboard*. When you add any code to a sprite, forcing it to rotate so that it always directly faces the camera as it moves around in the level, you create a Billboard. In short, a Billboard refers to a sprite that's always looking at the camera. It always rotates in synch with the camera so that the camera sees the sprite *head-on*. This eliminates any distortion and flatness arising from the camera seeing the sprite at other angles in perspective—because, with Billboards, the camera can only ever see the sprite from one angle and one angle only. In this section, then we'll code a `Billboard` class that we'll add to the Cash Power-Up (as well as all other power-ups) to solve the problem of sprite flatness. Create a new C# script file and begin with an empty class, which I've named `Billboard`. Then add this class as a component of the sprite object in the scene (see Listing 4-1).

Listing 4-1. Billboard.cs: The Beginnings of a Billboard Class

```
using UnityEngine;
using System.Collections;

public class Billboard : MonoBehaviour
{
}
```

Billboards and Cached Transforms

The critical feature of Billboard functionality is that it *rotates* a sprite to face the camera. Consequently, any Billboard class must access the Transform component of a GameObject on every frame, to achieve a permanent state of object rotation using any of Transform's members or functions, such as Transform.rotation, or Transform.Rotate, or Transform.RotateAround. These members and functions can be accessed easily for any component on a game GameObject by referencing its internal property, known as transform (lowercase t). For example, you may access an object's Transform and translate it in world space with the following code in Listing 4-2.

Listing 4-2. Using the transform Property

```
void Update()
{
        //Sets the object's world positon to 10, 10, 10
        transform.position = new Vector3(10, 10, 10);
}
```

Now, although the code in Listing 4-2 *works* and *achieves* its purpose, it can still be improved in terms of performance and efficiency, albeit marginally so. The main problem with the code is that, during Update, a reference to transform is being made, which is a *C# property* and *not* a *member variable*. This means that every call to *transform* indirectly invokes a function (Property), which *returns* a reference to the Transform component. transform does not, however, access an object's Transform directly, as a member variable would. Remember, C# properties were covered in depth in the previous chapter. Because transform is a property, there is a small optimization we can perform, known as *Cached Transforms*. Consider the refined Billboard class in Listing 4-3, which uses Cached Transforms.

Listing 4-3. The Billboard Class Prepared for Action with Cached Transforms

```
01 using UnityEngine;
02 using System.Collections;
03
04 public class Billboard : MonoBehaviour
05 {
06     private Transform ThisTransform = null;
07
08     // Use this for initialization
09     void Start ()
10     {
11             //Cache transform
12             ThisTransform = transform;
13     }
14 }
```

Listing 4-3 shows how, in just two lines of code, we can create a Cached Transform object. In essence, using the Start event (at line 09), we store a direct and local reference to an object's Transform component with the private Transform member ThisTransform. ThisTransform is a member variable and not a property, and gives us direct and immediate access to the transform component. Consequently, by using ThisTransform instead of transform on Update functions, we can reduce additional and unnecessary functional calls on every frame. This may initially seem a trivial optimization, hardly worth pursuing perhaps, but the aggregate improvements this can make over time, across many possible transform calls, can be considerable. So I recommend using Cached Transforms wherever possible; they're quick and easy to implement. We'll be using them here, for creating Billboards.

Billboards and Rotation

For a sprite to truly act as a Billboard, it needs to continually rotate (around the Y axis) to face the game camera, wherever it may be in the scene (see Figure 4-4). We don't need to worry about Z and X rotations for CMOD, since the player cannot crouch, jump, or roll over to see the sprite from underneath or above. Using Cached Transforms, we can achieve this rotation in only a few lines of code. (Listing 4-4 shows the complete `Billboard` class. Comments follow, and I recommend reading the code sample through a few times—it uses many different concepts that we'll explore.)

Figure 4-4. CMOD sprites will need to rotate around the Y axis (YAW)

Listing 4-4. Completing the Billboard Class

```
01 using UnityEngine;
02 using System.Collections;
03
04 public class Billboard : MonoBehaviour
05 {
06     private Transform ThisTransform = null;
07
08     // Use this for initialization
09     void Start ()
10     {
11             //Cache transform
```

```
12              ThisTransform = transform;
13      }
14
15      void LateUpdate()
16      {
17              //Billboard sprite
18              Vector3 LookAtDir = new Vector3 (Camera.main.transform.position.x - ThisTransform.
                position.x, 0, Camera.main.transform.position.z - ThisTransform.position.z);
19              ThisTransform.rotation = Quaternion.LookRotation(-LookAtDir.normalized, Vector3.up);
20      }
21 }
```

- **Line 15.** The Billboard rotation code occurs inside LateUpdate and not Update. Both events are called once each frame, so what's the difference? In short, LateUpdate is *always* called *after* Update. This is important, especially for cameras or objects that track the movement of other objects. For the Billboard, our sprite rotates based on camera movement. If we rotate inside Update, it's possible the Billboard Update will be called *before* the camera Update *(that is, before the camera is positioned and located physically in the game environment for that frame)*. If that happens, then our Billboard rotation will be invalidated because the camera will have moved since for that frame. If we use LateUpdate however, all update and movement functionality for the camera will have finalized before rotating the Billboard, allowing us use the latest camera position.

> **Note**   For more information on LateUpdate, see the online Unity documentation at http://docs.unity3d.com/430/Documentation/ScriptReference/MonoBehaviour. LateUpdate.html.

- **Line 18.** Here we use vector subtraction, subtracting the power-up position (as a Vector3) from the camera position (as a Vector3) to produce a resultant vector, expressing the difference between the two. This vector, in essence, describes the *direction* in which the power-up would have to be looking to face the camera. This line of code does not change the rotation of the sprite. It simply calculates the direction in which the sprite *should* be looking.

> **Note**   For more information on vector arithmetic, consult the Unity documentation at http://docs.unity3d.com/Documentation/Manual/UnderstandingVectorArithmetic.html.

- **Line 19**. Here we actually set the sprite rotation based on the LookAtDir vector calculated in the previous line. A quaternion structure is generated to describe the rotation a sprite must go through to be looking in the desired direction. *Quaternions* are specialized mathematical structures that describe *orientation*. They are a set of numbers telling you which way an object is oriented in 3D space. If you need to rotate or turn an object in Unity, or if you need to look at a specified location, then you'll almost always need to work with quaternions at some level.

Note   Quaternions can seem intimidating to many because they're surrounded by lots of mathematical jargon and depend on many other concepts and ideas that are beyond the scope of this book. But don't let them intimidate you for this reason. If you're new to quaternions, it can be helpful to approach them not with the intention of understanding their inward workings, but with an acceptance that they are simply a tool to use. Spend less time looking *inside* them, and more time looking at how to *use* them. However, this doesn't mean that developing a deeper understanding of their background and innards isn't useful or worthwhile. It only means that such knowledge isn't essential to getting started at using them. More information on quaternions can be found at http://unity3d.com/learn/tutorials/modules/intermediate/scripting/quaternions.

Go ahead and attach the Billboard component script to the Cash Power-Up sprite in the scene. When you do this, the sprite will now turn to face the camera as it moves during gameplay. In fact, with this short script, you can turn any sprite into a Billboard (see Figure 4-5)!

Figure 4-5. Billboards always rotate to face the camera

Billboards and Bobbing

We're making good progress with the Cash Power-Up, but it still needs "something more" than just the ability to act as a Billboard. To really "stand out" to the player as a collectible object, it needs to move. True, the power-up *technically* moves already, as it always rotates to face the camera, but this movement is *practically* imperceptible because it's perfectly synchronized with the camera. So to create perceptible movement, we'll need to translate the power-up to move it. Specifically, we'll add a bobbing motion, making the power-up gently move up and then down in a loop (see Figure 4-6 to see the planned motion).

Figure 4-6. Adding bobbing motion to the power-up to help it stand out as a collectible object

The act of vacillating continuously between two extremes, such as moving up and down repeatedly, is termed *PingPonging*. To create a PingPong for object movement, then, we'll need to create a new C# class and component. I'll call this class PingPongDistance, since it'll move the power-up up and down by a specified distance, back and forth. The development of this class will also introduce two highly important concepts in Unity—namely, *deltaTime* and *coroutines*. Let's start the class, as shown in Listing 4-5.

Listing 4-5. PingPongDistance.cs: Starting a PingPong Class for Animating Power-Up Movement

```
01 using UnityEngine;
02 using System.Collections;
03
04 public class PingPongDistance : MonoBehaviour
05 {
06     private Transform ThisTransform = null;
07
```

```
08      // Use this for initialization
09      void Start ()
10      {
11              //Cache transform
12              ThisTransform = transform;
13      }
14 }
```

Coroutines

Before proceeding with the power-up PingPong movement, we'll take a detour into the world of coroutines, which will come in useful for us soon. In Unity, coroutines *act like* threads or asynchronous functions, if you're familiar with those concepts. In short, typical functions in Unity and C# act *synchronously*. This means that, when an event (like Start) calls a function in a class, the function performs its behavior sequentially, line by line from top to bottom, and then finally terminates at the end, returning a value. When the function returns, the calling event will resume its execution at the next line. But coroutines don't seem to act that way. They act like they are asynchronous (although they are not truly so). When you call a coroutine, it starts execution and seems to "run in the background" *at the same time* as other functions. With this ability comes great power, as we'll see. Consider the following Listing 4-6, which uses a coroutine; comments follow.

Listing 4-6. Sample Coroutine

```
01 using UnityEngine;
02 using System.Collections;
03
04 public class PrintHelloWorld : MonoBehaviour
05 {
06      // Use this for initialization
07      IEnumerator Start ()
08      {
09              //Start Coroutine
10              StartCoroutine(Counter());
11
12              //Has finished
13              Debug.Log ("Counter Finished");
14
15              yield break;
16      }
17
18      IEnumerator Counter()
19      {
20              for(int i=0; i<10; i++)
21              {
22                      Debug.Log (i.ToString() + " Seconds have elapsed");
23                      yield return new WaitForSeconds(1.0f);
24              }
25      }
26 }
```

Before reading the following comments, execute this code in Unity and look inside the Console window to see what happens. The result is shown in Figure 4-7.

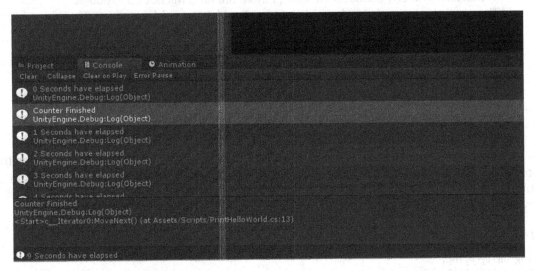

Figure 4-7. Using coroutines. Notice that the string "Counter Finished", which occurs inside Start on a line after the function Counter is called, is actually printed before the counter function completes!

- **Lines 07 and 18.** Both of these lines declare a coroutine. Notice that many Unity events, like Start, can be declared as a coroutine. They need not always return *void*. Coroutines are always declared with an IEnumerator return type, and they always feature a yield statement somewhere in their body. Technically, a function that returns a type of IEnumerator and has a yield statement in its body is a coroutine. So in Listing 4-6, both Start and Counter are coroutines.

- **Line 10.** In this class, the Start coroutine is invoked automatically by Unity, just as it invokes the normal Start event, but line 10 invokes a coroutine manually. Notice that a coroutine cannot be called like a regular function. Instead, the function StartCoroutine must be used to initiate the specified coroutine. If you've actually tested and run this code, you'll see from the output in the Console window, and from Figure 4-7, that the Counter coroutine is executed, but Start *does not* wait for it to finish before resuming execution on the next line at line 13. Line 13 is executed, and "Counter Finished" is printed to the console *before* the Counter coroutine is completed entirely. This demonstrates the asynchronous behavior of coroutines.

- **Line 15.** In the world of coroutines, `yield break` is equivalent to `return null` in the world of functions. In other words, `yield break` terminates the coroutine at that line, and any subsequent lines (if there are any) will not be executed. There's also another kind of `yield` statement, which is `yield return null`. This terminates execution of the coroutine for the current frame, but the coroutine will resume at the *next line* on the *next frame*. We'll see this form of `yield` in action shortly when creating the bobbing motion for our Cash Power-Up object.

- **Line 23.** This `yield WaitForSeconds` statement works like a `Sleep` function. In Listing 4-6, `yield WaitForSeconds` is used to suspend execution of the coroutine for 1 second before resuming on the next line. Since this statement is called inside a `For` loop, it executes once on each iteration.

There's another and interesting use of `yield`, however, which is not so widely documented. You may be wondering how we could fix the "asynchronous problem" in Listing 4-6 so that line 13 was truly executed *after* the Counter coroutine had completed entirely, and not sooner. To do that, consider the revised code, as shown in Listing 4-7.

Listing 4-7. Waiting for a Coroutine to Complete

```
01 using UnityEngine;
02 using System.Collections;
03
04 public class PrintHelloWorld : MonoBehaviour
05 {
06      // Use this for initialization
07      IEnumerator Start ()
08      {
09              //Start Coroutine
10              yield return StartCoroutine(Counter());
11
12              //Has finished
13              Debug.Log ("Counter Finished");
14
15              yield break;
16      }
17
18      IEnumerator Counter()
19      {
20              for(int i=0; i<10; i++)
21              {
22                      Debug.Log (i.ToString() + "Seconds have elapsed");
23                      yield return new WaitForSeconds(1.0f);
24              }
25      }
26 }
```

In short, the `yield` statement can be used inside a coroutine (such as `Start`) to wait for the termination of another coroutine (such as `Counter`). With this code, line 13 will not be executed until the `Counter` coroutine has ended. Before moving on, I recommend playing around with coroutines. They are powerful and we'll put them to good use in the next section to create an endless PingPong motion for power-ups.

> **Note** For more information on coroutines, consult the Unity documentation at
> http://docs.unity3d.com/Documentation/Manual/Coroutines.html.

Power-Up Motion with Coroutines and deltaTime

Listing 4-8 provides the complete class for PingPongDistance. And this class is also included in
the book companion files for this chapter at Chapter2/AssetsToImport. Rather than go into lengthy
descriptions here, let's first see the code, and then I'll offer comments.

Listing 4-8. PingPongDistance – Complete Class

```
01 using UnityEngine;
02 using System.Collections;
03 //--------------------------------------------------------------
04 public class PingPongDistance : MonoBehaviour
05 {
06     //Direction to move
07     public Vector3 MoveDir = Vector3.zero;
08
09     //Speed to move - units per second
10     public float Speed = 0.0f;
11
12     //Distance to travel in world units (before inverting direction and turning back)
13     public float TravelDistance = 0.0f;
14
15     //Cached Transform
16     private Transform ThisTransform = null;
17
18     //--------------------------------------------------------------
19     // Use this for initialization
20     IEnumerator Start ()
21     {
22             //Get cached transform
23             ThisTransform = transform;
24
25             //Loop forever
26             while(true)
27             {
28                     //Invert direction
29                     MoveDir = MoveDir * -1;
30
31                     //Start movement
32                     yield return StartCoroutine(Travel());
33             }
34     }
35     //--------------------------------------------------------------
36     //Travel full distance in direction, from current position
37     IEnumerator Travel()
38     {
```

```
39              //Distance travelled so far
40              float DistanceTravelled = 0;
41
42              //Move
43              while(DistanceTravelled < TravelDistance)
44              {
45                      //Get new position based on speed and direction
46                      Vector3 DistToTravel = MoveDir * Speed * Time.deltaTime;
47
48                      //Update position
49                      ThisTransform.position += DistToTravel;
50
51                      //Update distance travelled so far
52                      DistanceTravelled += DistToTravel.magnitude;
53
54                      //Wait until next update
55                      yield return null;
56              }
57      }
58      //-------------------------------------------------------------
59 }
```

- **Lines 16 and 20.** These should be familiar to us. In line 16 we declare a private ThisTransform object to cache the GameObject transform, ready to use either during coroutines or Update functions. In line 20, Start is declared as a coroutine rather than a regular function since we'll be waiting on Travel to complete in line 32. The Travel coroutine is used to move the power-up up and down.

- **Lines 07 and 29.** Line 07 declares a public Vector3 MoveDir, which should be set for each GameObject in the Object Inspector. This vector represents the starting direction in which an object should move for the specified distance TravelDistance (declared in line 13) and at the specified Speed (declared in line 10). This vector should be in a *normalized* form. By normalized here, I mean MoveDir is expected to use the values of 0 or 1 to indicate direction. Thus, if an object should move upward on the Y axis, the MoveDir vector would be (0,1,0). Movement on X would be (1,0,0), and on Z would be (0,0,1).

- **Lines 26–32.** Power-up objects should move up and down *endlessly in a loop*. This is where that high-level functionality happens. If MoveDir begins with a value of (0,1,0), then it's value is inverted at line 29 to (0,-1,0), and the *Travel* coroutine is called, to move the object downward at a specified speed and for a specified distance. On reaching the destination, the *Travel* coroutine completes, and MoveDir is inverted again. So (0,-1,0) becomes (0,1,0), and then the object moves up, and so on. Thus, through repeated inversion, we achieve PingPong.

- **Lines 37–55.** The Travel coroutine is responsible *moving* the power-up object *from* its current world space position, in the direction of MoveDir, at a specified *speed*, and until the total distance traveled exceeds TravelDistance. This is achieved especially with line 46, which calculates the amount to move in the direction MoveDir *for the current frame*. To calculate this, a Unity API variable Time.deltaTime is used. The next section discusses deltaTime further.

Exploring deltaTime

Every game relies either directly or indirectly on the concept of time to get its work done. If objects *move* or *animate* or *change*, then time is necessarily involved since every change must occur at a specified moment and at a specified speed. For an object to *change*, it must have been in a different state at an earlier time; otherwise, no change could be said to have occurred *now*. Thus, to represent any kind of change in-game, a concept and measure of time is needed. Measuring time has been problematic in games, however, historically speaking. Many older games measured time in terms of frames, but this resulted in performance inconsistency across hardware, because different computers could sustain different frame rates, and at different times. The result was that no two users on different computers could be guaranteed the same experience, even if they started playing the same game at the same time. So nowadays, many games measure time in a hardware-independent way, namely in terms of seconds. And Unity offers many such time-measuring features through the Time class.

> **Note** For more information on the Time class, see the Unity documentation at
> http://docs.unity3d.com/Documentation/ScriptReference/Time.html.

An important member variable of the Time class, which updates on each frame, is deltaTime. In mathematics and science, as well as video games, the term *delta* typically means "change in" or "difference." Thus, deltaTime refers to *time difference* or *change in time*. Specifically, the variable deltaTime expresses how much time (in seconds) has elapsed since the previous frame. For this reason, because video games typically display many frames per second, this value will almost always be a fractional value between 0 and 1, such as 0.03, or 0.5, or 0.111, and so forth. A value of 0.5 would mean that half a second has elapsed since the previous frame, and 1 would mean a whole second, and 2 would mean 2 seconds, and so on. Normally, larger values such as 1, and 2, and 3 are indicative of lag and problems in your game, because the hardware is clearly unable to sustain higher frame rates that would necessarily result in lower deltaTime values.

> **Note** For more information on deltaTime, see the Unity documentation at
> http://docs.unity3d.com/Documentation/ScriptReference/Time-deltaTime.html.

deltaTime is useful in Unity because it allows us to achieve frame-rate independence. Consider, for example, a GameObject (such as a spaceship) that should travel in a straight line. Let's say we want to translate the spaceship on the X axis, over time, to produce movement. One way to implement this behavior *without* deltaTime would be as shown in Listing 4-9.

Listing 4-9. Moving an Object Without deltaTime

```
01 void Update()
02 {
03     //Update spaceship position on x axis each frame
04     spaceship.position += new Vector3(5.0f,0,0);
05 }
```

This code increments the X position of the Player spaceship on each frame by five units. Over time, this will cause the spaceship to move. The problem, however, is that the *speed* of the spaceship entirely *depends* on the frequency with which Update is called. The more frequently Update is called, the faster the spaceship will move. Of course, we know in advance that Update is called on each and every frame, but frame rates differ across computers and even on the same computer at different times. For this reason, the code in Listing 4-9 will result in a spaceship that travels at different speeds on different computers, and even at different times on the same computer. This might not be a problem for us, if we don't care about spaceship speed in any way. But typically, we *do* care because we want to have some degree of control and understanding about the kind of experience gamers will have when they play our game. Now, we can solve this problem using deltaTime. Let's see how. Consider the following code in Listing 4-10, which improves on Listing 4-9.

Listing 4-10. Moving an Object with deltaTime

```
01 using UnityEngine;
02 using System.Collections;
03 //-----------------------------------------------------------------
04 public class Mover : MonoBehaviour
05 {
06     //Speed to move - units per second (5 units per second)
07     public float Speed = 5.0f;
08
09     //Cached Transform
10     private Transform ThisTransform = null;
11
12     //-----------------------------------------------------------
13     //Move spaceship
14     void Update()
15     {
16         //Update position
17         ThisTransform.position += new Vector3(Speed * Time.deltaTime, 0, 0);
18     }
19     //-----------------------------------------------------------
20 }
```

In Listing 4-10, the speed of the spaceship is defined in a ratio of units to seconds, namely *world units per second*. Further, we know that deltaTime expresses time as a fraction, based on how much time has elapsed since the previous frame. And lastly, we know that calculating the distance traveled for an object can be expressed using this formula: *Distance = Speed × Time*. Therefore, *Speed × deltaTime* results in the amount of world units the spaceship should travel. This allows you to move the spaceship not only a constant speed during gameplay, but a constant speed between different computers. The lesson here, then, is *for moving objects use deltaTime*!

Completing Power-Up Bobbing

We've now seen deltaTime in action, for creating a sample case of a spaceship moving forward along the X axis over time at a consistent speed. We've also seen in Listing 4-7 how deltaTime can be applied to the PingPongDistance class to create motion for power-ups. This means we can now move further with the Cash Power-Up. So, back in the Unity Editor, just drag and drop the

PingPongDistance script onto the power-up object, adding it as a component. I've positioned the Cash Power-Up in the scene, and set values for the properties for PingPongDistance in the Object Inspector. You may need to play around with these values if your level or power-up object differs from mine (see Figure 4-8 for the values I've used).

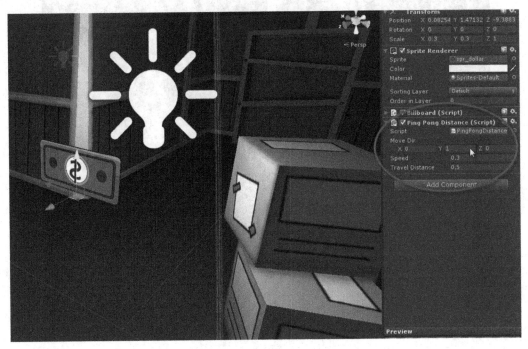

Figure 4-8. Adding a PingPongDistance component to the Cash Power-Up, making it bob up and down. Notice the MoveDir vector specified as (0, 1, 0) for the power-up move direction

Power-Up Collision

Things are looking good for the Cash Power-Up created so far. It exhibits Billboard functionality using the Billboard class, and also bobs gently up and down to accentuate its collectability, thanks to the PingPongDistance class. But all of these behaviors are essentially cosmetic features, and none of them actually make the power-up collectible. To truly round-off and complete the power-up object, we'll want it to disappear from the level when collected by the player. And the player collects the power-up simply by *walking through it*. That is, by colliding with it. Therefore, to implement power-up collection behavior, we'll need to work with Physics Colliders, to detect when the Player controller intersects the power-up bounding volume. So, before getting started at implementing this, make sure Collider Visibility is enabled for the Scene viewport, allowing us to see colliders when we create them. To do this, click the Gizmo button from the Scene toolbar and enable the *BoxCollider* check box, if it's not enabled already (see Figure 4-9 to see how to do this).

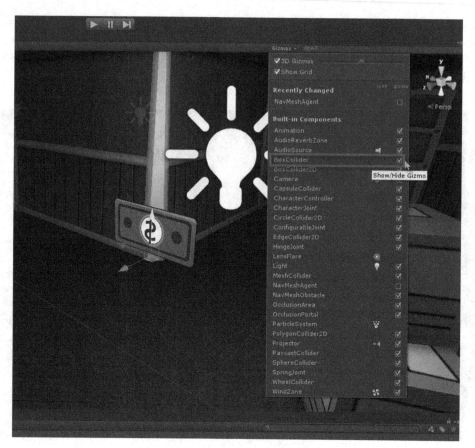

Figure 4-9. *Enabling BoxCollider visibility in the Scene viewport. If disabled, no colliders will be visible*

After Collider visibility is enabled, add a new BoxCollider component to the power-up object in the scene. To do that, select the power-up object, and choose **Component ➤ Physics ➤ Box Collider** from the main application menu. Once added, use the collider *Size* property, in the Object Inspector, to size the collider, surrounding the power-up and leaving some margin of space around the fringes. Be careful to give the collider some depth, too, even though the power-up object is really a flat sprite. It'll need depth for collisions to work properly (see Figure 4-10).

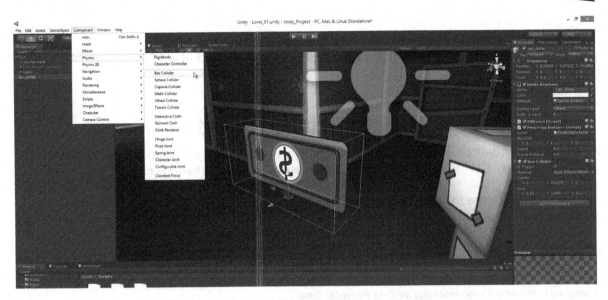

Figure 4-10. *Adding a Physics Collider to the Cash Power-Up to detect collisions with the Player*

Now the object is *almost* configured for collision detection with the Player. There's still one more step. For this object, and all power-ups, we want Unity to notify us explicitly in the script as and when collisions occur between the Player and Power-Ups, so we can respond appropriately, such as by removing the power-up object from the scene and increasing the collected cash score. Right now, Unity won't notify us by default. But we can easily configure the collider to do so. Just enable the *Is Trigger* check box from the Collider component in the Object Inspector. Enabling this will force Unity to send an event notification (a function call) to *all* components on the object whenever a collision occurs, if any (see Figure 4-11).

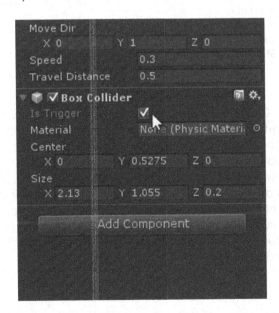

Figure 4-11. *Enable "Is Trigger" to receive collision notifications in the script when collisions happen*

> **Note**   More information on Unity colliders can be found at
> http://docs.unity3d.com/Documentation/ScriptReference/Collider.html.

Handling Collision Events: Getting Started

By using the Collider component of an object as a trigger volume, Unity can send all components on an object an event call for each and every unique collision, allowing us to code custom responses to the events when they happen. For Player collisions with the Cash Power-Up, we'll want to do the following: first, *increase the amount of cash collected* in total for the Player; second, *play a collection sound*; and third, *remove the power-up from the scene* so the Player cannot collect it more than once. To handle this behavior, we'll code a new class that I'll call Powerup_Dollar. To implement this, then, create a C# script file in the project named Powerup_Dollar.cs. Be sure to add this script as a component of the Cash Power-Up in the scene. A good start for this class might look like Listing 4-11.

Listing 4-11. Powerup_Dollar.cs: Starting the Cash Power-Up Class

```
01 //------------------------------------------------------------
02 using UnityEngine;
03 using System.Collections;
04 //------------------------------------------------------------
05 public class Powerup_Dollar : MonoBehaviour
06 {
07     //Amount of cash to give player
08     public float CashAmount = 100.0f;
09
10     //Audio Clip for this object
11     public AudioClip Clip = null;
12
13     //Audio Source for sound playback
14     private AudioSource SFX = null;
15     //------------------------------------------------------------
16 }
```

- **Lines 07-14.** The Cash Power-Up declares three variables, of which one is private. CashAmount is a float expressing how much cash should be awarded to the player when the power-up is collected. This allows us to specify different values for each power-up, if we need to. The Clip variable will specify which audio file to play when the power-up is collected. In Chapter 2, audio assets were imported into the project, and for this power-up I'll be using the audio file powerup_collect.wav. This file is included in the book companion files, but you can use any audio file you want. Finally, the SFX variable refers to an *Audio Source component*, the component to play the Clip audio file. This component acts like a media player.

Collisions and Responses

Let's move further with the Powerup_Dollar class to handle collision events. For Unity game objects with Trigger components, the OnTriggerEnter event is fired for the object when either a RigidBody object or another *collider*, such as the Player character, moves inside the trigger area (or volume). The extents of the trigger are defined by the BoxCollider. There is also a partner OnTriggerExit event, which is invoked when the collider *leaves* the trigger volume. However, in this book, we'll only need to deal with OnTriggerEnter. Listing 4-12 shows the almost complete Powerup_Dollar class (which can be found in the chapter companion files in Chapter04/AssetsToImport/); comments follow.

Listing 4-12. Moving Forward with Powerup_Dollar.cs

```
01 //-----------------------------------------------------------------
02 using UnityEngine;
03 using System.Collections;
04 //-----------------------------------------------------------------
05 public class Powerup_Dollar : MonoBehaviour
06 {
07     //Amount of cash to give player
08     public float CashAmount = 100.0f;
09
10     //Audio Clip for this object
11     public AudioClip Clip = null;
12
13     //Audio Source for sound playback
14     private AudioSource SFX = null;
15     //-----------------------------------------------------------------
16     void Start()
17     {
18         //Find sound object in scene
19         GameObject SoundsObject = GameObject.FindGameObjectWithTag("sounds");
20
21         //If no sound object, then exit
22         if(SoundsObject == null) return;
23
24         //Get audio source component for sfx
25         SFX = SoundsObject.GetComponent<AudioSource>();
26     }
27     //-----------------------------------------------------------------
28     //Event triggered when colliding with player
29     void OnTriggerEnter(Collider Other)
30     {
31         //Is colliding object a player? Cannot collide with enemies
32         if(!Other.CompareTag("player")) return;
33
34         //Play collection sound, if audio source is available
35         if(SFX){SFX.PlayOneShot(Clip, 1.0f);}
36
37         //Hide object from level so it cannot be collected more than once
38         gameObject.SetActive(false);
39
```

```
40              //Get PlayerController object and update cash
41              PlayerController PC = Other.gameObject.GetComponent<PlayerController>();
42
43              //If there is a PC attached to colliding object, then update cash
44              if(PC) PC.Cash += CashAmount;
45      }
46      //-------------------------------------------------------------
47 }
```

Note   More information on Unity trigger events can be found at http://docs.unity3d.com/
Documentation/ScriptReference/MonoBehaviour.OnTriggerEnter.html and
http://docs.unity3d.com/Documentation/ScriptReference/MonoBehaviour.
OnTriggerExit.html.

■ **Lines 16–25.** The Start event demonstrates an important and useful function
in Unity, namely GameObject.FindGameObjectWithTag. Using this function, the
purpose of Start is to *search* through all game objects *in the scene*, finding an
object with a *tag* of "sounds", and then to retrieve a reference to its AudioSource
component, if it has one. This component will be used to play back any sounds
associated with this power-up when it's collected. The success of this function
depends on there actually being an object in the scene that has a tag of
"sounds" and an AudioSource component. Thus, if there isn't such an object,
be sure to add one. Thankfully, however, this power-up has been coded so
that if no such object is present, the power-up will simply not play a sound on
collection, as opposed to throwing an error or exception.

Note   I recommend taking a look at the FindGameObjectWithTag function on the Unity online
documentation. It can be really useful for retrieving references to objects at runtime by object
tags (see http://docs.unity3d.com/Documentation/ScriptReference/GameObject.
FindGameObjectsWithTag.html).

■ **Lines 29–32.** The OnTriggerEnter function is inherited from Component, and is
executed automatically by Unity as an event, whenever a collision is detected
with the trigger. Here is where we should code a response to collision events.
The function argument Other is a reference to the object that is colliding with us,
and it's an important parameter for validating a collision. The power-ups for this
game should be collected by the Player only, and *not* by wandering Enemies.
But since both the Player and the Enemies will have colliders, both of them will
be able to collide with, and possibly collect, the power-up—unless we validate
the Other object! This validation occurs in line 32, where we check to see if the
colliding object is marked with the "player" tag. If it's not, then the event is
ignored. Consequently, for the collision functionality to work here, the Player
object must be marked with the tag "player".

- **Line 38.** Here the power-up is hidden (or removed) from the scene using the SetActive function. SetActive does not technically delete or remove an object from the scene, because any deactivated object can always be reactivated. Objects can be deleted permanently with the function DestroyImmediate. However, for performance reasons, I've avoided using that here. Instead, I'd recommend getting into the habit of caching and batching your objects. That is, create objects altogether in *one large batch* (such as a Scene Start), and then just hide them when they're not supposed to be in the scene, instead of creating and destroying objects as and when required during gameplay.

- **Lines 41–44.** These lines retrieve a PlayerController component from the colliding Player object, to increase the collected cash. The PlayerController class hasn't been created yet—it'll be made in the next chapter. But that's not a critical issue, because for now you can comment out these lines until we develop the class. The key issue to see is the OnTriggerEnter function will increment the player's collected cash.

Introducing the GameManager

The Powerup_Dollar class implements the event OnTriggerEnter to respond to player collisions. This program structure and functionality works well insofar as it goes, but it really doesn't go far enough. While it's useful for the Powerup_Dollar class to respond to collision events as it does, there may potentially be other classes that'll want to respond to and handle power-up collection. Perhaps, right now, we cannot conceive clearly of what those classes might be and how they might work exactly, but it'd be a good idea to structure our code now so that in the future, any other class has, at least, the potential and opportunity to respond directly to power-up collection events, should they need to. Thankfully, we already have the beginnings of a solution to this problem through the NotificationsManager class, created in the previous chapter. This class allows an event-receiver, such as Powerup_Dollar, to post event notifications to the NotificationsManager, which then relays all notifications to all registered listener objects by way of function calls.

However, an important consideration arises here. Our CMOD project doesn't yet have any valid instance of the NotificationsManager attached to an object in the scene. This means our project has no valid instance of NotificationsManager to receive or broadcast events, even though the script file is in our Project panel. I've deliberately put off discussing NotificationsManager instantiation until now. This is because the NotificationsManager is a managerial, overarching class that applies not to any one *particular instance* of an object, but to all objects generally throughout the game. It needs to receive and post event notifications between potentially *all* objects in scene and a game. This general and overarching quality is also likely to be shared by a range of other managerial classes. One particular class is the GameManager.

The GameManger is a special class in the sense that it's the highest level class in a game. If we want to restart or quit the game, then we'll need a GameManager. If we want to save or load game states, we'll need a GameManager. And if we want an instance of NotificationsManager for handling events throughout a game, then it'll be a member instance of GameManager. In short, any high-level, game-wide functionality that we'll need should be implemented in GameManager. It's effectively the "boss" of our game's logic. Given this, then, we'll now start to implement GameManager, and in doing this we'll be able to handle game-wide events with NotificationsManager. So let's get started by creating a new C# script file GameManager.cs.

GameManager and Singletons

The GameManager is a general, managerial and overarching class of special significance in practically every game. It has the single duty of representing and coordinating all high-level functionality, including game restarts, game exits, load-and-save states, game pauses, and more. It's notable here, too, that I've referred to GameManager in terms of "the GameManager" (singular)—as in the *one and only* GameManager—as opposed to "a GameManager" (where the possibility of *multiple* instances is admitted). This is for good reason because, in general, we'll *never need* more than one instance of GameManager throughout the duration of gameplay. The gamer can only play *one instance* of our game at any time, and that active instance is represented entirely by a single GameManager, which is created at game-start and is terminated at game-end.

Allowing for multiple GameManager instances would be confusing and game-breaking, since multiple instances would necessarily conflict and fight for controlling the same game. Therefore, we can safely establish here that not only will we never need more than one GameManager instance at any one time, but there's also good reason to create the class so that multiple instantiations of it are not possible. This will be especially useful if other programmers should work on our code. This kind of object, where only one instance can be made, is known as a Singleton. Classes designed to produce Singleton objects are said to use the *Singleton design pattern*. Thus, our GameManager object should be a Singleton. But how can we create such an object?

There are multiple solutions or methods for creating Singletons. The method illustrated here will be through *static members*. Let's see this process, step by step (see Listing 4-13).

Listing 4-13. Starting the Singleton Class

```
01 //-------------------------------------------------------------------
02 using UnityEngine;
03 using System.Collections;
04 //-------------------------------------------------------------------
05 public class GameManager : MonoBehaviour
06 {
07     //Internal reference to single active instance of object - for singleton behaviour
08     private static GameManager instance = null;
09 }
```

Start by adding a *private static* member of type GameManager (line 08 in Listing 4-13). Being static, the value of this member *would* be shared across *all* instances of GameManager. This variable will be null if there's no valid instance of GameManager active in the scene; otherwise, it'll be a reference to a previously declared instance of GameManager. Next, see Listing 4-14.

Listing 4-14. Expanding on the Singleton Class

```
01 //-------------------------------------------------------------------
02 using UnityEngine;
03 using System.Collections;
04 //-------------------------------------------------------------------
05 public class GameManager : MonoBehaviour
06 {
07     //-------------------------------------------------------------------
08     //C# property to retrieve currently active instance of object, if any
```

```
09        public static GameManager Instance
10        {
11                get
12                {
13                        if (instance == null) instance = new GameObject ("GameManager").
                        AddComponent<GameManager>(); //create game manager object if required
14                        return instance;
15                }
16        }
17
18        //----------------------------------------------------------------
19        //Internal reference to single active instance of object - for singleton behaviour
20        private static GameManager instance = null;
21 }
```

Here we add a *public* and *static* C# property, called Instance. The name is not essential, but its purpose is to return a reference to the active GameManager instance. If there is no currently active instance at the time of the call, then one is created and a reference to that instance is returned. As we'll see, most other classes in our game will use this property to retrieve a reference to the active GameManager instance whenever they need to access and invoke functions on the Game Manager. Now consider Listing 4-15.

Listing 4-15. Completing the Singleton Class

```
01 //----------------------------------------------------------------
02 using UnityEngine;
03 using System.Collections;
04 //----------------------------------------------------------------
05 public class GameManager : MonoBehaviour
06 {
07        //----------------------------------------------------------------
08        //C# property to retrieve currently active instance of object, if any
09        public static GameManager Instance
10        {
11                get
12                {
13                        if (instance == null) instance = new GameObject ("GameManager").
                        AddComponent<GameManager>(); //create game manager object if required
14                        return instance;
15                }
16        }
17
18        //----------------------------------------------------------------
19        //Internal reference to single active instance of object - for singleton behaviour
20        private static GameManager instance = null;
21
22        //----------------------------------------------------------------
23        // Called before Start on object creation
24        void Awake ()
25        {
26                //Check if there is an existing instance of this object
27                if((instance) && (instance.GetInstanceID() != GetInstanceID()))
```

```
28                         DestroyImmediate(gameObject); //Delete duplicate
29              else
30              {
31                         instance = this; //Make this object the only instance
32                         DontDestroyOnLoad (gameObject); //Set as do not destroy
33              }
34      }
35 }
```

> **Note**   There are many ways to check for equality between objects, to determine if two references to an
> object refer to one and the same object. You can use == equality, but I prefer Object.GetInstanceID.
> The ID for each instance is *guaranteed* to be unique for a single session (see Unity documentation).

Finally, after Listing 4-15, the Singleton magic is completed, and we're left with a Singleton object. Listing 4-15 adds an Awake event, which is called for the instance automatically by Unity on object creation (before the Start function). Inside this function we test the private static member *instance* to see if an active instance of this object already exists, and if it does, we *delete* the current instance (lines 27 and 28), since it must be a duplicate. Notice, in this case we don't simply hide or deactivate the object, as we did when hiding the cash power-up when collected in Listing 4-12. Here, we really do delete the object, if required, using the API function DestroyImmediate, restricting the active instance to just one. And that's it! Here, we've created a singleton GameManager. To test, I recommend adding this class as a component to an empty GameObject in the scene, and then see what happens you try to instantiate more instances in script, using the *new* keyword or the AddComponent function. It shouldn't be possible, thanks to the Singleton functionality (see Figure 4-12).

Figure 4-12. Adding the GameManager component as a Singleton to an empty GameObject

> **Note**   For more information on AddComponent, see the online Unity documentation at
> http://docs.unity3d.com/Documentation/ScriptReference/GameObject.AddComponent.html.

GameManager and Event Handling

GameManager, right now, doesn't implement any high-level functionality, such as Save-Game and Restart-Game. It will do so later in this book. But for now, it just acts a Singleton, and that's fine. Often, while developing high-level classes like Game Managers and Notification Managers, it'll be necessary to jump back and forth between many classes, developing some parts sooner and some later. This is normal and is usually required—and need not be any cause for concern or the result of bad planning. Many classes implemented so far, such as the NotificationsManager and PingPongDistance were sufficiently generic and "low-level" that they never depended on other classes and implementations to achieve their own functionality. But we don't have that luxury with the GameManager. It'll have to be an ongoing project throughout CMOD development. One feature, however, that we should implement right away into GameManager because it affects most other classes, is event-handling functionality. Most classes will need to post or receive events, and they'll do this via GameManager; let's see how in Listing 4-16. This code contains three major additions that make use of the NotificationsManager; comments follow.

Listing 4-16. Integration NotificationsManager into GameManager

```
01 //------------------------------------------------------------
02 using UnityEngine;
03 using System.Collections;
04 [RequireComponent (typeof (NotificationsManager))] //Component for sending and receiving
   notifications
05 //------------------------------------------------------------
06 public class GameManager : MonoBehaviour
07 {
08     //------------------------------------------------------------
09     //C# property to retrieve currently active instance of object, if any
10     public static GameManager Instance
11     {
12         get
13         {
14             if (instance == null) instance = new GameObject ("GameManager").
               AddComponent<GameManager>(); //create game manager object if required
15             return instance;
16         }
17     }
18     //------------------------------------------------------------
19     //C# property to retrieve notifications manager
20     public static NotificationsManager Notifications
21     {
22         get
23         {
```

```
24                    if(notifications == null) notifications =  instance.GetComponent
                      <NotificationsManager>();
25                    return notifications;
26            }
27    }
28    //----------------------------------------------------------------
29    //Internal reference to single active instance of object - for singleton behaviour
30    private static GameManager instance = null;
31
32    //Internal reference to notifications object
33    private static NotificationsManager notifications = null;
34
35    //----------------------------------------------------------------
36    // Called before Start on object creation
37    void Awake ()
38    {
39            //Check if there is an existing instance of this object
40            if((instance) && (instance.GetInstanceID() != GetInstanceID()))
41                    DestroyImmediate(gameObject); //Delete duplicate
42            else
43            {
44                    instance = this; //Make this object the only instance
45                    DontDestroyOnLoad (gameObject); //Set as do not destroy
46            }
47    }
48 }
```

- **Line 04.** The RequiresComponent line is a Unity-specific command that can be inserted into your classes to designate component dependence and relationships. In this case, the GameManager class is said to require the NotificationsManager. In practice, this means that every instance of GameManager requires its host GameObject to also have a NotificationsManager component. If you add a GameManager component to a GameObject without a NotificationsManager already attached, then Unity will automatically add a NotificationsManager.

- **Line 33.** Here, we've declared an internal private reference to a NotificationsManager component, which the GameManager will use for managing events. In essence, this variable is a reference to the NotificationsManager object that all other objects will use for sending and receiving events.

- **Lines 20–27.** A static C# Notifications property has been added to the GameManager, offering global access to the NotificationsManager to all objects in the game—meaning that all objects can send and receive notifications. We'll see the class in use shortly.

Note   You could of course implement the NotificationsManager as a Singleton class, separate from the GameManager, as opposed to being a member variable of it. However, in terms of class and object organization, I prefer to have all global classes accessed as members of a single, singleton Game Manager object.

So we've now created a singleton Game Manager class that exposes a Notifications Manager property to which all objects may send and receive application-wide event notifications, if they need to. Let's put these classes to the test in a practical context for CMOD. To prepare for this process in the Unity Editor, first ensure an empty GameObject is created in the scene. I've named it *GameManager*. This object should contain both a GameManager and a NotificationsManager component. Remember, due to the RequiresComponent keyword, you don't need to add both components manually. You can just add a GameManager component to an object, and Unity automatically adds a NotificationsManager if one doesn't already exist. Having done this, our scene is configured for using the GameManager as a globally accessible Singleton. We'll see how to use it in the next section.

Completing the Cash Power-Up

Back in Listing 4-12, we coded a Cash Power-Up object to respond directly to an OnTriggerEnter event, to handle player collisions. However, we also need this event to integrate with NotificationsManager to notify all listener objects, in case they, too, need to respond when it happens. In other words, the event OnTriggerEnter of Powerup_Dollar needs to be amended to post a notification to the NotificationsManager. In this context, the NotificationsManager is accessible as a static member variable of the globally accessible GameManager singleton. Consider the completed Powerup_Dollar class in Listing 4-17, which posts an event notification.

Listing 4-17. Completed Cash Power-Up

```
01 //------------------------------------------------------------
02 using UnityEngine;
03 using System.Collections;
04 //------------------------------------------------------------
05 public class Powerup_Dollar : MonoBehaviour
06 {
07      //Amount of cash to give player
08      public float CashAmount = 100.0f;
09
10      //Audio Clip for this object
11      public AudioClip Clip = null;
12
13      //Audio Source for sound playback
14      private AudioSource SFX = null;
15      //------------------------------------------------------------
16      void Start()
17      {
18           //Find sound object in scene
19           GameObject SoundsObject = GameObject.FindGameObjectWithTag("sounds");
20
21           //If no sound object, then exit
22           if(SoundsObject == null) return;
23
24           //Get audio source component for sfx
25           SFX = SoundsObject.GetComponent<AudioSource>();
26      }
27      //------------------------------------------------------------
28      //Event triggered when colliding with player
```

```
29      void OnTriggerEnter(Collider Other)
30      {
31              //Is colliding object a player? Cannot collide with enemies
32              if(!Other.CompareTag("player")) return;
33
34              //Play collection sound, if audio source is available
35              if(SFX){SFX.PlayOneShot(Clip, 1.0f);}
36
37              //Hide object from level so it cannot be collected more than once
38              gameObject.SetActive(false);
39
40              //Get PlayerController object and update cash
41              PlayerController PC = Other.gameObject.GetComponent<PlayerController>();
42
43              //If there is a PC attached to colliding object, then update cash
44              if(PC) PC.Cash += CashAmount;
45
46              //Post power up collected notification, so other objects can handle this
                event if required
47              GameManager.Notifications.PostNotification(this, "PowerupCollected");
48      }
49      //-------------------------------------------------------------
```

■ **Line 47.** This line represents a fantastic feature of static members and
  Singletons! This is where they are a real joy to use, because in an important
  sense they evade variable-scope considerations. To access the GameManager
  and the NotificationsManager as global objects here, we didn't need to declare
  an internal variable for Powerup_Dollar. Nor did we need to find a game object
  in the scene with GameObject.Find to retrieve its GameManager component.
  Nor did we need to add a GameManager public variable or NotificationsManager
  public variable to the Powerup_Dollar class to reference the active Singleton.
  Instead, we simply use the convention, GameManager.Notifications. This gives
  us direct access to the static member *Notifications*. In just one line, therefore,
  we always access the NotificationsManager attached to the GameManager
  singleton. Using this logic, we can also access the Singleton instance of the
  GameManager by using the GameManager.Instance property. And this works
  not just for the Powerup_Dollar class. In *every* class and *every* line *throughout*
  our project, we can access the GameManager singleton instance using
  this technique. No extra lines of coding are required. More on this powerful
  technique will be seen throughout subsequent chapters!

Making a Prefab from the Completed Power-Up

The Cash Power-Up in the scene is now completed in terms of code and GameObject component
structure (see Figure 4-13). The final code for the power-up is given in Listing 4-17. However, at
this stage of development, we have only *one* power-up object, whereas our scene and the game
design requires us to have more. We could add further Cash Power-Ups in the *existing* scene
by simple object duplication (*Ctrl+D*), but these power-ups should also appear in *other* scenes,
and perhaps other *games*. To achieve this, then, the Power-Up should be turned into a Prefab for
infinite reusability.

*Figure 4-13. The completed Cash Power-Up*Note: *Before creating the Prefab for the Cash Power-Up. Don't forget to attach an audio clip from the Project panel into the* Powerup_Dollar.Clip *member, as shown in Figure 4-13*

To create a Prefab from the Cash Power-Up, select **Assets ➤ Create ➤ Prefab** from the application menu (see Figure 4-14).

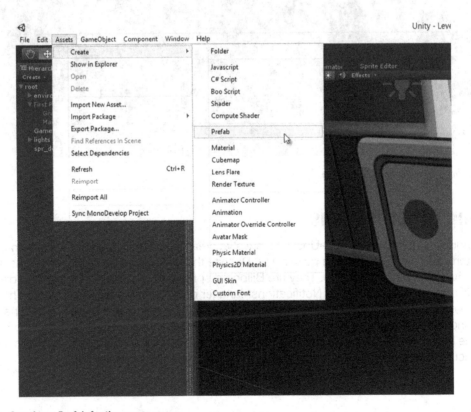

Figure 4-14. Creating a Prefab for the power-up

Once created, drag and drop the power-up object in the Hierarchy panel onto the newly created Prefab in the Project panel. Doing this completes Prefab creation. The Prefab can now be duplicated in the same scene, as well as different scenes and projects (see Figure 4-15).

Figure 4-15. Completing the power-up Prefab

Creating Other Prefabs

CMOD features not just Cash Power-Ups, which we've created in this chapter, but also ammo-restore, health-restore, and weapon-upgrade power-ups. Despite the differences in these power-ups, however, they share the same basic mechanic. They are Billboard sprites with colliders that respond directly to player collisions, interacting with the NotificationsManager on a GameManager singleton. The chief difference between them rests not in their mechanics, but in their responses to collisions. The Cash Power-Up increases Player cash, while health-restore affects Player health, and weapon-upgrade changes the Player weapon, and so on. Their differences rest in what they actually *do* when a Player collision occurs, but not in how collisions are fundamentally detected and handled.

For this reason, their implementation specifics need not be examined here, because creating them follows the same basic process in which the Cash Power-Up was created. The classes are, however, included in the book companion project files, should you wish to explore them and examine their source code further. Specifically, the classes are Powerup_Ammo (ammo restore), Powerup_Burger (health restore), and Powerup_Weapon (weapon upgrade). More information on these power-ups can be found in Chapter 1, including Figures 1-5, 1-6, 1-7, and 1-8.

Conclusion

This chapter was primarily dedicated to creating a Cash Power-Up object, and in so doing, we've seen a lot of critical C# and scripting concepts. There's a lot more work going on with our power-ups than there might seem at first glance. Once you open them and explore their innards, we see they rely on physics, colliders, events, singletons, deltaTime, coroutines, and a host of other Unity conventions. Having reached this far, however, we're now in a strong position to begin development of the Player character. This is considered in the next chapter. At this stage, you should be able to do the following:

- Create C#-based power-ups for your own projects

- Understand what Billboards are and how they work

- Understand coroutines and yield statements

- Use deltaTime to create frame-rate independent motion and animation

- Apply basic vector arithmetic and quaternion rotation

- Use the Unity Time class

- Understand the Singleton design pattern

- Create Singleton objects using static members

- Understand how the Unity RequiresComponent works

- Integrate NotificationsManager into your own games via Singletons

- Make Prefabs for your scenes

Chapter 5

Player Controller

FPS games (first-person shooter games) are played, unsurprisingly, from a *first-person perspective*. This means that game events, and the game world, are seen through the eyes of the main game character—as though *you* were that person in that world. This perspective is perhaps one of the most common kinds in contemporary video games. It's used in some of the famous and biggest selling games in history, including *Call of Duty*, *Halo*, *Skyrim*, and others. CMOD too will be an FPS game. Consequently, we'll need first-person behavior. Thankfully, lots of the underpinning coding work for this is created for us, from the standard Unity Character Controller packages (specifically the *First Person Controller*). However, this package features important limitations that we'll want to overcome for CMOD. Throughout this chapter, we'll examine the First Person Controller further, refining and adapting it by creating our own customized `PlayerController` class with first-person functionality and more besides.

Character Controllers and the First Person Controller

The ready-made First Person Controller that ships with Unity is included in the *Character Controllers* asset package, which can be imported into any project by selecting **Assets ➤ Import Package ➤ Character Controller** from the application main menu. This package is included in both the Free and Pro versions of Unity (see Figure 5-1).

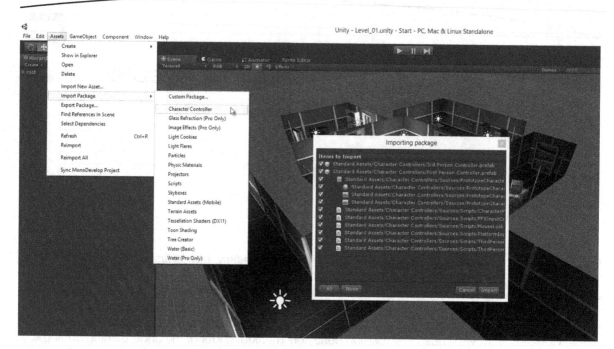

Figure 5-1. *Importing a First Person Controller (from the Character Controller package) into the Unity project*

> **Note**   This chapter assumes you're resuming work from where we left off in the previous chapter, or else you can begin from the starting project associated with this chapter, included in the book companion files inside folder Chapter04/Start.

After the Character Controller package is fully imported, you can easily add first-person functionality to your game, simply by dragging and dropping the First Person Controller from the Project panel into the scene. The First Person Controller is really a *Prefab* object. Adding this will typically override any existing cameras in the scene, replacing them as the default scene camera. When running the game with a First Person Controller, you may receive a printed error or warning in the console, complaining about multiple audio listeners. The error usually reads: "There are 2 audio listeners in the scene. Please ensure there is always exactly one audio listener in the scene," (see Figure 5-2). This normally happens when two or more cameras, each with an *AudioListener* component, are active in the scene simultaneously. This causes sound/audio conflict because each AudioListener represents a separate *ear point* or location from which sound is heard. To solve the problem, you can delete any unnecessary cameras (always delete *unnecessary* objects!), or you can remove the AudioListener component, or you can deactivate the AudioListener (if it'll be needed at a later time). The key point is: there should be *no more* than *one* AudioListener component active in the current scene at any one time.

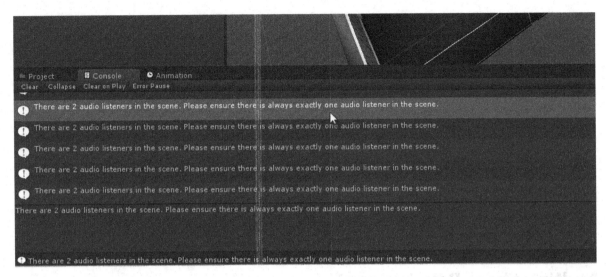

Figure 5-2. Multiple audio listeners warning

Note   If you're having trouble finding an asset in the Project panel, or an object in the Hierarchy panel, you can always use the Search field to find them using the "t:" syntax. For example, to find all objects in the scene with an AudioListener component, enter **t:audiolistener**.

The First Person Controller is already configured, through script, to respond to user input. The input is default or typical first-person controls: WASD for navigation (forward, left, back, and right) and mouse movement for head rotation. In general, the controller works well: *it does what it's supposed to do*. But still, there are two main areas where we could want improvement.

- **Platform specific.** If you're making a desktop game for Windows, Mac, or Linux, then the standard First Person Controller will serve most of your needs. But if you try running the controller on a mobile device, such as iOS or Android, you'll find that it fails. The standard First Person Controller is not configured to work from mobile input. It simply doesn't respond to any mobile input. There is, however, a separate and independent First Person Controller suited for mobile input (included in the Standard Assets (Mobile) package). But this Prefab has nothing to do with the standard First Person Controller. This can make cross-platform first-person input tedious. Instead, it'd be great if we, as developers, never had to worry about dealing with these two separate Prefabs. It'd be ideal if we had just *one universal* First Person Controller; a Prefab that worked across multiple platforms *automatically*—desktop and mobile. We'll see how to achieve this shortly.

> **Note**   CMOD is not specifically a mobile game. We won't be exploring mobile development in depth in this book. Nonetheless, here (at the stage of input development) is an opportunity where we may configure and prepare our game in an important way to be cross-platform, should we wish to pursue mobile development later.

▪ **Head bobbing.** The second problem relates to first-person camera movement and believability. Specifically, both the mobile and desktop First Person Controllers offer no native support for head bobbing. Whenever a human or biped moves by walking, the overall "kinematics" of the legs and body in motion typically causes the head to move involuntarily up and down. This motion is not included in the default First Person Controllers, but it can add an extra level of believability and realism to a game. In later sections, we'll see how to add this using sine waves.

Multiplatform Development

To get started creating a cross-platform (universal) First Person Controller, let's examine platform support in Unity and the general cross-platform workflow for games. Unity *can* build for many platforms, including Windows, OS X, iOS, Android, Windows Phone, and more. The word *can* is important here, because despite the platforms officially *supported* by Unity, *deploying* to them actually involves additional considerations and issues *for you* as a developer. Not just technical considerations about optimization and tweaking, but also economical and logistic considerations. For example, to build and deploy to iOS devices, you'll need an *Apple Developer License*, as well as a *Mac* computer—you can't build for iOS devices on a Windows PC, even with Unity Pro! Similarly, to develop for Android, you'll need to download and install the freely available *Android SDK*, whether you're developing on Windows or Mac. Without these requisites, you won't be able to develop and properly test mobile applications—so it's important to be aware of them.

More information on developing for iOS can be found in the Unity official documentation at `http://docs.unity3d.com/Documentation/Manual/iphone-GettingStarted.html`.

More information on developing for Android can be found at `https://docs.unity3d.com/Documentation/Manual/android-GettingStarted.html`.

Once you're configured and set to go for mobile development, you can start testing your game for your chosen platform in Unity via the *Build Settings* dialog. By choosing **File ➤ Build Settings...** from the application menu, you'll display the Build settings. From here, you select your platform of choice, and choose *Switch Platform*. Doing this forces Unity to apply all relevant platform settings to your project. Consequently, the next time you hit Play on the Unity toolbar, your game behaves as though it were running on the chosen mobile device (see Figure 5-3). With mobile apps such as *Unity Remote* installed on your device, you can also *control* your game using a mobile device, such as a tablet or phone.

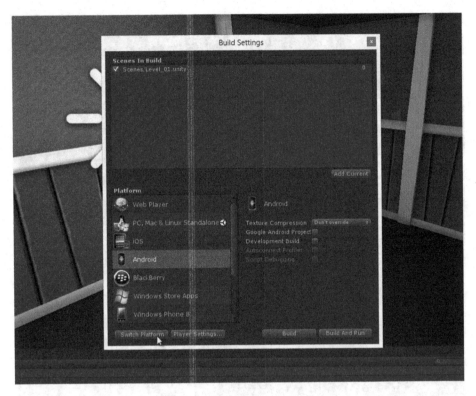

Figure 5-3. Switching platforms from the Build Settings dialog

Note   Unity Remote can be downloaded for Android from the PlayStore at
`https://play.google.com/store/apps/details?id=com.unity3d.androidremote`.

For iOS, Unity Remote can be downloaded from the App Store at
`https://itunes.apple.com/gb/app/unity-remote-3/id394632904?mt=8`.

Notice also that Unity offers *per-platform* settings for many features, including *texture* assets (see Figure 5-4). Each platform tab in the Object Inspector allows you to control and specify settings for an asset on a per-platform basis. This means, for example, that a texture can be sized and compressed differently and optimally for *each* platform. Whenever the Build Settings dialog is used to switch platform, as shown in Figure 5-3, Unity automatically switches and applies the appropriate settings for all assets and features, according to their configuration. This makes cross-platform developing a lot easier!

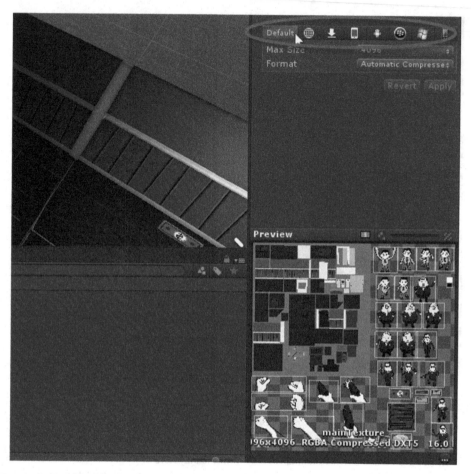

Figure 5-4. Per-platform texture settings

Beginning the Universal First Person Controller

Unity ships with two First Person Controller prefabs, the default First Person Controller included in the Standard Assets (Character Controller) package, and the mobile First Person Controller, included in the Standard Assets (Mobile) package. The crucial difference between these two controllers is their handling of user input. The desktop controller expects user input from keyboards and mice exclusively, and the mobile controller from mobile devices exclusively; and neither accepts input from the other method. Our aim here, therefore, is to forge a bridge between these two controllers, resulting in a new controller prefab that automatically handles input from any device, desktop or mobile. Before getting started, be sure to import both the desktop and mobile First Person Controllers into your project, if they're not imported already (see Figure 5-5).

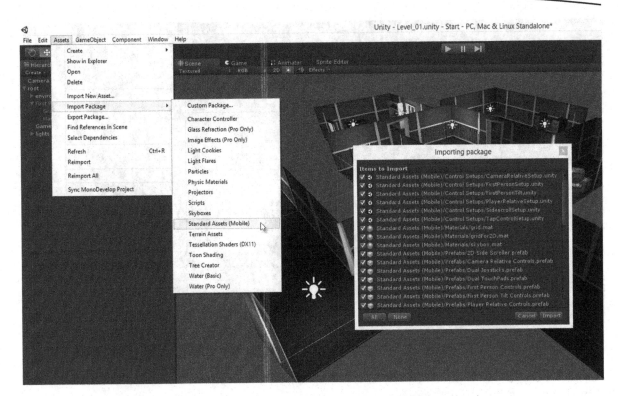

Figure 5-5. *Importing the mobile First Person Controller from the Standard Assets (Mobile) asset package*

To create a *universal* first-person Prefab, we'll add one instance of each First Person Controller to the scene (one desktop and one mobile) and then we'll explore the *Platform Dependent Compilation* feature of Unity and C# to automatically switch to the appropriate controller for the active platform. Start by adding the First Person Controllers to the scene, dragging and dropping them from the Project panel to the scene. The desktop First Person Controller can be found in the `Standard Assets/Character Controllers` folder. The mobile controller can be found in the `Standard Assets (Mobile)/Prefabs` folder (see Figure 5-6).

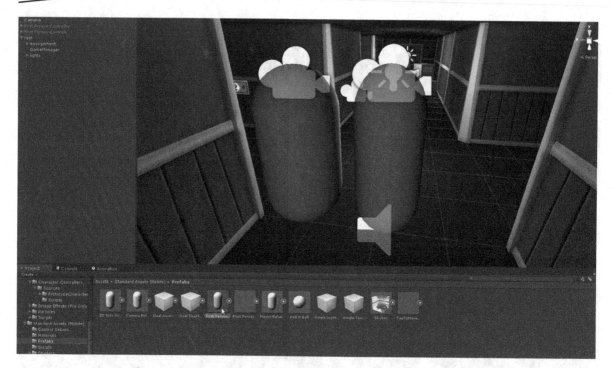

Figure 5-6. Importing the desktop and mobile First Person Controllers into the active scene

> **Note**   Remember to delete any other cameras in the scene, if there are any. We won't need them since our
> game is exclusively first-person.

Obviously, we're going to write some C# script to switch between these two controllers at level-start, on a per-platform basis—the desktop controller used for desktop games, and the mobile controller for mobile games. But first, let's apply some *GameObject* organization to the scene, as opposed to simply leaving the two newly added controllers as separate objects. I want to *organize* both controllers under a *single* GameObject umbrella that eventually, when taken as a whole, will become a Player prefab—an object we'll reuse as often as we need for other scenes and levels. The First Person Controller prefabs we've created will only form a part of that Player object—because the Player can do more than just move around the scene. To get started, I'll create two new and empty GameObjects: Player and Controls. These are created using the menu item **GameObject ➤ Create Empty**. The Player GameObject represents the *root* object for the Player prefab. Beneath this (as a child game object) will be the Controls object. Then I'll add both First Person Controller objects as children of the Controls object. The hierarchy looks like Figure 5-7.

Figure 5-7. Creating a GameObject hierarchy for adding universal first-person controls to a Player prefab

Note   I've also overlapped the two First Person Controller objects in the scene, so each starts from the same position. Since we'll only need *one* of these two controllers, depending on the platform, their overlapping won't matter in terms of physics or collision. The other, unneeded, controller will be deactivated automatically at level start (as we'll see soon).

Note   Take care to position the mobile controller at the *world origin* (0, 0, 0). Due to its implementation, the screen position of the *left* and *right* touch pads for mobile input are based on the controller's start position in the world. If a different world position is used, then, the mobile inputs will be offset on-screen.

Next, let's rename the First Person Controller objects to differentiate the desktop and mobile controllers. I've used the names *DesktopController* and *MobileControls* (see Figure 5-8).

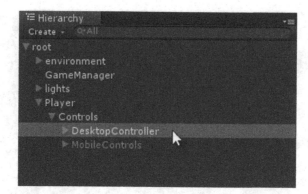

Figure 5-8. Renaming the First Person Controllers

In Listing 4-11 in the previous chapter, we examined collision detection with Cash Power-Ups. In that sample, the OnTriggerEnter event was used to detect the intersection of a rigid body with the power-up. While coding that event, we were aware that, in the future, there would be several rigid bodies moving around the level during gameplay, namely the Player *and* Enemies. Since we wanted to avoid enemies collecting power-ups, we coded OnTriggerEnter to verify the colliding objects' tag, ensuring it was marked as *player*. To ensure our player object, and its First Person Controllers, work in conjunction with that functionality, we'll need to tag the relevant objects as player. Since the desktop and mobile First Person Controllers are implemented slightly differently, we'll need to tag different GameObjects in each one. For the desktop First Person Controller, the root object DesktopController should be marked as player (since it features the physics-based CharacterController component). For the MobileController, it should be the object named player, which is a child object embedded deep within the Mobile prefab—again, this object features the CharacterController component (see Figure 5-9).

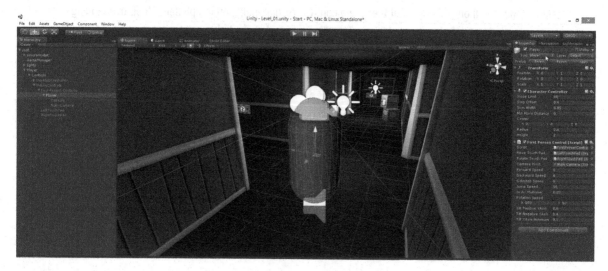

Figure 5-9. Tagging objects in First Person Controllers to work with power-up collision

Platform Dependent Compilation

The desktop and mobile controllers are now added and configured successfully in the scene. If you run the game now, however, both controllers will be active and operational—working simultaneously: desktop input controlling the desktop controller, and mobile input controlling the mobile controller. That's not what we want. The aim now is to code a C# script to deactivate the redundant controller at scene start-up, leaving us with the relevant controller, based on the target platform. This can be achieved using a Unity C# feature known as *Platform Dependent Compilation*. To see this in action, create a new C# script file, ControlSwitcher.cs, and attach this as a component to the Controls GameObject, created in the previous section (see Figure 5-10). Then take a look at Listing 5-1 for ControlSwitcher.cs, after which comments follow.

Figure 5-10. Attaching a ControlSwitcher script to the Controls object. This script will deactivate the redundant First Person Controller on scene start-up

Listing 5-1. ControlSwitcher.cs: Deactivates Redundant First Person Controller

```
01 //-------------------------------------------------
02 using UnityEngine;
03 using System.Collections;
04 //-------------------------------------------------
05 public class ControlSwitcher : MonoBehaviour
06 {
07      //-------------------------------------------------
08      //Reference to desktop first person controller (default)
09      public GameObject DesktopFirstPerson = null;
10
11      //Reference to mobile first person controller
12      public GameObject MobileFirstPerson = null;
13
14      //-------------------------------------------------
15      //Select appropriate first person control for platform
```

```
16      void Awake()
17      {
18          //If mobile platform, then use mobile first person controller
19          #if UNITY_IPHONE || UNITY_ANDROID || UNITY_WP8
20          DesktopFirstPerson.SetActive(false);
21          MobileFirstPerson.SetActive(true);
22          #endif
23      }
24      //------------------------------------------------
25 }
```

- **Lines 09–12.** This class defines two public variables: DesktopFirstPerson and MobileFirstPerson. These are references to each of the controllers, one of which should be disabled on Awake.

- **Lines 19–22.** The Awake event is called implicitly before Start, when the scene begins. Line 19 uses the Platform Dependent Compilation syntax to define two subsequent lines that should execute, only if the platform is iPhone, Android, or Windows Phone. The global flag UNITY_IPHONE encompasses all iOS devices, such as iPads and iPhones. In this sample, if the platform is a mobile device, then the desktop controller is deactivated and the mobile controller is activated. Notice there is no branch for a desktop platform. Why? We can simply avoid coding this branch by deactivating the mobile First Person Controller *by default in the Unity Editor*. This way, the default configuration saves us coding and time!

It's important to understand both what *is* happening and *is not* happening regarding Platform Dependent Compilation. Line 19 of Listing 5-1 is *not* executed every time the game runs on *every* platform. The Awake function is *not* performing a runtime check for the active Unity platform, and then acting accordingly. The #if directive is *not* the same as an if statement. The #if directive works at the *compilation* level and not at a *runtime* level. In practice, Listing 5-1 means that when the Unity platform is switched to desktop, the compiler recompiles the *ControlSwitcher* script and treats lines 19–22 as *code comments*, since the active platform is not a mobile one. The compiler only recognizes lines 19–22 as valid when the active platform is mobile.

Go ahead and give this code a try—the result is a universal First Person Controller. Whether you're on desktop or mobile, your scene now has a First Person Controller ready to use!

> **Note**   If you just want to make a runtime check for the active Unity platform, then use Application. platform. See the online Unity documentation at https://docs.unity3d.com/Documentation/ ScriptReference/Application-platform.html.

Head Bobbing and Sine Waves

Whenever the First Person Controller walks forward or backward, we want the camera to bob or oscillate up and down smoothly in the Y axis. This is to simulate the involuntary head movement that occurs naturally whenever most bipeds, like humans, move using their legs. We could, of course, implement this behavior by resorting to the familiar bobbing motion technique created for the Cash Power-Up in the previous chapter. But this motion was decidedly *linear* and *mechanical*. That is, the Cash Power-Up moves up and down at a *constant* speed and in a *straight* line. Head motion, however, isn't really like this: its movement upward is slightly slower than its movement downward. There's a smooth ease-in and ease-out motion that unravels with our heads whenever we walk around. In fact, if this motion could be plotted on a line graph, in terms of the camera Y position over time, it would probably create a *curve* and not a straight line. This curve, when repeated in sequence, would look like a *wave*. In real life, our head motion may not really form a completely smooth and repeating curve, but it could be approximated believably in a video game by using such a curve. One type of curve that creates repeated oscillation is a *sine wave* (see Figure 5-11).

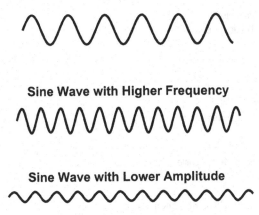

Figure 5-11. *Sine waves are useful for creating smooth oscillations in motion*

Mathematically, there are two main parts to a sine wave—at least, the two parts of interest *to us* in creating head bobbing; these are the *frequency* and the *amplitude* of the wave (see Figure 5-11). The amplitude refers to the tallness of the wave—it represents how strong the head bob should be. Higher amplitude values will produce higher and lower head bobs—more extreme offsets from a default center. The frequency refers to the size or horizontal length of one complete wave cycle (known as a *period*). The higher the frequency, the more wibbly-wobbly the wave is! In other words, higher frequencies will make the head bob happen more often and quickly. The general formula for producing a sine wave is *sin(angle × frequency) × amplitude*. If frequency is 1, then a range of 0–360 degrees for angle will produce one complete period for the wave. Values outside this range (higher or lower) will simply produce repetitions of the *same* wave—so you never need to worry about clamping between 0–360 for sine waves.

Now let's code a C# class that can be attached to the First Person Controller to add head-bob motion. I'll call this class HeadBob.cs (see Listing 5-2; comments follow).

Listing 5-2. HeadBob.cs: Script to Add Head-Bob Motion to Camera Through Sine Waves

```
01 //--------------------------------------------------
02 //Class to make first person camera bob gently up and down while walking
03 using UnityEngine;
04 using System.Collections;
05 //--------------------------------------------------
```

```
06 public class HeadBob : MonoBehaviour
07 {
08        //Strength of head bob - amplitude of sine wave
09        public float Strength = 1.0f;
10
11        //Frequency of wave
12        public float BobAmount = 2.0f;
13
14        //Neutral head height position
15        public float HeadY = 1.0f;
16
17        //Cached transform
18        private Transform ThisTransform = null;
19
20        //Elapsed Time since movement
21        private float ElapsedTime = 0.0f;
22
23        //-------------------------------------------------
24        void Start()
25        {
26                //Get transform
27                ThisTransform = transform;
28        }
29        //-------------------------------------------------
30        // Update is called once per frame
31        void Update ()
32        {
33                //If input is not allowed, then exit
34                if(!GameManager.Instance.InputAllowed) return;
35
36                //Get player movement if input allowed
37                float horizontal = Mathf.Abs(Input.GetAxis("Horizontal"));
38                float vertical = Mathf.Abs(Input.GetAxis("Vertical"));
39
40                //Total movement
41                float TotalMovement = Mathf.Clamp(horizontal + vertical,0.0f,1.0f);
42
43                //Update elapsed time
44                ElapsedTime = (TotalMovement > 0.0f) ? ElapsedTime += Time.deltaTime : 0.0f;
45
46                //Y Offset for headbob
47                float YOffset = Mathf.Sin (ElapsedTime * BobAmount) * Strength;
48
49                //Create position
50                Vector3 PlayerPos = new Vector3(ThisTransform.position.x, HeadY + YOffset *
                   TotalMovement, ThisTransform.position.z);
51
52                //Update position
53                ThisTransform.position = PlayerPos;
54        }
55        //-------------------------------------------------
56 }
```

- **Lines 09 and 12.** The public class members `Strength` and `BobAmount` define the amplitude and frequency of the sine wave, respectively. They can be used to control and customize the sine wave to affect head bobbing.

- **Line 15.** The `HeadY` value will represent the camera Y position in the scene *when at rest*. During movement, the camera Y position will be offset from this center as a result of the sine wave.

- **Line 34.** I've added a Boolean member to the GameManager `InputAllowed`, which can be set to false to disable user input. All input-reading classes should verify this variable before processing input.

- **Lines 37 and 38.** Together these lines will result in two variables, either 1 or 0, indicating whether the user is moving the First Person Controller (1=Yes, 0=No). If yes, then we'll need to apply head-bob movement; otherwise, the camera should be at its default Y position.

- **Line 44.** The `ElapsedTime` variable keeps track of the total elapsed time in seconds since the Player started moving. This value will be used for calculating the sine wave.

- **Line 47.** Finally, the amount of Y offset for the camera on the current frame is calculated using the `Mathf.Sin` function, along with the amplitude and frequency parameters.

Now add the HeadBob.cs script to the *First Person Controllers*, and then take them for a test run in-game. Your First Person Controller should now display a distinct head bob when walking. The final details can be tweaked using the class public member variables from the Object Inspector (see Figure 5-12).

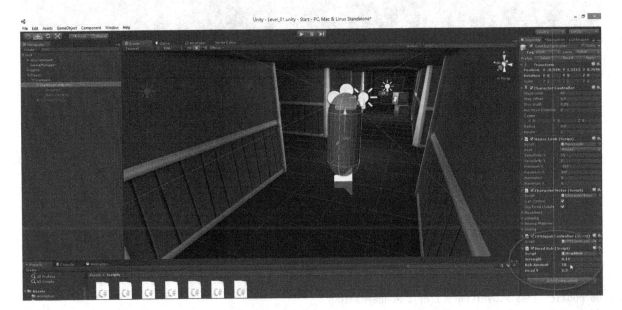

Figure 5-12. Assigning the HeadBob script to First Person Controllers

First-Person Capsule Mesh

Next, let's get to work on creating a general `PlayerController.cs` class for handling most high-level player functionality. The first issue to address with this class concerns the player controllers. Both the desktop and mobile First Person Controllers feature a renderable capsule mesh, which is both visible in the Unity Editor *and* at runtime. Normally, the capsule mesh is *not* visible during gameplay, but this is only because the controller camera is positioned in a specific way. In theory, the capsule *could* be seen if reflective materials were used in the scene or if the camera were offset through animation (and it will be later). There's nothing either in principle or practice to prevent the capsule mesh from being seen, and normally we don't want it to be seen. So let's hide it at runtime using a C# script, as opposed to disabling it in the editor. This lets us continue seeing the capsule mesh in the editor at design time. To get started, create a `PlayerController.cs` file. This will be added to each First Person Controller object—attached to the same object as the HeadBob script—the object marked with the *player* tag (see Figure 5-13). This is important for later because this script will also handle Player collision events with power-ups: specifically, cash allocation (see Listing 5-3; comments follow).

Figure 5-13. Adding the PlayerController script to First Person Controller objects

Listing 5-3. PlayerController.cs: Disabling Capsule Meshes for First Person Controllers

```
01 //------------------------------------------------
02 using UnityEngine;
03 using System.Collections;
04 using System.Collections.Generic;
05 //------------------------------------------------
06 public class PlayerController : MonoBehaviour
07 {
08        //------------------------------------------------
```

```
09        //Reference to transform
10        private Transform ThisTransform = null;
11
12        //-----------------------------------------------
13        //Called when object is created
14        void Start()
15        {
16            //Get First person capsule and make non-visible
17            MeshRenderer Capsule = GetComponentInChildren<MeshRenderer>();
18            Capsule.enabled = false;
19
20            //Get cached transform
21            ThisTransform = transform;
22        }
23 }
```

- **Line 17.** Here, the GetComponentInChildren API function is called to search through the GameObject hierarchy, from the current object downward, to find the first mesh renderer component. For First Person Controllers, there's only one mesh renderer—the capsule collider. Line 18 disables the render, hiding the collider.

Note More information on GetComponentInChildren can be found in the Unity documentation at https://docs.unity3d.com/Documentation/ScriptReference/Component.GetComponentInChildren.html.

Handling Cash Collection

Before proceeding, jump back to the previous chapter and consider Listing 4-11, especially lines 41 and 44. This sample implements the Cash Power-Up OnTriggerEnter event, which is called each and every time the Player collides with the power-up in the scene. Lines 41 and 44 retrieve a PlayerController component, attached to the Player GameObject, and increases its *Cash* member. In other words, the PlayerController needs to implement a Cash variable to maintain its collected cash, and this member should be increased for each Cash Power-Up collected. The Cash member should be implemented as a *property*, and not a public variable. Doing this is consistent with the event-handling functionality coded in Chapter 3, because properties allow us to *validate* the assignment of values to variables, giving us the opportunities to call functions and invoke event notifications. For cash collection, we'll need to verify whether the *collected cash* exceeds or meets the *total cash* available in the level. Remember, when the Player collects all available cash, the level is completed! The PlayerController class can be amended to support cash collection using the code in Listing 5-4.

Listing 5-4. Changing PlayerController.cs to Handle Cash Collection

```
01 //--------------------------------------------------
02 using UnityEngine;
03 using System.Collections;
04 using System.Collections.Generic;
05 //--------------------------------------------------
06 public class PlayerController : MonoBehaviour
07 {
08         //--------------------------------------------------
09         //Amount of cash player should collect to complete level
10         public float CashTotal = 1400.0f;
11
12         //Amount of cash for this player
13         private float cash = 0.0f;
14
15         //Reference to transform
16         private Transform ThisTransform = null;
17
18         //--------------------------------------------------
19         //Called when object is created
20         void Start()
21         {
22                 //Get First person capsule and make non-visible
23                 MeshRenderer Capsule = GetComponentInChildren<MeshRenderer>();
24                 Capsule.enabled = false;
25
26                 //Get cached transform
27                 ThisTransform = transform;
28         }
29         //--------------------------------------------------
30         //Accessors to set and get cash
31         public float Cash
32         {
33                 //Return cash value
34                 get{return cash;}
35
36                 //Set cash and validate, if required
37                 set
38                 {
39                         //Set cash
40                         cash = value;
41
42                         //Check collection limit - post notification if limit reached
43                         if(cash >= CashTotal)
44                                 GameManager.Notifications.PostNotification(this, "CashCollected");
45                 }
46         }
47         //--------------------------------------------------
48 }
```

- **Lines 10 and 13.** Two variables have been added: `TotalCash` representing the total amount of cash to collect in the level, and `cash`, a private variable representing the amount of cash actually collected. The `TotalCash` variable could instead be added to the GameManager or to a separate `Level` class since it relates specifically *to the level*, as opposed to the player.

- **Lines 31–46.** The `Cash` property gets and sets the private `cash` variable for the PlayerController. If all cash has been collected, then a `CashCollected` event is fired. Typically, the GameManager will listen for and handle this event to end the current level and move to the next.

After adding this code to the First Person Controllers, be sure to test it by running the game in-editor and collecting power-ups. Use `Debug.Log` statements to help determine program flow. Get into the habit of testing often. Don't simply write many pages of code without testing, even if you're confident there are no mistakes. It's easy to overlook even typographical errors. Instead, add some lines of code, test them, and then fix, if required. Back and forth between coding and testing. This helps you to eliminate bugs before they even get introduced.

For testing cash collection, I'd temporarily turn the `Cash` variable into public, as opposed to private, so I can see its value in the Object Inspector. Then I'd play-test in-editor, observing the Cash value in the Object Inspector as power-ups are collected. Remember, the Object Inspector is a powerful debugging tool (see Figure 5-14) as well! Don't forget to switch Cash back to private once you're done.

Figure 5-14. Using the Object Inspector as a debugging tool to observe cash collection behavior

Life and Death: Getting Started

Historically and philosophically, there's much of interest to be said about the way video games implement life and death. Here, CMOD uses the "traditional" approach where Player life or health is expressed quantitatively as an integer between 0–100; 0 is death and 100 is full health. Similarly, in keeping with retro side-scrollers where you can attack a phone booth and get a health-restoring turkey out of it, CMOD allows you to pick up floating, restorative hamburger power-ups to restore health. These tasty burgers have the power-up to heal bullet wounds and punch attacks. Death, however, comes upon the Player when health reaches 0 or below; and this typically happens because of enemy attacks. Here again, CMOD takes the traditional approach to death: when death arrives, the scene is restarted and the Player respawns back to the level origin, allowing a resurrection *ad infinitum*. So let's start implementing these concepts now, starting with a consideration of death.

When the Player dies, I'd like to play a small death-sequence before restarting the level in the form of a camera animation. Specifically, the camera should roll over and fall to the ground. This simple transformation-style animation can be recorded using the Unity Animation Editor, through **Window ➤ Animation**. This editor works through key framing (see Figure 5-15). There I've defined two key frames for rotation and position, defining the motion for the camera as it falls to the ground. I'm going to apply the animation to a newly created empty game object, `AnimatedCamera`, which has been parented to the First Person Controller camera (as we'll see shortly), to keep the translation and rotation *separate* from the camera transformations themselves. When the animation is saved from the editor, it's added automatically as an animation clip asset in the Project panel. I've named the asset *CameraDeath*.

Figure 5-15. Creating a basic camera fall animation using the Legacy Animation Editor

> **Note**   More information on the Unity Legacy Animation Editor can be found at `https://docs.unity3d.com/Documentation/Components/animeditor-UsingAnimationEditor.html`.
>
> Remember, the animation and completed project for this chapter are included in the chapter companion files at `Chapter05/Completed`.

The animation asset itself just defines a generic animation sequence in terms of key frames and transformations; these could apply to any GameObject. For the death sequence, I'll first create empty objects (named `AnimatedCamera`), added to the First Person Controller, as parents of the Camera objects. Make sure their transformations are set to 0 for all positions and rotations (see Figure 5-16). Then add *Animator* components to the objects, which will handle the animation functionality through the Mecanim system. Animator components can be added from the main menu by choosing **Component ➤ Miscellaneous ➤ Animator**.

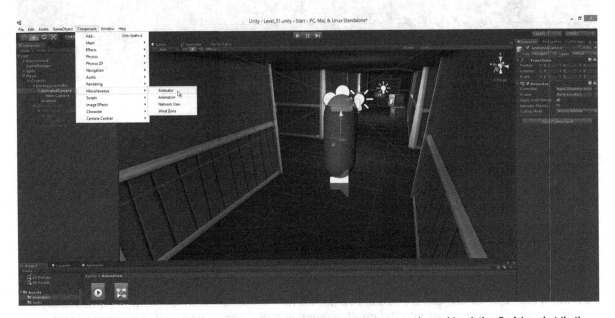

Figure 5-16. Adding animations to camera parent objects. Doing this may break connections with existing Prefabs—but that's fine in this case

The added Animator component begins empty, without any associations to animation. We'll fix that now. Specifically, we'll create an *AnimationController* asset that will drive the camera death animation when health reaches less than 0. To do this, create a new AnimationController asset, right-clicking in the Project panel and choosing **Create ➤ Animation Controller** from the context menu. View the Animation Controller (see Figure 5-17) using the *Animator* window (*not* the *Animation* window).

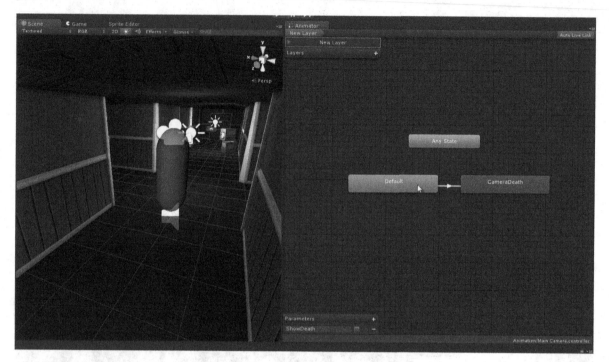

Figure 5-17. Using the Animator window to control animation logic

> **Note**   Personally, I'm not entirely convinced the term *Animator* is appropriate for this editor. It's not wholly descriptive of what it actually does. Specifically, it's a node editor and a form of visual programming that's concerned with wiring-up animation sequences into a logical arrangement to control their playback under specific conditions. I think that *animation dynamics* or *animation nodes* would be more descriptive names. But anyway, *Animator* is the name currently assigned to the editor by Unity Technologies; and I'll use this name throughout the rest of the book, where applicable.

To control the logic for camera animation I've added two states: a *default* state, with no associated animation clip, that transitions into the *death* animation state, associated with the CameraDeath animation clip. The transition between the default and death state is controlled by a Death trigger parameter. This means that when the Death trigger is set to true, the camera death animation will play (see Figure 5-18). For this trigger to fire, a script must be used.

Figure 5-18. Building a transition from the default state to the death state

Making Death: Scripting with Mecanim

Together, the animation clip and the Animation Controller define the animation key frames and general playback logic. But still, the act of triggering and playing the animation when death occurs needs to be coded. This will be achieved by amending the PlayerController.cs script (see Listing 5-5 for further PlayerController refines, followed by comments).

Listing 5-5. Refining PlayerController for a Death Animation

```
01 //-----------------------------------------------
02 using UnityEngine;
03 using System.Collections;
04 using System.Collections.Generic;
05 //-----------------------------------------------
06 public class PlayerController : MonoBehaviour
07 {
08      //-----------------------------------------------
09      //Amount of cash player should collect to complete level
10      public float CashTotal = 1400.0f;
11
```

```
12       //Amount of cash for this player
13       private float cash = 0.0f;
14
15       //Reference to transform
16       private Transform ThisTransform = null;
17
18       //Respawn time in seconds after dying
19       public float RespawnTime = 2.0f;
20
21       //Get Mecanim animator component in children
22       private Animator AnimComp = null;
23
24       //-----------------------------------------------
25       //Called when object is created
26       void Start()
27       {
28            //Get First person capsule and make non-visible
29            MeshRenderer Capsule = GetComponentInChildren<MeshRenderer>();
30            Capsule.enabled = false;
31
32            //Get Animator
33            AnimComp = GetComponentInChildren<Animator>();
34
35            //Get cached transform
36            ThisTransform = transform;
37       }
38       //-----------------------------------------------
39       //Accessors to set and get cash
40       public float Cash
41       {
42            //Return cash value
43            get{return cash;}
44
45            //Set cash and validate, if required
46            set
47            {
48                 //Set cash
49                 cash = value;
50
51                 //Check collection limit - post notification if limit reached
52                 if(cash >= CashTotal)
53                      GameManager.Notifications.PostNotification(this, "CashCollected");
54            }
55       }
56       //-----------------------------------------------
57       //Function called when player dies
58       public IEnumerator Die()
59       {
60            //Disable input
61            GameManager.Instance.InputAllowed = false;
62
63            //Trigger death animation if available
```

```
64          if(AnimComp) AnimComp.SetTrigger("ShowDeath");
65
66          //Wait for respawn time
67          yield return new WaitForSeconds(RespawnTime);
68
69          //Restart level
70          Application.LoadLevel(Application.loadedLevel);
71      }
72      //-----------------------------------------
73 }
```

- **Lines 19 and 22**. The Respawn time variable is effectively a waiting period used by the Die coroutine. It expresses the amount of time in seconds to wait before restarting the level, allowing enough time for the death animation to play. The AnimComp member is an internal reference to the camera's Animator component; used for controlling and invoking animation states in the Animator Controller. A reference to this component is retrieved in the class Start event, at line 33.

- **Lines 58–72**. The Die coroutine is currently not called by anything in the class. It will be invoked later when Player health reduces to 0 or less, to invoke the death animation. When the coroutine is called, the *ShowDeath* trigger is set in the AnimationController—notice the name "ShowDeath" matches exactly the trigger name in the Animation Controller. When this trigger is set, the camera death animation will be played. In addition, the Application.LoadLevel API function is called to reload the level (respawn behavior).

Note   More information in Application.LoadLevel can be found in the Unity online documentation at http://docs.unity3d.com/Documentation/ScriptReference/Application.LoadLevel.html. There are also variations of this function, including LoadLevelAsync and LoadLevelAdditive.

Implementing Health

The Player needs a health feature to keep track of his lifeline in-game. This feature is also important for determining whether a death and respawn are required. Take a look at Listing 5-6 to see how PlayerController is refined to implement health and death in full. Relevant changes are highlighted in bold. Then, in subsequent sections, we'll explore the code deeper to see how it works more thoroughly. The full PlayerController.cs file is included in the chapter companion files.

Listing 5-6. PlayerController, Life and Death

```
001 //-----------------------------------------
002 using UnityEngine;
003 using System.Collections;
004 using System.Collections.Generic;
005 //-----------------------------------------
```

```
006 public class PlayerController : MonoBehaviour
007 {
008        //--------------------------------------------------
009        //Amount of cash player should collect to complete level
010        public float CashTotal = 1400.0f;
011
012        //Amount of cash for this player
013        private float cash = 0.0f;
014
015        //Reference to transform
016        private Transform ThisTransform = null;
017
018        //Respawn time in seconds after dying
019        public float RespawnTime = 2.0f;
020
021        //Player health
022        public int health = 100;
023
024        //Get Mecanim animator component in children
025        private Animator AnimComp = null;
026
027        //Private damage texture
028        private Texture2D DamageTexture = null;
029
030        //Screen coordinates
031        private Rect ScreenRect;
032
033        //Show damage texture?
034        private bool ShowDamage = false;
035
036        //Damage texture interval (amount of time in seconds to show texture)
037        private float DamageInterval = 0.2f;
038        //--------------------------------------------------
039        //Called when object is created
040        void Start()
041        {
042                //Get First person capsule and make non-visible
043                MeshRenderer Capsule = GetComponentInChildren<MeshRenderer>();
044                Capsule.enabled = false;
045
046                //Get Animator
047                AnimComp = GetComponentInChildren<Animator>();
048
049                //Create damage texture
050                DamageTexture = new Texture2D(1,1);
051                DamageTexture.SetPixel(0,0,new Color(255,0,0,0.5f));
052                DamageTexture.Apply();
053
054                //Get cached transform
055                ThisTransform = transform;
056        }
```

```
057        //--------------------------------------------------
058        //Accessors to set and get cash
059        public float Cash
060        {
061                //Return cash value
062                get{return cash;}
063
064                //Set cash and validate, if required
065                set
066                {
067                        //Set cash
068                        cash = value;
069
070                        //Check collection limit - post notification if limit reached
071                        if(cash >= CashTotal)
072                                GameManager.Notifications.PostNotification(this, "CashCollected");
073                }
074        }
075        //--------------------------------------------------
076        //Accessors to set and get health
077        public int Health
078        {
079                //Return health value
080                get{return health;}
081
082                //Set health and validate, if required
083                set
084                {
085                        health = value;
086
087                        //Playe Die functionality
088                        if(health <= 0) gameObject.SendMessage("Die",SendMessageOptions.
                        DontRequireReceiver);
089                }
090        }
091        //--------------------------------------------------
092        //Function to apply damage to the player
093        public IEnumerator ApplyDamage(int Amount = 0)
094        {
095                //Reduce health
096                Health -= Amount;
097
098                //Post damage notification
099                GameManager.Notifications.PostNotification(this, "PlayerDamaged");
100
101                //Show damage texture
102                ShowDamage = true;
103
104                //Wait for interval
105                yield return new WaitForSeconds(DamageInterval);
106
```

```
107              //Hide damage texture
108              ShowDamage = false;
109          }
110      //-----------------------------------------------
111      //ON GUI Function to show texture
112      void OnGUI()
113      {
114              if(ShowDamage){GUI.DrawTexture(ScreenRect,DamageTexture);}
115      }
116      //-----------------------------------------------
117      //Function called when player dies
118      public IEnumerator Die()
119      {
120              //Disable input
121              GameManager.Instance.InputAllowed = false;
122
123              //Trigger death animation if available
124              if(AnimComp) AnimComp.SetTrigger("ShowDeath");
125
126              //Wait for respawn time
127              yield return new WaitForSeconds(RespawnTime);
128
129              //Restart level
130              Application.LoadLevel(Application.loadedLevel);
131      }
132      //-----------------------------------------------
133      void Update()
134      {
135              //Build screen rect on update (in case screen size changes)
136              ScreenRect.x = ScreenRect.y = 0;
137              ScreenRect.width = Screen.width;
138              ScreenRect.height = Screen.height;
139      }
140      //-----------------------------------------------
141  }
```

Health and Damage: Procedural Textures

Listing 5-6 implemented the bulk of the PlayerController class. This class features a health value, defined as private integer member health (line 22). Access to this value is controlled through the public Health property, which validates the health value each time it's updated or changed. When (and if) it reaches 0 or below, the Player death functionality is executed, as shown in line 87. Notice, however, that additional functions and variables were added to PlayerController, besides simply a Health property. Of special significance is the ApplyDamage coroutine, which can be called to damage the Player. Damage in this sense might seem merely a matter of just reducing Player health, but typically we want to do more. When the Player is damaged, we may want to play a sound and flash the screen red to offer graphical feedback that damage has been taken. These effects are not essential, but they emphasize a point to the gamer that something bad happened. The ApplyDamage coroutine achieves this effect by fading a red texture into view. Let's examine further exactly how it does this (see Listing 5-7, which is an extract from Listing 5-6).

Listing 5-7. Creating Textures

```
039     //Called when object is created
040     void Start()
041     {
042         //Get First person capsule and make non-visible
043         MeshRenderer Capsule = GetComponentInChildren<MeshRenderer>();
044         Capsule.enabled = false;
045
046         //Get Animator
047         AnimComp = GetComponentInChildren<Animator>();
048
049         //Create damage texture
050         DamageTexture = new Texture2D(1,1);
051         DamageTexture.SetPixel(0,0,new Color(255,0,0,0.5f));
052         DamageTexture.Apply();
053
054         //Get cached transform
055         ThisTransform = transform;
056     }
```

The Start event for PlayerController has been amended to create a texture in code to be used as a red damage texture when damage is taken. This red texture could have been created manually in an image editor and imported as a texture asset; but when bold-color textures are required (often red, black, and white) it's usually more convenient to generate them from code. Here, a texture of size 1×1 pixel in dimensions is created, and the SetPixel method of Texture2D is used to fill the texture with the RGB value for red. Notice that the Apply method has also been called to confirm the SetPixel operation. This code doesn't actually display the texture on-screen; texture display is covered in the next section. More information on Texture2D can be found in the Unity documentation at http://docs.unity3d.com/Documentation/ScriptReference/Texture2D.html.

Note   Although the red texture is generated at 1×1 pixels, it doesn't have to display on-screen at that size; textures can be *stretched*. This means a 1×1–pixel red texture can be upsized to the screen dimensions to fill the screen with red. Normally, the upsizing of textures is to be avoided due to quality loss caused by resampling, but this is an exceptional case. Quality loss doesn't apply to a texture filled with a single color.

GUIs

The previous section demonstrated how fill textures can be generated procedurally. This section explores how we can show textures on-screen quickly using the native GUI functionality. The Unity GUI classes are designed to display GUI elements in screen space. And we can use them here to fill a red texture across the screen. This happens in the native event OnGUI (see Listing 5-8, which is an extract of Listing 5-6).

Listing 5-8. Displaying Textures

```
110     //-------------------------------------------------
111     //ON GUI Function to show texture
112     void OnGUI()
113     {
114             if(ShowDamage){GUI.DrawTexture(ScreenRect,DamageTexture);}
115     }

        //[...]

132     //-------------------------------------------------
133     void Update()
134     {
135             //Build screen rect on update (in case screen size changes)
136             ScreenRect.x = ScreenRect.y = 0;
137             ScreenRect.width = Screen.width;
138             ScreenRect.height = Screen.height;
139     }
140     //-------------------------------------------------
```

Here, the Update function is used to size a rectangle structure (ScreenRect) to the screen dimensions (in pixels). This rect is updated on each frame, instead of being generated at application-start, since it's possible, in some circumstances, for the display size to change during gameplay. For example, the user could change the screen resolution or resize the game window. The OnGUI function is where the texture is drawn or flashed to the display for a few seconds while damage is taken, using a call to GUI.DrawTexture. The OnGUI function is called implicitly by Unity *several times per frame*. This means OnGUI is usually called more regularly than Update, making it one of the most computationally expensive events and a frequent source of performance problems. In short, you'll almost *never* want to do anything in OnGUI, except draw graphical elements using the native GUI class. And there are even developers who recommend never using OnGUI at all, even for *GUIs*. For my part, while the GUI class and OnGUI events can be useful for drawing limited GUIs (such as showing flashing red textures), I almost never use it for GUIs, because I find it often causes performance issues on mobile devices. Sometimes workarounds can be used, but later in this book we'll see an alternative method for GUIs. In this case, however, OnGUI can be used profitably to display a damage animation.

> **Note**   Don't just take my word that this code works. Test it for yourself. Temporarily edit the Update event, for example, so that a key press triggers the ApplyDamage event, to see the damage functionality in action!

Conclusion

So, reaching this far, we've created a working and flexible `PlayerController` class offering universal first-person functionality that works on both desktop and mobile devices, and can also collect power-ups whenever it intersects them in the scene. Further, the controller implements health and death functionality. By now, you should be able to do the following:

- Create a universal First Person Controller

- Understand Platform Dependent Compilation

- Understand sine waves and smooth motion

- Create a head-bob animation for a camera

- Integrate the PlayerController into the event and notification system

- Handle collision events

- Maintain collected cash

- Generate procedural textures

- Understand the limitations of GUIs and OnGUI

- Use Mecanim and the Animator to define the logic for animations

- Maintain Player health

Weapons

Let's quickly recap what we've done so far in CMOD. At this stage, we've created a complete game environment with rooms and corridors, collectable power-up objects for health restore and cash bonuses, a notifications manager class to send and dispatch events to game objects, and a universal player controller for desktops and mobiles, including first-person functionality with a complementary head bob. In this chapter, we'll build on this existing work by adding weapons for the Player character—specifically, a short-range fists/punch weapon (the default weapon) and a long-range gun weapon, which can be collected through a weapons power-up. The purpose of these weapons is to damage Enemy characters. Of course, *right now*, we haven't created any enemies for CMOD—they'll be coded in the *next* chapter. But here we'll at least make a start with weapons. In creating these, a wide range of Unity and C# concepts will be explored in depth; specifically, sprite and object animation, physics and rays, *object orientation*, *class inheritance* and *polymorphism*. So let's get started...

Weapons Overview

CMOD features a total of two weapons that can be used by the Player character; though only one weapon may be active and in use at any one time. These weapons are *fists that punch* (as shown in Figure 6-1) and a *gun* (as shown in Figure 6-2). These weapons are considered in more detail next.

Figure 6-1. The default fists/punch weapon

Figure 6-2. The collectable gun weapon

> **Note**   This chapter assumes you're resuming work from where we left off in the previous; or else you can begin from the starting project associated with this chapter, included in the book companion files inside folder `Chapter06/Start`.

- **Fists/punch.** Perhaps the most common default weapon in any FPS shooter (as well as the weakest) is the fists/punch. The fists/punch is the "old reliable" weapon: short-ranged, weak, and typically used only as a last resort—when all other weapons have expired. The main advantage of the fists/punch is their *infinite reusability*: they *never* run out of ammo, simply because they're not the kind of weapon to require ammo. In CMOD, the Player begins with the fists/punch weapon.

- **Gun.** Now, if the gamer is smart or just very, very lucky, then he'll collect the gun weapon, which is a marked improvement over the fists/punch. The gun allows ranged attack and deals heavier damage than fists/a punch. But, its ammo is *limited*. This means, it has a *finite* number of uses. After all bullets have been fired, the weapon expires and remains unusable—*unless* more ammo is collected. If the gun expires, the gamer must resort to the next best weapon, which will be fists/punch in our work here, since we're only making two weapons.

Object Orientation: Classes and Instances

This book assumes you're already familiar with the basics of C# and coding in Unity. Part of that fundamental knowledge includes a general understanding of objects and object orientation. Indeed, we've already made extensive use of these concepts in creating many classes over previous chapters, such as classes for events, power-ups, and player controllers. But before proceeding further, let's revisit object orientation to reinforce our understanding. Object orientation will be critical for our work with weapons.

Object orientation begins with the concept of a *class*. But what exactly is that? Of course, we've coded classes before in previous chapters using C# script files—and they all worked! But it's important to understand more deeply the *mechanics* or *underpinning philosophy* of *how* it works. It's not enough to follow along with examples in a book and to copy and paste code. In short, a class is an *abstract* or *template* entity—something that exists in *theory* or in *principle*. We when look at the world around us, the analytical mind restlessly breaks things down into neat categories or groups in search of a deeper understanding. We don't just observe a random flux of atoms; instead, we see tables, and chairs, and trees, and people, and discrete objects that have clear beginnings and endings. We recognize all these things when we see them *because* of a general or abstract picture we hold in our minds.

For example, we *recognize a* table when we see one, because we have an abstract understanding of *a table*. That is, we *know enough* about everything tables have *in common* to recognize individual *instances* of a table when we see them in the real world. There is, in our minds, a general template or pattern of an ideal table. And this helps us to recognize particular real-world tables when we see them. The ideal table is a *class*. And the real-world specific tables are *instances* or *instantiations* of that class. In Unity, classes are defined in *script files*. Instances are made in the scene by way of *components*—that is, classes are instantiated in the scene as *components* on a game object. We just drag and drop scripts into the scene to make instantiations. Now, perhaps none of this is news to you—you may already know about objects and instances, but everything we've said so far poses a logistical problem for us when creating weapons. Let's see what that is.

Object Orientation: Inheritance

CMOD supports two weapon types, as we've seen. This immediately suggests that we need to create two separate C# classes: one for the fists/punch (Weapon_Punch.cs) and another for the gun (Weapon_Gun.cs). This is correct, but a problem introduces itself regarding code and feature duplication. The problem is that although the fist and gun weapons are separate and distinct objects, there are still many similarities between the weapon types. Specifically, both are *weapons*, both deal a specified amount of *damage* to enemies, both have a *recovery rate* (the amount of time that should elapse before the weapon can be reused after being fired), and both have a range (the distance from the enemy at which the weapon is effective). These are numerous and significant features held *in common*, and not just across the two weapons we're creating for CMOD in *this* book, but across almost *all* weapons imaginable. We could, of course, disregard these similarities entirely and simply jump into implementing our weapons straightaway, coding these properties *for each* weapon. This approach, however, is inefficient because it means we're adding the *same* kinds of properties to two *separate* classes. We're unnecessarily duplicating our workload and increasing the size of our code. Instead, we can solve this problem using *class inheritance* to develop a *base class* for all weapons.

Whenever we identify two separate classes—*X* and *Y*—that share lots of behavior and functionality in common, we've usually found good candidates for inheritance. Class inheritance allows you to create a third class, *Z*, known as a *base class*, which defines all behaviors common to X and Y. The classes X and Y (*subclasses*) can then *inherit* that functionality from the *base class* Z, to save you having to code it twice, once for X and again for Y. Base class Z is therefore a distillation of all commonalities between X and Y. It's not a class intended to be instantiated *on its own*. Its purpose is to be *inherited* by other classes that wish to *reuse* and recycle its behavior as though it were their own. This kind of class is more formally known as an *abstract base class*. So, let's start coding the Player weapons here, with the base class (see Listing 6-1, which demonstrates a base class Weapon.cs; comments follow).

Listing 6-1. Weapon.cs: Abstract Base Class for Player Weapons

```
01 //---------------------------------------------------
02 using UnityEngine;
03 using System.Collections;
04 //---------------------------------------------------
05 public class Weapon : MonoBehaviour
06 {
07          //Custom enum for weapon types
08          public enum WEAPON_TYPE {Punch=0, Gun=1};
09
10          //Weapon type
11          public WEAPON_TYPE Type = WEAPON_TYPE.Punch;
12
13          //Damage this weapon causes
14          public float Damage = 0.0f;
15
16          //Range of weapon (linear distance outwards from camera) measured in world units
17          public float Range = 1.0f;
18
19          //Amount of ammo remaining (-1 = infinite)
20          public int Ammo = -1;
21
22          //Recovery delay
23          //Amount of time in seconds before weapon can be used again
24          public float RecoveryDelay = 0.0f;
25
26          //Has this weapon been collected?
27          public bool Collected = false;
28
29          //Is this weapon currently equipped on player
30          public bool IsEquipped = false;
31
32          //Can this weapon be fired
33          public bool CanFire = true;
34
35          //Next weapon in cycle
36          public Weapon NextWeapon = null;
37 }
```

■ **Line 05.** Notice that practically any class definition in Unity always involves inheritance. Even our abstract base class Weapon derives from MonoBehaviour, a Unity API class used as a base for Components. Other weapon classes, such as Fists/Punch and Gun will derive from Weapon. This means there are multiple chains of inheritance happening here: Guns ➤ Weapon ➤ MonoBehaviour. And even MonoBehaviour derives from Behaviour, which derives from Component, which finally derives from Object—an ultimate ancestor class.

> **Note** More information on the ultimate API ancestor class, Object, can be found online in the Unity documentation at `https://docs.unity3d.com/Documentation/ScriptReference/Object.html`.

- **Lines 14, 17, 20, and 24.** These public class variables define Damage, Range, Ammo, and RecoveryDelay properties. Every weapon deals *damage* to an Enemy within its *range*, and can be used only so long as there is sufficient *ammo* remaining. Once used, however, there is a short *recovery/delay* time (measured in seconds) during which the Player cannot fire again. He must instead wait for the recovery period to expire before a second attack may be made. This is to simulate real-world recovery times when using weapons.

- **Line 27.** This is a Boolean determining whether the weapon has been collected by the Player. For all weapons except fists/punch, this value should begin as *false*.

- **Line 30.** This Boolean specifies whether a collected weapon is currently active and being used by the Player right now. Consequently, only one weapon may have this flag set to true at any one time.

- **Line 33.** CanFire is a Boolean describing whether the collected and equipped weapon can be fired right now. If this is *false*, then it's because the weapon RecoveryDelay has not yet expired.

So how would we inherit two new weapons from this abstract base class? Simply by creating two new script files, one for each new weapon, and specifying the Weapon class as the *ancestor*, instead of MonoBehaviour. In doing this, both classes inherit all Weapon behavior and functionality: that is, Weapon public properties also become public properties for the derived classes (see Listings 6-2 and 6-3 for Weapon_Punch.cs and Weapon_Gun.cs, respectively, configured for inheritance and ready for further refinement and coding).

Listing 6-2. Weapon_Punch.cs: Punch Weapon Derived from Weapon Base Class

```
01 //-------------------------------------------------
02 using UnityEngine;
03 using System.Collections;
04 //-------------------------------------------------
05 public class Weapon_Punch : Weapon
06 {
07 }
```

Listing 6-3. Weapon_Gun.cs: Gun Weapon Derived from Weapon Base Class

```
01 //-------------------------------------------------
02 using UnityEngine;
03 using System.Collections;
04 //-------------------------------------------------
05 public class Weapon_Gun : Weapon
06 {
07 }
```

Animations, Frames, and Prefabs

Before moving further, refining the derived gun classes to implement extended and specialized functionality for each weapon, we'll take a detour into animation. This might initially seem a misplaced detour. But animation will play an important role for our two weapon classes, because both must display a fire or attack animation each time the weapon is used. Consider Figures 6-1 and 6-2, which show not only each weapon, but also the frames of animation that should play when fired. When the gamer presses the Fire button, we'll want the active weapon to cycle through its frames of animation, returning back to the original, neutral frame when completed. To achieve this, a new class must be coded. Specifically, this class will accept an array of sprite objects in the scene (each sprite representing a *single frame* in an animation sequence) and it will hide and show all related sprites (frames) in sequence to play back the complete animation, frame by frame. Take a look at the class in Listing 6-4, called SpriteShowAnimator.cs. Comments follow.

Listing 6-4. SpriteShowAnimator.cs: Class to Display a Sprite Animation

```
01 //This class maintains a collection of sprite objects as frames of animation
02 //It shows and hides those frames according to a set of playback settings
03 //--------------------------------------------------------------------
04 using UnityEngine;
05 using System.Collections;
06 //--------------------------------------------------------------------
07 public class SpriteShowAnimator : MonoBehaviour
08 {
09         //--------------------------------------------------------------------
10         //Playback types - run once or loop forever
11         public enum ANIMATOR_PLAYBACK_TYPE {PLAYONCE = 0, PLAYLOOP = 1};
12
13         //Playback type for this animation
14         public ANIMATOR_PLAYBACK_TYPE PlaybackType = ANIMATOR_PLAYBACK_TYPE.PLAYONCE;
15
16         //Frames per second to play for this animation
17         public int FPS = 5;
18
19         //Custom ID for animation - used with function PlaySpriteAnimation
20         public int AnimationID = 0;
21
22         //Frames of animation
23         public SpriteRenderer[] Sprites = null;
24
25         //Should auto-play?
26         public bool AutoPlay = false;
27
28         //Should first hide all sprite renderers on playback? or leave at defaults
29         public bool HideSpritesOnStart = true;
30
31         //Boolean indicating whether animation is currently playing
32         bool IsPlaying = false;
```

```
33          //---------------------------------------------------------------
34          void Start()
35          {
36                  //Should we auto-play at start up?
37                  if(AutoPlay){StartCoroutine(PlaySpriteAnimation(AnimationID));}
38          }
39          //---------------------------------------------------------------
40          //Function to run animation
41          public IEnumerator PlaySpriteAnimation(int AnimID = 0)
42          {
43                  //Check if this animation should be started. Could be called via SendMessage or
                    BroadcastMessage
44                  if(AnimID!= AnimationID) yield break;
45
46                  //Should hide all sprite renderers?
47                  if(HideSpritesOnStart)
48                  {
49                          foreach(SpriteRenderer SR in Sprites)
50                                  SR.enabled = false;
51                  }
52
53                  //Set is playing
54                  IsPlaying = true;
55
56                  //Calculate delay time
57                  float DelayTime = 1.0f/FPS;
58
59                  //Run animation at least once
60                  do
61                  {
62                          foreach(SpriteRenderer SR in Sprites)
63                          {
64                                  SR.enabled = !SR.enabled;
65                                  yield return new WaitForSeconds(DelayTime);
66                                  SR.enabled = !SR.enabled;
67                          }
68                  }
69                  while(PlaybackType == ANIMATOR_PLAYBACK_TYPE.PLAYLOOP);
70
71                  //Stop animation
72                  StopSpriteAnimation(AnimationID);
73          }
74          //---------------------------------------------------------------
75          //Function to stop animation
76          public void StopSpriteAnimation(int AnimID = 0)
77          {
78                  //Check if this animation can and should be stopped
79                  if((AnimID!= AnimationID) || (!IsPlaying)) return;
80
81                  //Stop all coroutines (animation will no longer play)
82                  StopAllCoroutines();
83
```

```
84                //Is playing false
85                IsPlaying = false;
86
87                //Send Sprite Animation stopped event to gameobject
88                gameObject.SendMessage("SpriteAnimationStopped", AnimID,
                  SendMessageOptions.DontRequireReceiver);
89            }
90            //-------------------------------------------------------------
91  }
```

■ **Line 23.** The public array member *Sprites* references a collection of *SpriteRenderer* components in the scene, together representing all frames for an animation. The order of the SpriteRenderers in the array is important; the order defines the direction and flow of the animation, with the first element corresponding to the first frame, and the last element to the last frame. Notice how this animation class works: it accepts a collection of preinstantiated SpriteRenderers in the scene, and *shows* or *hides* them during animation playback—showing only the current and active frame, while hiding all other frames. This animation class will *not* edit or adjust sprite UVs.

■ **Line 17.** The FPS public member defines the animation speed. Specifically, it defines the number of sprites in the array SpriteRenderer that should be processed (or shown) *per second* during animation playback.

■ **Line 41.** The PlaySpriteAnimation coroutine should be called to start animation playback. If the member *PlaybackType* is set to *PLAYLOOP*, the coroutine will repeat endlessly unless StopSpriteAnimation is called.

Let's now put this animation class to the test by assembling a new weapon Prefab object in the scene, starting with the fists/punch weapon. To do this, I'll drag the four punch sprite frames from the atlas texture into the scene (each a unique frame of animation for the fists/punch weapon), making sure all sprites are positioned at exactly the same world position, overlapping one another. The sprites are *Spr_Punch_01*, *Spr_Punch_02*, *Spr_Punch_03*, and *Spr_Punch_04*. Overlapping their position is important to maintain frame consistency across the animation. It doesn't matter for appearances that the sprites overlap, since only one sprite will be shown at any one time (see Figure 6-3). The sprites will probably appear huge in comparison to the rest of the scene. Don't worry about this for now; we'll fix it later.

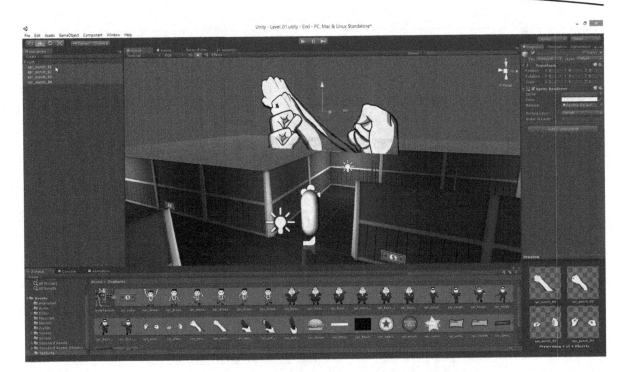

Figure 6-3. Adding the punch sprite frames into the scene; preparing to create a punch weapon prefab

Now parent all frame objects under a new, empty game object (Weapon_Punch). To this object, add the *SpriteShowAnimator* component and define the animation as shown in Figure 6-4. I've specified a *Playback Type* of loop for now, simply for testing purposes to observe the sprite animation in the Scene viewport, playing back endlessly as opposed to just once. For the final weapon prefab, the playback type will be set to *PlayOnce*, since an animation should play only once for each attack. Give this configuration a test to see the animation in action.

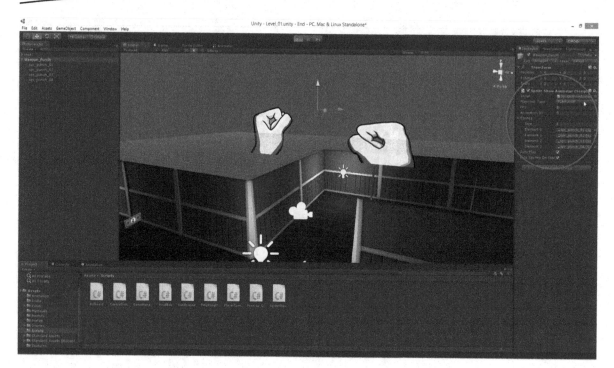

Figure 6-4. Playing the attack animation

> **Note**   Remember, all code in this chapter is included in the book companion files at
> Chapter06/AssetsToImport/.

Cameras: Layers and Rendering

If you take a look at Figures 6-3 and 6-4, you'll likely see a potential problem emerging for the Player weapons. Specifically, the Player weapons (whether a fists/punch or a gun) should (1) always appear at the screen middle-bottom, and (2) appear at a consistent and believable size (see Figure 6-5 for an example). Right now, Figures 6-3 and 6-4 show just how large the weapon sprites appear in relation to the scene. And if the scene is played right now, the weapons are not appropriately aligned on the screen either. Let's address the second problem first.

Figure 6-5. Weapons should appear at a consistent size and at the bottom-middle of the screen

No matter where the First Person Controller moves or looks in the scene during gameplay, the gun sprite should always follow, being aligned to the bottom-middle of the screen, exactly where we'd expect to find the Player's hand holding a weapon. There are many ways to achieve this functionality: you could, for example, use GameObject parenting to create transformation dependencies. But in this chapter, we'll use a layered camera technique, effectively rendering all scene geometry from the default first-person camera, and the weapon from a second and orthographic camera layered on top of the original rendering. To get started, I'll adjust the scene hierarchy somewhat for clearer organization.

Specifically, I'll create a new GameObject (called Weapons), adding this as a child of the Player object, and then add a new Camera object (WeaponCamera) as a child of the Weapons object, and finally, I'll add the Weapon_Punch object as a child of WeaponCamera. In addition, I'll also remove all components from the Camera object (including the AudioListener), leaving only the Camera component (see Figure 6-6 for clarification on this process).

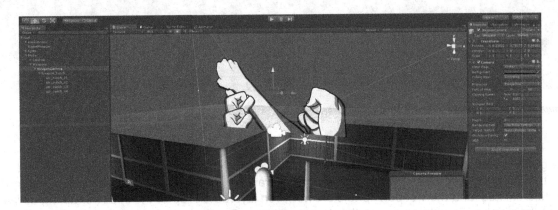

Figure 6-6. Housekeeping game objects and creating a second camera

> **Note**   Cameras are created by selecting **GameObject ➤ Create Other ➤ Camera** from the
> application menu.

After adding a second camera, change its *Projection Type* from *Perspective* to *Orthographic*.
Perspective cameras are useful for rendering 3D geometry in which objects are seen in perspective;
distant objects appear smaller and objects further to the camera edges are distorted from
foreshortening. Orthographic cameras, in contrast, are useful for rendering 2D graphics drawn
directly in screen space, such as 2D weapon sprites. After changing the camera projection, translate
the camera (along with its children) outside the main scene area—at a distance where it doesn't
collide with or intersect scene geometry. It doesn't ultimately matter where it's moved; this step is
mainly for *our* benefit, to avoid confusion with other game objects and to facilitate easier selection
from the viewport (see Figure 6-7). Notice that I've adjusted the punch sprites to be in view of the
camera, as shown in the camera preview window.

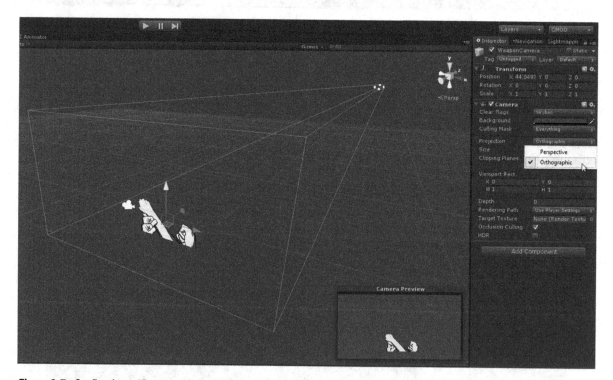

Figure 6-7. Configuring a 2D camera for rendering weapon sprites

The camera is now almost configured for rendering the weapon punch sprites. But, if you play
the game right now, you'll still see only the First Person Controller camera being rendered, and
not the newly created weapon camera. From appearances, the user would never know a second
camera existed, and the weapon sprites are not even layered on top of the initial rendering as we
want them to be. To fix this, change the WeaponCamera *Depth* property to *1*, and the *Clear Flags*

property to *Depth Only*, as shown in Figure 6-8. The *MainCamera* on the First Person Controller has a default Depth property of 0. Cameras with higher depth values are layered *on top* of lower-order ones. The Clear Flags property defines how the camera background should be rendered: Depth Only renders the background as transparent and allows the First Person Controller camera to appear beneath the WeaponCamera (see Figure 6-8).

Figure 6-8. Layering the weapon camera onto of the scene camera using the Depth and Clear Flag properties

Configuring the camera this way is not all we *should* do, however. Although the layered weapon camera now renders weapon sprites *on top* of the first-person camera, as we intended, it will still render any scene geometry and other objects, *if they ever come into its view*. This could produce confusing results leading to scene geometry being rendered twice or strange overlapping scenarios, depending entirely on what enters the camera view. To *restrict* the WeaponCamera to render *only* weapon sprites, and nothing else, we can use *layers*. Taking this extra precaution is highly recommended. Start by creating a new layer (*weapon_layer*), and assigning all weapon sprites to it from the Object Inspector. Layers are created from the *Tags and Layers* menu, accessed by selecting *Add New Layer* from the *Layer* drop-down menu at the top-right corner of the Object Inspector (see Figure 6-9).

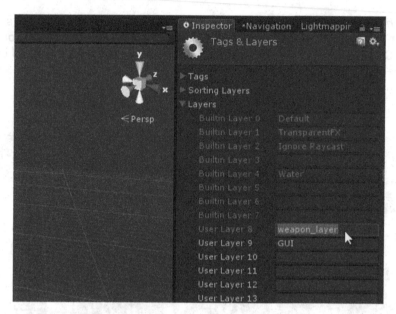

Figure 6-9. Creating a weapon camera layer to restrict camera rendering to weapon objects

After creating the layer, assign all Weapons objects to it. This can be achieved in just one cascaded operation, by selecting the root Weapons object, beneath the Player object, and assigning it to the weapon_layer, allowing the assignment to be applied to all child objects downward in the hierarchy (see Figure 6-10).

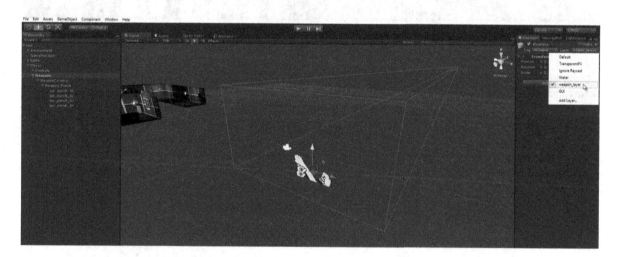

Figure 6-10. Assigning Weapon objects to a render layer

Finally, the *WeaponCamera* can be configured to render only from the weapon_layer, through the *CullingMask* member. Select *CullingMask* from the Object Inspector, picking only the weapon_layer from the drop-down (see Figure 6-11). Once selected, this restricts rendering to only the selected layer.

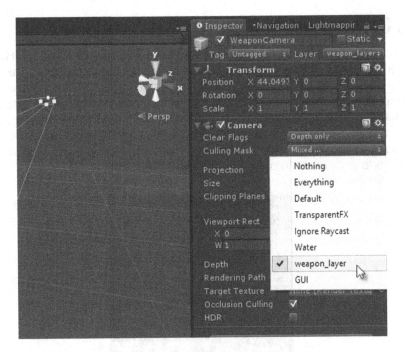

Figure 6-11. Restricting camera rendering using Culling Masks

Good work! Progress is being made. But still, the punch weapon is probably not looking quite right. Perhaps it's not positioned where you want it to be, and it's probably not the size you need either (see Figure 6-12). You could, of course, use the Scale tool to up- or downsize the objects by eye, but sometimes you'll need pixel precision for extra control. We'll explore that next.

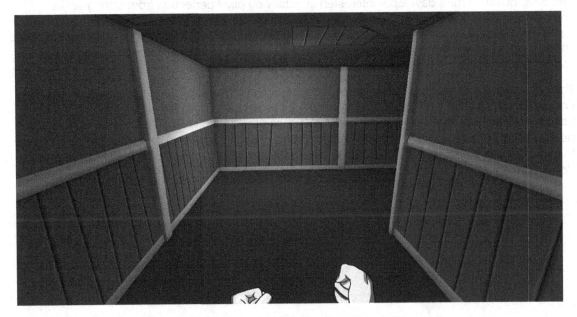

Figure 6-12. Almost there! But the punch weapon is not rendered at an appropriate size. Too small!

Cameras: Orthographic Size

Perhaps the most common question I'm asked about 2D development in Unity is, "How can I make a sprite appear on-screen at its true pixel size, minus all perspective distortion?" This question is, in essence, about *pixel perfection*. Perhaps you've created an image in Photoshop or GIMP, and you want it to display in an orthographic camera at exactly the same size as the image file—pixel for pixel. This section explores this issue as we scale and size the punch weapon to fit the weapon camera. In short, the ultimate render size of an orthographic camera is controlled using the Size member—although this member works in conjunction with other settings, as we'll see. This member determines how *world units* relate to *pixels* (see Figure 6-13).

Figure 6-13. The size member of orthographic cameras controls the size of graphical elements on-screen

The main question for a developer interested in achieving pixel perfection from orthographic cameras is, "What value should *size* be for an orthographic camera?" To achieve a 1:1 ratio between world units and pixels, the *size* value should be *half the vertical height of the game window in pixels* (That is: *Size = pxHeight/2*). Thus, for games with a resolution of 1024×768, a size value of 384 (768/2) is correct. This seems simple enough: but give it a try for CMOD.

There's a problem. Even if we set the camera size to 384 and the resolution to 1024×768 from the Game tab, the weapon sprite appears too small—it's barely visible. We know something is wrong because the game texture size is 4096×4096 pixels, and the punch weapon within that texture has been explicitly sized for a 1920×1080 HD display. This means, the weapon should appear much larger than it does with a camera setting of 384, where 1 unit should equate to 1 pixel (see Figure 6-14). So what's wrong?

Figure 6-14. Weapon sprite too small at 1:1 orthographic size

The answer is, by default, Unity applies *additional scaling* to all 2D sprites. To examine this, select the main texture in the Project panel and examine the *Pixels to Units* field in the Object Inspector. For the CMOD texture, this value is 200. This means all sprites are scaled automatically such that 200 texels (texture pixels) are mapped to 1 world unit. For this reason, a 1:1 orthographic size for a camera will render the sprites and textures *200* times *too small* for pixel perfection. Therefore, to create pixel-perfect mapping, we'll need to revise the orthographic size formula to: *Size = pxHeight/2/SpriteScale*. Thus, for a 1024×768 game, it should be *768 / 2 / 200*. Take a look at Figure 6-15, where things are looking better, and pixel-perfect. But don't celebrate just yet! There's still an issue to resolve...

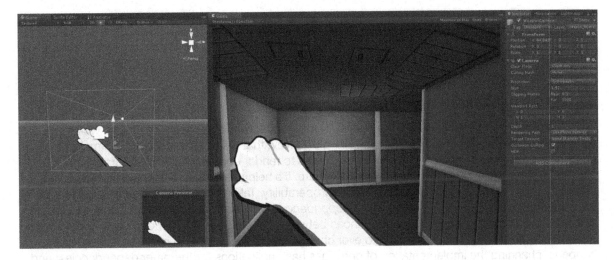

Figure 6-15. Pixel-perfect weapons!

The problem that exists now is that despite being pixel perfect, the punch weapon appears too large for the resolution of 1024×768. But even if you change the resolution to 1920×1080, the punch weapon appears too large to the same degree. This is because the orthographic *size* is resolution dependent. If we change the resolution from one size to another, we'll also need to recalculate the *Size* value. If we don't, then the Size value always *scales* the graphics at that size to fit the target resolution, whatever it may be. This gives us a critical clue to achieving a certain kind of resolution independence for CMOD. Since we know the weapon should show pixel-perfect at 1920×1080, the size should be set to *1080 / 2 / 200*. By using and keeping this value, regardless of the game resolution, we'll always know the Player's weapons will appear at the correct size and scale (see Figure 6-16). Of course, this can involve a nonuniform scaling issue concerning *aspect ratio*. We'll return to that issue later in the book, in Chapter 8, when considering GUIs.

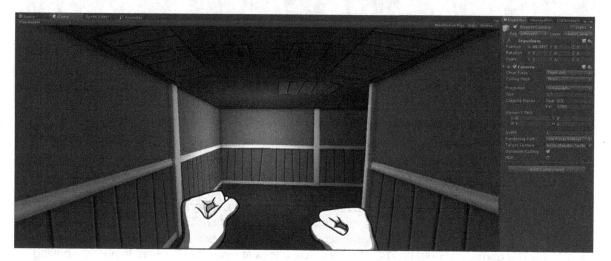

Figure 6-16. Weapons now display correctly

> **Note**   Repeat this process for the gun weapon, too.

Weapon Implementation: Punching

Let's now return to the specific implementation of the punch weapon (Weapon_Punch.cs), which we started coding earlier in the chapter, in Listing 6-2. Now that we've coded a sprite animation component, as well as configured the weapon sprites to render correctly for an orthographic camera, we can make progress. Sometimes, like here, it's helpful to develop multiple classes in parallel, jumping back and forth, testing their interoperability. Take care when doing this, however, as interoperability between classes can lead to *dependency injection*. In other words, it can lead you to create inhibiting and unnecessary dependences between classes, leaving your code scattered across multiple source files, so that it's difficult to ever change one of the classes in isolation. When that happens, changing the implementation of one class has implications for the other dependencies, and so on. This can cause a nightmare of spaghetti logic. Try, *wherever possible*, to make your classes as independent and self-contained as possible. Achieving this is actually easier said than done; but with patience and practice, it gets a lot easier to spot ways of doing it.

Right now, if you've been following along with the chapter, the punch weapon simply plays a relatively simple punch animation on a loop, just for testing purposes. But the weapon should really do more than this for the final game. Specifically, the punch weapon should *remain in an idle state*, displaying an attack animation *only* when the gamer manually launches an attack by pressing the Fire button. When this happens, the weapon should also determine whether an Enemy has been hit and, if so, to apply damage. Take a look at Listing 6-5; comments follow.

Listing 6-5. Weapon_Punch.cs: Adding Attack Functionality to the Punch Weapon

```
001 //------------------------------------------------------
002 using UnityEngine;
003 using System.Collections;
004 //------------------------------------------------------
005 //Inherits from Weapon class
006 public class Weapon_Punch : Weapon
007 {
008         //------------------------------------------------------
009         //Default Sprite to show for weapon when active and not attacking
010         public SpriteRenderer DefaultSprite = null;
011
012         //Sound to play on attack
013         public AudioClip WeaponAudio = null;
014
015         //Audio Source for sound playback
016         private AudioSource SFX = null;
017
018         //Reference to all child sprite renderers for this weapon
019         private SpriteRenderer[] WeaponSprites = null;
020         //------------------------------------------------------
021         void Start()
022         {
023                 //Find sound object in scene
024                 GameObject SoundsObject = GameObject.FindGameObjectWithTag("sounds");
025
026                 //If no sound object, then exit
027                 if(SoundsObject == null) return;
028
029                 //Get audio source component for sfx
030                 SFX = SoundsObject.GetComponent<AudioSource>();
031
032                 //Get all child sprite renderers for weapon
033                 WeaponSprites = gameObject.GetComponentsInChildren<SpriteRenderer>();
034         }
035         //------------------------------------------------------
036         // Update is called once per frame
037         void Update ()
038         {
039                 //If not equipped then exit
040                 if(!IsEquipped) return;
041
```

```
042                    //If cannot accept input, then exit
043                    if(!GameManager.Instance.InputAllowed) return;
044
045                    //Check for fire button input
046                    if(Input.GetButton("Fire1") && CanFire)
047                            StartCoroutine(Fire());
048            }
049    //-------------------------------------------------
050    //Coroutine to fire weapon
051    public IEnumerator Fire()
052    {
053                    //If can fire
054                    if(!CanFire || !IsEquipped) yield break;
055
056                    //Set refire to false
057                    CanFire = false;
058
059                    //Play Fire Animation
060                    gameObject.SendMessage("PlaySpriteAnimation", 0,
                       SendMessageOptions.DontRequireReceiver);
061
062                    //Calculate hit
063
064                    //Get ray from screen center target
065                    Ray R = Camera.main.ScreenPointToRay(new Vector3(Screen.width/2,
                       Screen.height/2,0));
066
067                    //Test for ray collision
068                    RaycastHit hit;
069
070                    if(Physics.Raycast(R.origin, R.direction, out hit, Range))
071                    {
072                            //Target hit - check if target is enemy
073                            if(hit.collider.gameObject.CompareTag("enemy"))
074                            {
075                                    //Play collection sound, if audio source is available
076                                    if(SFX){SFX.PlayOneShot(WeaponAudio, 1.0f);}
077
078                                    //Send damage message (deal damage to enemy)
079                                    hit.collider.gameObject.SendMessage("Damage",Damage,
                                       SendMessageOptions.DontRequireReceiver);
080                            }
081                    }
082
083                    //Wait for recovery before re-enabling CanFire
084                    yield return new WaitForSeconds(RecoveryDelay);
085
086                    //Re-enable CanFire
087                    CanFire = true;
088            }
```

```
089          //-------------------------------------------------
090          //Called when animation has completed playback
091          public void SpriteAnimationStopped()
092          {
093                  //If not equipped then exit
094                  if(!IsEquipped) return;
095
096                  //Show default sprite
097                  DefaultSprite.enabled = true;
098          }
099          //-------------------------------------------------
100 }
```

> **Note** Notice that, due to class inheritance, the Weapon_Punch class is using inherited variables, such as CanFire, as though they were its own. No declaration for them is provided in the Weapon_Punch.cs file.

- **Line 10.** The DefaultSprite public variable refers a SpriteRenderer component to be used as the default, idle state for the weapon. This value should be specified from the Unity Editor, via the Object Inspector, before running the code. In short, whenever the weapon is equipped but not being fire, the *DefaultSprite* will show at the bottom-middle of the screen.

- **Line 46.** Notice that gamer input is read using a virtual button with the Input.GetButton function, as opposed to reading directly from the keyboard with Input.GetKeyDown. This allows input mapping to be changed without breaking the code—a great technique for allowing the gamer customizable controls.

- **Line 51.** The Fire behavior is coded as a coroutine for resetting the CanFire variable back to true after the recovery delay.

- **Line 59.** The punch animation is initiated by sending a message to the GameObject with SendMessage. This allows animation playback using the *SpriteAnimator* component *without* the Weapon class ever needing to know the data type or interface details of the SpriteAnimator! SendMessage is sometimes a great way to establish relationships and interaction between classes. But it does have performance implications, which are considered in the last chapter.

Physics and Damage Dealing

In Listing 6-5, the Weapon class (Weapon_Punch.cs) responded to gamer input and applies damage to enemies within range of an attack whenever an attack is launched. The specific details of detecting whether an Enemy is hit is handled using the physics system, and covers lines 62–82. These are reproduced in Listing 6-6 and warrant further discussion.

Listing 6-6. Detecting Enemy Hits

```
062 //Calculate hit
063
064 //Get ray from screen center target
065 Ray R = Camera.main.ScreenPointToRay(new Vector3(Screen.width/2,
    Screen.height/2,0));
066
067 //Test for ray collision
068 RaycastHit hit;
069
070 if(Physics.Raycast(R.origin, R.direction, out hit, Range))
071 {
072         //Target hit - check if target is enemy
073         if(hit.collider.gameObject.CompareTag("enemy"))
074         {
075                 //Play collection sound, if audio source is available
076                 if(SFX){SFX.PlayOneShot(WeaponAudio, 1.0f);}
077
078                 //Send damage message (deal damage to enemy)
079                 hit.collider.gameObject.SendMessage("Damage",Damage,
                        SendMessageOptions.DontRequireReceiver);
080         }
081 }
082
```

Collision detection and damage dealing begins by constructing a *ray*. A ray is a mathematical structure representing an imaginary straight line, projected from the screen into the scene space ahead. In our case, the ray will act as an imaginary beam cast outward from the tip of our weapon (assumed to be screen-center). Line 65 uses the Unity camera function ScreenPointToRay to construct a ray that begins from the screen center and is projected forward, away from the camera and inward into the scene.

> **Note**   More information on ScreenPointToRay can be found in the online Unity documentation at http://docs.unity3d.com/Documentation/ScriptReference/Camera.ScreenPointToRay.html.

After a ray has been constructed and cast into the scene, the Physics.Raycast function is used to access the *first* collidable GameObject intersecting the ray. This object is the nearest collidable object *to us*.

> **Note**   More information on Physics.Raycast can be found in the online Unity documentation at http://docs.unity3d.com/Documentation/ScriptReference/Physics.Raycast.html.

Finally, line 73 validates whether the nearest hit object was an Enemy by using its tag (enemy implementation is considered in the next chapter). Notice from line 79 that damage is applied to the enemy using a SendMessage function, creating a degree of independence between the weapon and enemy classes, because the weapon class needs knowledge of the enemy data type or interface specifics. We just send the enemy object a SendMessage command.

Now go ahead and take this component for a test ride (see Figure 6-17 for the component settings I've used). You should not have a functional punch weapon. Although this chapter has covered only the punch weapon so far, the gun weapon can be created using almost the same approach. The crucial difference between the punch and the gun rests in having finite ammo, the weapon range, and the damage inflicted.

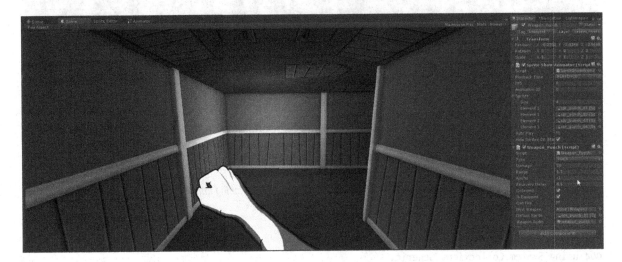

Figure 6-17. BLAM! The punch weapon in action!

Weapon Changing and Polymorphism

As soon as the Player collects more than one weapon, he'll want the ability to change or cycle between them on demand. Doing this requires some coding changes both to the weapon classes and to the PlayerController class, and we'll see an Object Orientation feature, known as *polymorphism*, at work. The PlayerController will need to maintain a list of collected weapons and make only one of them active for the Player at any one time. The weapons too will need to be notified when they have become the active weapon and when deactivated. Before proceeding further, however, this section assumes you have both a fists/punch and a gun weapon configured, with their sprites set up to render in an orthographic camera (see Figure 6-18 for the GameObject setup that I'm using). Remember, you can always load up the Start or End projects included in the book files to follow along (found in Chapter06/Start and Chapter06/End).

Figure 6-18. *Preparing to create weapon-change functionality. Notice that I've hidden all sprite renderers for the gun, to prevent multiple frames showing at the same time. The PlayerController and Weapon classes handle which sprites should be shown, and when*

To implement weapon changing for the PlayerController, consider the revised controller class in Listing 6-7, with changes highlighted in bold. Remember, the PlayerController class was first created in the previous chapter. Comments follow.

Listing 6-7. PlayerController.cs: Revised PlayerController Class with Weapon Switching Implemented

```
001 //-------------------------------------------------
002 using UnityEngine;
003 using System.Collections;
004 using System.Collections.Generic;
005 //-------------------------------------------------
006 public class PlayerController : MonoBehaviour
007 {
008         //-----------------------------------------------
009         //Amount of cash player should collect to complete level
010         public float CashTotal = 1400.0f;
011
012         //Amount of cash for this player
013         private float cash = 0.0f;
014
015         //Reference to transform
016         private Transform ThisTransform = null;
017
018         //Respawn time in seconds after dying
019         public float RespawnTime = 2.0f;
020
021         //Player health
022         public int health = 100;
023
024         //Get Mecanim animator component in children
025         private Animator AnimComp = null;
026
```

```
027        //Private damage texture
028        private Texture2D DamageTexture = null;
029
030        //Screen coordinates
031        private Rect ScreenRect;
032
033        //Show damage texture?
034        private bool ShowDamage = false;
035
036        //Damage texture interval (amount of time in seconds to show texture)
037        private float DamageInterval = 0.2f;
038
039        //Default player weapon (Punch)
040        public Weapon DefaultWeapon = null;
041
042        //Currently active weapon
043        public Weapon ActiveWeapon = null;
044        //-------------------------------------------------
045        //Called when object is created
046        void Start()
047        {
048                //Register controller for weapon expiration events
049                GameManager.Notifications.AddListener(this, "AmmoExpired");
050
051                //Activate default weapon
052                DefaultWeapon.gameObject.SendMessage("Equip", DefaultWeapon.Type);
053
054                //Set active weapon
055                ActiveWeapon = DefaultWeapon;
056
057                //Get First person capsule and make non-visible
058                MeshRenderer Capsule = GetComponentInChildren<MeshRenderer>();
059                Capsule.enabled = false;
060
061                //Get Animator
062                AnimComp = GetComponentInChildren<Animator>();
063
064                //Create damage texture
065                DamageTexture = new Texture2D(1,1);
066                DamageTexture.SetPixel(0,0,new Color(255,0,0,0.5f));
067                DamageTexture.Apply();
068
069                //Get cached transform
070                ThisTransform = transform;
071        }
072        //-------------------------------------------------
073        //Accessors to set and get cash
074        public float Cash
075        {
076                //Return cash value
077                get{return cash;}
078
```

```
079                       //Set cash and validate, if required
080                       set
081                       {
082                               //Set cash
083                               cash = value;
084
085                               //Check collection limit - post notification if limit reached
086                               if(cash >= CashTotal)
087                                       GameManager.Notifications.PostNotification(this, "CashCollected");
088                       }
089               }
090               //-----------------------------------------------
091               //Accessors to set and get health
092               public int Health
093               {
094                       //Return health value
095                       get{return health;}
096
097                       //Set health and validate, if required
098                       set
099                       {
100                               health = value;
101
102                               //Playe Die functionality
103                               if(health <= 0) gameObject.SendMessage("Die",SendMessageOptions.
                                  DontRequireReceiver);
104                       }
105               }
106               //-----------------------------------------------
107               //Function to apply damage to the player
108               public IEnumerator ApplyDamage(int Amount = 0)
109               {
110                       //Reduce health
111                       Health -= Amount;
112
113                       //Post damage notification
114                       GameManager.Notifications.PostNotification(this, "PlayerDamaged");
115
116                       //Show damage texture
117                       ShowDamage = true;
118
119                       //Wait for interval
120                       yield return new WaitForSeconds(DamageInterval);
121
122                       //Hide damage texture
123                       ShowDamage = false;
124               }
125               //-----------------------------------------------
126               //ON GUI Function to show texture
127               void OnGUI()
128               {
129                       if(ShowDamage){GUI.DrawTexture(ScreenRect,DamageTexture);}
130               }
```

```
131            //---------------------------------------------------
132            //Function called when player dies
133            public IEnumerator Die()
134            {
135                    //Disable input
136                    GameManager.Instance.InputAllowed = false;
137
138                    //Trigger death animation if available
139                    if(AnimComp) AnimComp.SetTrigger("ShowDeath");
140
141                    //Wait for respawn time
142                    yield return new WaitForSeconds(RespawnTime);
143
144                    //Restart level
145                    Application.LoadLevel(Application.loadedLevel);
146            }
147            //---------------------------------------------------
148            void Update()
149            {
150                    //Build screen rect on update (in case screen size changes)
151                    ScreenRect.x = ScreenRect.y = 0;
152                    ScreenRect.width = Screen.width;
153                    ScreenRect.height = Screen.height;
154
155                    if(Input.GetKeyDown(KeyCode.Period))
156                            EquipNextWeapon();
157            }
158            //---------------------------------------------------
159            //Equip next available weapon
160            public void EquipNextWeapon()
161            {
162                    //No weapon found yet
163                    bool bFoundWeapon = false;
164
165                    //Loop until weapon found
166                    while(!bFoundWeapon)
167                    {
168                            //Get next weapon
169                            ActiveWeapon = ActiveWeapon.NextWeapon;
170
171                            //Activate weapon, if possible
172                            ActiveWeapon.gameObject.SendMessage("Equip", ActiveWeapon.Type);
173
174                            //Is successfully equipped?
175                            bFoundWeapon = ActiveWeapon.IsEquipped;
176                    }
177            }
```

```
178      //--------------------------------------------------
179      //Event called when ammo expires
180      public void AmmoExpired(Component Sender)
181      {
182              //Ammo expired for this weapon. Equip next
183              EquipNextWeapon();
184      }
185      //--------------------------------------------------
186 }
```

- ■ **Lines 40 and 43.** There are some important features in this code. First, notice that PlayerController supports weapon switching between both weapon types, and yet it never references any one of the derived classes directly, either Weapon_Punch or Weapon_Gun. It uses the super-class Weapon to reference weapon objects.

- ■ **Lines 160–185.** This is where the core functionality of weapon-switching occurs. When the gamer presses the period (.) key on the keyboard, and is carrying more than one eligible weapon, the active weapon is switched to the next. This is achieved using the NextWeapon variable coded into the Weapon class. This value should be specified in the Object Inspector for all weapons, allowing any weapon to reference the next weapon in the cycle. For our purposes, the punch weapon refers to the gun as its next. And further, because we wanted to cycle around the weapons in a loop, the gun refers back to the punch weapon as its next. But notice again (lines 169 and 175) that the EquipNextWeapon function works with the Weapon super-class and not any of its derivatives.

Both comments for Listing 6-7 point to *polymorphism* at work. In short, whenever multiple classes derive from a common ancestor class using *inheritance*, such as the weapon classes deriving from Weapon, you can still loop through and work with those classes together by using only references to their base or ancestor class (see lines 166–176). This means that PlayerController can maintain a complete array of different weapon types, using only the base type Weapon. Because of *polymorphism*, C# sees only the *commonalities* between these classes through their ancestor, seeing them as being fundamentally alike and interchangeable, and it ignores their differences implemented from deriving. The practical value of this means that many different objects, regardless of their type, can be treated alike if they share a common ancestor class somewhere in their lineage. It becomes possible to loop through and iterate over objects of multiple types stored together in a single array of only one type.

Note   For more information on polymorphism, see the MSDN C# documentation at http://msdn.microsoft.com/en-us/library/ms173152.aspx.

Completing the Punch and Gun Weapons

The PlayerController has been sufficiently prepared and modified to support weapon switching. It's now time to update the two weapon classes themselves to support this behavior. Doing this is required because the PlayerController.EquipNextWeapon method calls on an Equip function in the Weapon class, to equip the weapon for the Player (line 172). This method is invoked not on the Weapon class itself, but by using a SendMessage function, allowing the derived classes to respond. And it's called for any newly equipped weapon, each and every time it's equipped, giving it the opportunity to perform any initialization code, such as displaying the default, idle sprite. Listing 6-8 lists the completed Weapon_Punch code, with additions highlighted in bold.

Listing 6-8. Weapon_Punch.cs: Completed Punch Weapon

```
001 //--------------------------------------------------
002 using UnityEngine;
003 using System.Collections;
004 //--------------------------------------------------
005 //Inherits from Weapon class
006 public class Weapon_Punch : Weapon
007 {
008         //--------------------------------------------------
009         //Default Sprite to show for weapon when active and not attacking
010         public SpriteRenderer DefaultSprite = null;
011
012         //Sound to play on attack
013         public AudioClip WeaponAudio = null;
014
015         //Audio Source for sound playback
016         private AudioSource SFX = null;
017
018         //Reference to all child sprite renderers for this weapon
019         private SpriteRenderer[] WeaponSprites = null;
020         //--------------------------------------------------
021         void Start()
022         {
023                 //Find sound object in scene
024                 GameObject SoundsObject = GameObject.FindGameObjectWithTag("sounds");
025
026                 //If no sound object, then exit
027                 if(SoundsObject == null) return;
028
029                 //Get audio source component for sfx
030                 SFX = SoundsObject.GetComponent<AudioSource>();
031
032                 //Get all child sprite renderers for weapon
033                 WeaponSprites = gameObject.GetComponentsInChildren<SpriteRenderer>();
034
035                 //Register weapon for weapon change events
036                 GameManager.Notifications.AddListener(this, "WeaponChange");
037         }
```

```
038          //-------------------------------------------------------------
039          // Update is called once per frame
040          void Update ()
041          {
042                  //If not equipped then exit
043                  if(!IsEquipped) return;
044
045                  //If cannot accept input, then exit
046                  if(!GameManager.Instance.InputAllowed) return;
047
048                  //Check for fire button input
049                  if(Input.GetButton("Fire1") && CanFire)
050                          StartCoroutine(Fire());
051          }
052          //-------------------------------------------------
053          //Coroutine to fire weapon
054          public IEnumerator Fire()
055          {
056                  //If can fire
057                  if(!CanFire || !IsEquipped) yield break;
058
059                  //Set refire to false
060                  CanFire = false;
061
062                  //Play Fire Animation
063                  gameObject.SendMessage("PlaySpriteAnimation", 0,
                     SendMessageOptions.DontRequireReceiver);
064
065                  //Calculate hit
066
067                  //Get ray from screen center target
068                  Ray R = Camera.main.ScreenPointToRay(new Vector3(Screen.width/2,
                     Screen.height/2,0));
069
070                  //Test for ray collision
071                  RaycastHit hit;
072
073                  if(Physics.Raycast(R.origin, R.direction, out hit, Range))
074                  {
075                          //Target hit - check if target is enemy
076                          if(hit.collider.gameObject.CompareTag("enemy"))
077                          {
078                                  //Play collection sound, if audio source is available
079                                  if(SFX){SFX.PlayOneShot(WeaponAudio, 1.0f);}
080
081                                  //Send damage message (deal damage to enemy)
082                                  hit.collider.gameObject.SendMessage("Damage",Damage,
                                     SendMessageOptions.DontRequireReceiver);
083                          }
084                  }
085
```

```
086                          //Wait for recovery before re-enabling CanFire
087                          yield return new WaitForSeconds(RecoveryDelay);
088
089                          //Re-enable CanFire
090                          CanFire = true;
091                  }
092          //-------------------------------------------------
093          //Called when animation has completed playback
094          public void SpriteAnimationStopped()
095          {
096                          //If not equipped then exit
097                          if(!IsEquipped) return;
098
099                          //Show default sprite
100                          DefaultSprite.enabled = true;
101          }
102          //-------------------------------------------------
103          //Equip weapon
104          public bool Equip(WEAPON_TYPE WeaponType)
105          {
106                          //If not this type, then exit and no equip
107                          if((WeaponType != Type) || (!Collected) || (Ammo == 0) || (IsEquipped))
                             return false;
108
109                          //Is this weapon. So equip
110                          IsEquipped = true;
111
112                          //Show default sprite
113                          DefaultSprite.enabled = true;
114
115                          //Activate Can Fire
116                          CanFire = true;
117
118                          //Send weapon change event
119                          GameManager.Notifications.PostNotification(this, "WeaponChange");
120
121                          //Weapon was equipped
122                          return true;
123          }
124          //-------------------------------------------------
125          //Weapon change event - called when player changes weapon
126          public void WeaponChange(Component Sender)
127          {
128                          //Has player changed to this weapon?
129                          if(Sender.GetInstanceID() == GetInstanceID()) return;
130
131                          //Has changed to other weapon. Hide this weapon
132                          StopAllCoroutines();
133                          gameObject.SendMessage("StopSpriteAnimation", 0,
                             SendMessageOptions.DontRequireReceiver);
134
```

```
135                //Deactivate equipped
136                IsEquipped = false;
137
138                foreach(SpriteRenderer SR in WeaponSprites)
139                        SR.enabled = false;
140        }
141        //-------------------------------------------------
142 }
```

- **Line 36.** This weapon class registers for a WeaponChange event. When this event occurs, the NotificationsManager will invoke the WeaponChange function (line 126), which typically will hide the weapon sprites for the active weapon, when it becomes deactivated as the Player changes to a different weapon.

- **Line 104.** The EquipWeapon function is called by the PlayerController class when the weapon becomes activated for the Player—that is, when it becomes the currently selected weapon. Notice, this function also raises a WeaponChange event at line 119.

Let's also take a look over the Weapon_Gun class, as shown in Listing 6-9. Notice that its implementation is *very similar* to the punch weapon in Listing 6-8. It simply features extra code to handle limited and expired ammo. In fact, the Weapon_Gun class is so similar to Weapon_Punch, that one might even be tempted to insert an additional level of class inheritance, creating a new base class between Weapon and its derivatives Weapon_Gun and Weapon_Punch. This class would define more behavior common to Weapon_Punch and Weapon_Gun, but without "infecting" the original Weapon class. Decisions about class inheritance and where functionality belongs is critical to designing a solid class framework for your games.

Listing 6-9. Weapon_Gun.cs: Completed Gun Weapon

```
001 //-------------------------------------------------
002 using UnityEngine;
003 using System.Collections;
004 //-------------------------------------------------
005 public class Weapon_Gun : Weapon
006 {
007        //-------------------------------------------------
008        //Default Sprite to show for weapon when active and not attacking
009        public SpriteRenderer DefaultSprite = null;
010
011        //Sound to play on attack
012        public AudioClip WeaponAudio = null;
013
014        //Audio Source for sound playback
015        private AudioSource SFX = null;
016
017        //Reference to all child sprite renderers for this weapon
018        private SpriteRenderer[] WeaponSprites = null;
019
```

```
020             //-----------------------------------------------
021             // Use this for initialization
022             void Start ()
023             {
024                     //Find sound object in scene
025                     GameObject SoundsObject = GameObject.FindGameObjectWithTag("sounds");
026
027                     //If no sound object, then exit
028                     if(SoundsObject == null) return;
029
030                     //Get audio source component for sfx
031                     SFX = SoundsObject.GetComponent<AudioSource>();
032
033                     //Get all child sprite renderers for weapon
034                     WeaponSprites = gameObject.GetComponentsInChildren<SpriteRenderer>();
035
036                     //Register weapon for weapon change events
037                     GameManager.Notifications.AddListener(this, "WeaponChange");
038             }
039             //-----------------------------------------------
040             // Update is called once per frame
041             void Update ()
042             {
043                     //If not equipped then exit
044                     if(!IsEquipped) return;
045
046                     //If cannot accept input, then exit
047                     if(!GameManager.Instance.InputAllowed) return;
048
049                     //Check for fire button input
050                     if(Input.GetButton("Fire1") && CanFire)
051                             StartCoroutine(Fire());
052             }
053             //-----------------------------------------------
054             //Coroutine to fire weapon
055             public IEnumerator Fire()
056             {
057                     //If can fire
058                     if(!CanFire || !IsEquipped || Ammo <= 0) yield break;
059
060                     //Set refire to false
061                     CanFire = false;
062
063                     //Play Fire Animation
064                     gameObject.SendMessage("PlaySpriteAnimation", 0,
                        SendMessageOptions.DontRequireReceiver);
065
066                     //Play collection sound, if audio source is available
067                     if(SFX){SFX.PlayOneShot(WeaponAudio, 1.0f);}
068
```

```
069                    //Calculate hit
070
071                    //Get ray from screen center target
072                    Ray R = Camera.main.ScreenPointToRay(new Vector3(Screen.width/2,
                       Screen.height/2,0));
073
074                    //Test for ray collision
075                    RaycastHit hit;
076
077                    if(Physics.Raycast(R.origin, R.direction, out hit, Range))
078                    {
079                            //Target hit - check if target is enemy
080                            if(hit.collider.gameObject.CompareTag("enemy"))
081                            {
082                                    //Send damage message (deal damage to enemy)
083                                    hit.collider.gameObject.SendMessage("Damage",Damage,
                                       SendMessageOptions.DontRequireReceiver);
084                            }
085                    }
086
087                    //Reduce ammo
088                    --Ammo;
089
090                    //Check remaining ammo - post empty notification
091                    if(Ammo <= 0) GameManager.Notifications.PostNotification(this, "AmmoExpired");
092
093                    //Wait for recovery before re-enabling CanFire
094                    yield return new WaitForSeconds(RecoveryDelay);
095
096                    //Re-enable CanFire
097                    CanFire = true;
098            }
099    //----------------------------------------------------
100    //Called when animation has completed playback
101    public void SpriteAnimationStopped()
102    {
103                    //If not equipped then exit
104                    if(!IsEquipped) return;
105
106                    //Show default sprite
107                    DefaultSprite.enabled = true;
108    }
109    //----------------------------------------------------
110    //Equip weapon
111    public bool Equip(WEAPON_TYPE WeaponType)
112    {
113                    //If not this type, then exit and no equip
114                    if((WeaponType != Type) || (!Collected) || (Ammo == 0) || (IsEquipped))
                       return false;
115
```

```
116                    //Is this weapon. So equip
117                    IsEquipped = true;
118
119                    //Show default sprite
120                    DefaultSprite.enabled = true;
121
122                    //Activate Can Fire
123                    CanFire = true;
124
125                    //Send weapon change event
126                    GameManager.Notifications.PostNotification(this, "WeaponChange");
127
128                    //Weapon was equipped
129                    return true;
130            }
131        //-------------------------------------------------
132        //Weapon change event - called when player changes weapon
133        public void WeaponChange(Component Sender)
134        {
135                    //Has player changed to this weapon?
136                    if(Sender.GetInstanceID() == GetInstanceID()) return;
137
138                    //Has changed to other weapon. Hide this weapon
139                    StopAllCoroutines();
140                    gameObject.SendMessage("StopSpriteAnimation", 0, SendMessageOptions.
                       DontRequireReceiver);
141
142                    //Deactivate equipped
143                    IsEquipped = false;
144
145                    foreach(SpriteRenderer SR in WeaponSprites)
146                            SR.enabled = false;
147            }
148        //-------------------------------------------------
149 }
```

Before going further, be sure to implement both weapon classes into your project and take stock over just how far we've come. Figure 6-19 shows the completed project up and running with weapon functionality! Remember, the completed project for this chapter can be found in the book companion files at Chapter06/End.

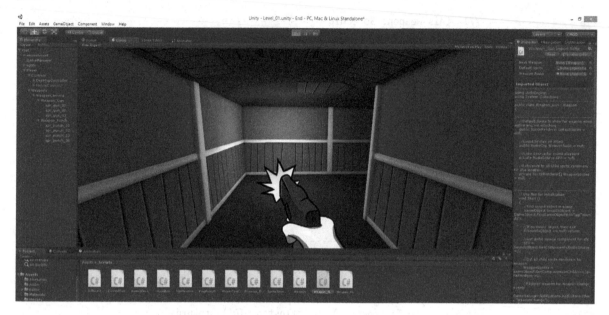

Figure 6-19. CMOD so far, with completed weapon functionality

Note One issue to consider here, regarding both the punch and the gun weapons, concerns code duplication across multiple classes. These classes, as given here, duplicate some functionality, especially within the `Fire` method. In general, code duplication is not recommended practice, unless essential, because it leads to lengthy source files and increases the possibility of error.

One way to solve this here would be by moving some of the common functionality into the base class, allowing both classes to inherent the behavior. But doing this puts greater restrictions on what weapons can be, and makes the base class "heavier" in terms of functionality. Further, we might want to add new weapons later that do not share this behavior and which work entirely differently. You could solve this by introducing more classes and levels of inheritance, or by overriding functions differently.

In short, finding the right balance between inheritance, levels of inheritance, and code duplication (where unavoidable) is part of creating a suitable class hierarchy for your project.

Don't forget to create a weapon power-up that gives the Player the -weapon when collected (see book companion files, if you're not sure how to do that). Or else, enable the `Weapon_Gun.Collected` public member for the gun in the Object Inspector, to assign the gun to the Player automatically at level start-up. Don't forget to set the gun ammo to 0 or above, and not –1; the gun cannot fire infinitely! See Chapter 4 for more information on how to create collectable power-ups.

Conclusion

In this chapter we've implemented a complete weapon system. This includes the full implementation of a punch and gun weapon, as well as a system for switching between weapons after both have been collected. By now, your trigger finger is probably getting itchy to shoot some baddies and test the damage code. We'll see that in action in the upcoming chapter as we explore intelligent enemies. By now, you should be able to do the following:

- Create weapon prefabs

- Understand object orientation and inheritance

- Understand how to create base classes and derived classes

- Code weapons from a common abstract base class

- Create basic sprite animation

- Create orthographic cameras

- Understand how to control camera depth and rendering

- Understand how to achieve pixel-perfection with orthographic size

- Create weapon cycling with polymorphism

- Understand how using SendMessage creates object independence

- Create classes that work nicely with the event system

Chapter 7

Enemies

Right now, CMOD is really starting to take shape. By investing extra time and forethought, as we've been doing, in carefully applying well-established C# and Unity-scripting principles, CMOD not only *works,* but *works solidly*. That is, it's easy to expand upon and difficult to break. When game development seems to flow like that, one stage naturally coming out of the previous and moving smoothly in a logical sequence, we may generally take that as a "good sign." Thus far, we've created a complete game environment, an event system, a First Person Controller, head-bobbing behavior, collectible power-ups, and damage-dealing weapons. But we're still missing Enemy characters, and that's a crucial ingredient for CMOD and practically any shooter game.

Essentially, we're missing the *things* we can actually shoot at, and which can also shoot us back, if we're not quick enough to defend ourselves. So now it's time to fix this serious omission. Specifically, we'll develop enemies that can both take and deal damage with weapons, and who also exhibit a degree of "intelligence," to guide their behavior and actions during gameplay, making them appear animated and alive. In achieving this, we'll cover a lot of technical ground, and some of it highly controversial in game development and beyond, exploring subjects such as artificial intelligence, finite state machines, and pathfinding and navigation. So, let's go!

Meet the Bad Guys

As discussed in Chapter 1 of this book, CMOD will feature a total three different Enemy types, all of whom are dangerous to the Player in different ways. These are *the Drone* (see Figure 7-1), *the Tough Guy* (see Figure 7-2), and *Mr. Big Cheese* (see Figure 7-3).

Figure 7-1. *The Drone: The weakest enemy. Has short-range attack*

Figure 7-2. *The Tough Guy: Nasty! Has a power handgun and long-range attack*

Figure 7-3. *Mr Big Cheese: The head honcho, the big fish, numero uno! There's only one of this guy in each level. His attack is short-range, but he hits very hard*

It may come as no surprise to you by now that all three of these Enemy characters will be implemented as Prefab objects. This will allow us to group together all graphics, assets, and script files into a complete package—one we can reuse as necessary, filling the level with as many enemies as we need. Let's start by creating the *enemy Drone* prefab, a process that can be repeated afterward to create all the remaining character prefabs.

Note   In case you're interested in how the enemies were drawn: I used the "three box" character design method. That is, I started by drawing three empty squares on top of one another on a sketch pad, arranged vertically. I then sized the boxes to represent the leg, torso, and head regions of the character. And then I filled the boxes using only basic primitive shapes, such as squares, circles, and rectangles. These represent the main forms of the character—and details can be added to these, such as a nose, eyes, and mouth, and so forth. Try it for yourself, allowing only 5–7 minutes for each character.

Starting the Enemy Drone Prefab

First, create a new and empty GameObject in the scene (named *Drone*), to represent the basis for the Drone enemy character. As seen before, new objects are created with the shortcut key *Ctrl+Shift+N*, or by selecting **GameObject ➤ Create Empty** from the menu. Often, however, the new object is not centered at the world origin as you'd expect, but is positioned at an offset. Now, this isn't really problematic, because it's easy to reset an object's position by simply typing in *0, 0, 0* into the *X, Y,* and *Z* fields of the *Transform* component in the Object Inspector. But, there's an even quicker method still. Just click the *Cog* icon in the Transform component, and choose *Reset* from the context menu, to reset the Transform component to its default values (see Figure 7-4).

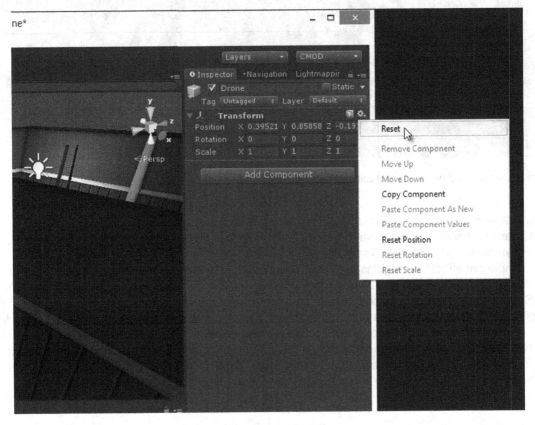

Figure 7-4. A game object can be reset to zeroed values by choosing Reset from the component cog menu

Next, drag and drop all Drone-related *sprites* from the atlas texture in the project panel onto the newly created empty in the scene, ensuring all sprite instances are added as child objects. Be sure to drag and drop the sprites into the Hierarchy panel, and not the Scene viewport. Remember, the hierarchical arrangement of objects in this way (many objects grouped as children beneath a common parent) is crucial for easily generating Prefab objects further along the line. Prefabs expect a single parent ancestor (see Figure 7-5).

Figure 7-5. Adding all Drone sprites to a common parent object

As with the weapon objects created in the previous chapter, the sprite instances added here will act as *frames of animation* for when the Enemy walks around the level or attacks the Player. These frames will be shown using the *SpriteShowAnimator* component (coded in the previous chapter). This component effectively toggles the visibility of sprite objects over time, ensuring only one frame is visible at once. The result is a flipbook animation effect. For the enemy object, however, we'll need two SpriteShowAnimator components, one for each animation type: *Attack* and *Walk*. Each Enemy will either be *walking around* or *attacking* the Player. More on these states later when we explore finite state machines. But here, it's enough to confirm that each Enemy relies on two animations: so let's add two SpriteShowAnimator components and configure each one. The move animation consists of four frames: *spr_drone_run_01*, *spr_drone_run_02*, *spr_drone_run_03*, and *spr_drone_run_04*. The attack animation consists of two frames: *spr_drone_attack*, and *spr_drone_neutral* (see Figure 7-6).

Figure 7-6. Configuration animations for the Enemy objects using SpriteShowAnimator components

> **Note** I've given each SpriteShowAnimator component a unique ID number. Further, the Walk animation has an FPS of 12, and the Attack animation has an FPS of 3. You don't need to maintain exactly the IDs I've used here, nor the FPS values I've chosen; so long as you choose consistent IDs and FPS values, choose what works best in your view and with your assets.

Be sure to tag the Enemy object as an *enemy*; a value we'll use later when detecting collisions. That is, use the *Tags* drop-down in the Object Inspector to label the object as an Enemy. In addition, hide all the added sprite objects by deactivating their Sprite Renderer components, leaving only the default (neutral) sprite visible as the main sprite and frame for the Enemy in all cases when it's not animating. This prevents all frames of animation from being seen at the same time when the level begins; only one frame should be visible at once. Finally, to complete the basic configuration, add both a *Billboard* component and a *Box Collider* component to the enemy object; the former keeps the Enemy sprite aligned to the camera, and the second ensures that the Enemy has a basic volume and bounding area for collision detection (see Figure 7-7).

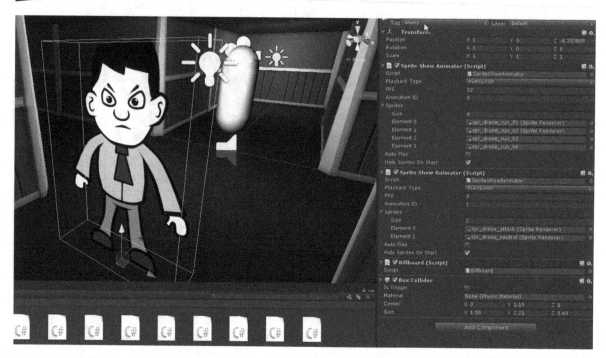

Figure 7-7. Configuring the Drone enemy with a Billboard component and a BoxCollider component

> **Tip**   Billboard and Box Collider objects were considered in depth for power-up objects in Chapter 4.

Coding Enemy Damage

The preliminaries taken so far have established the basics for the Drone prefab, but lots more awaits us in terms of C# coding. Let's start by considering the issue of *dealing damage* to the Enemy. When the Player fires a weapon at an Enemy that's in range, the Enemy should take damage unless there's an overriding reason not to (such as an invincibility shield), and further, the Enemy should be destroyed if the dealt damage reduces its health to 0 or below. In this game, we won't need to consider invincibility shields and other damage-reducing factors. I mention it here primarily because for many games *it is* a consideration. To implement the damage receiving functionality for the Drone, as well as its other behaviors, we'll code two classes, and we'll use the object-oriented concept of *class inheritance* to make them work together. Inheritance was introduced in the previous chapter when considering weapon implementation. I'll call these classes Enemy (the base class for *all* Enemies generally), and Enemy_Drone (the derived class implementing *Drone-specific* functionality). These classes will be added in the C# script files Enemy.cs and Enemy_Drone.cs, respectively. Go ahead and add these script files now, as shown in Figure 7-8.

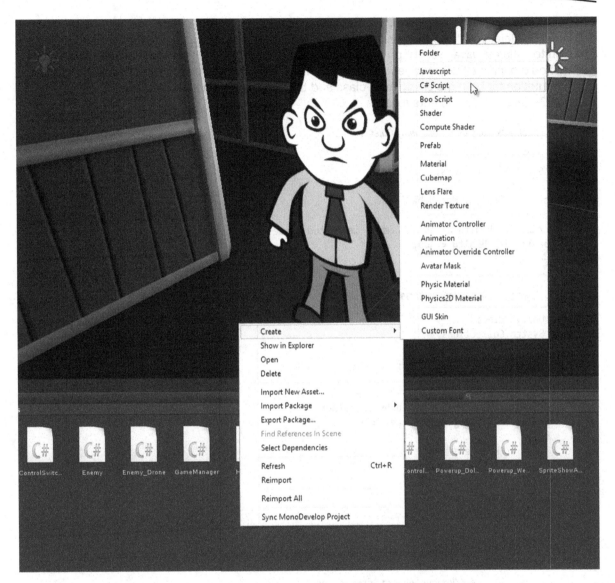

Figure 7-8. *Adding an Enemy base class and an Enemy_Drone derived class to create Drone-specific functionality*

Note Be sure to add the Enemy_Drone class as a component to the Drone object in the scene. Remember, you don't need to add the Enemy base class as a component, because the functionality of this class is inherited automatically *by* Enemy_Drone.

For now, let's turn back to the previous chapter (Chapter 6) for creating weapons, and view Listing 6-8 (line 78). Here, you'll see that when a weapon strikes an enemy object, it uses the SendMessage function to initiate a Damage event on the Enemy object being hit, if such an event exists. The Damage event should handle all damage-receiving functionality. With this in mind, let's consider the starting implementation for both the Enemy base class and the Enemy_Drone derived class, as shown in Listings 7-1 and 7-2; comments follow.

Listing 7-1. Enemy.cs: Base Class for Enemy Objects

```
01 using UnityEngine;
02 using System.Collections;
03
04 public class Enemy : MonoBehaviour
05 {
06     //Current health of this enemy - inherited by descendent classes
07     public int Health = 100;
08 }
```

Listing 7-2. Enemy_Drone.cs: Derived Class for Drone Objects

```
01 using UnityEngine;
02 using System.Collections;
03
04 public class Enemy_Drone : Enemy
05 {
06     //-------------------------------------------------
07     //Event called when damaged by an attack
08     public void Damage(int Damage = 0)
09     {
10         //Reduce health
11         Health -= Damage;
12
13         //Check if dead
14         if(Health <= 0)
15         {
16             //Send enemy destroyed notification
17             GameManager.Notifications.PostNotification(this, "EnemyDestroyed");
18
19             //Remove object from scene
20             DestroyImmediate(gameObject);
21
22             //Clean up old listeners
23             GameManager.Notifications.RemoveRedundancies();
24         }
25     }
26     //-------------------------------------------------
27 }
```

- **Listing 7-1. Line 07**. The base Enemy class defines a Health variable, common to all enemies. Using this, derived classes may keep track of Enemy health.

- **Listing 7-2. Line 08**. The Enemy_Drone class implements a Damage event, which will be called every time the Player strikes the Enemy with a weapon: either a punch with fists or a gun.

- **Listing 7-2. Lines 11–23**. Here, the Enemy's health is reduced by the weapon damage amount, specified by the function argument Damage. Further, if Enemy health is reduced to 0 or below, the Enemy object is destroyed using the DestroyImmediate function, and the NotificationsManager is updated to remove all redundant listeners.

Let's give this code a test run to confirm it works as intended. Run the game in Editor, selecting the Drone object in the scene. As you attack the Enemy with your weapon, observe his Health variable in the Object Inspector. For each successful strike you make, the Enemy's health will be reduced by the damage appropriate for your weapon. The gun weapon deals the most damage. Congratulations! We've now established an important connection between objects; specifically, the Player, Weapons, Enemies, and the NotificationsManager (see Figure 7-9).

Figure 7-9. Damaging enemies with weapons!

Improving Damage Dealing: Feedback

Right now the Player deals damage to the Enemy, but we (as developers) only have the live-preview of variable values in the Object Inspector to confirm that this behavior is truly working as intended at runtime. There's currently no visual or graphical indication *for the gamer* that damage has been sustained by the Enemy. Some might not regard this as a very big deal—after all, it works, and isn't that enough? However, this dismissal might be premature. Many academic studies have been made about the emotional influence of graphical and audible feedback in software, and especially in games. It seems possible that the aggregate effects of even the smallest tokens of feedback, such as a ping or swoosh sound played when achievements are made, can contribute toward a more rewarding and satisfying feeling in-game, leading to greater emotional attachments between the gamer and the game.

But even without these studies and theories, I'm guessing most of us have felt emotionally rewarded and gratified firsthand whenever a game acknowledges our successes or correct moves. At least, I know I have! So, let's add some visual feedback to CMOD for enemy damage events by making the Enemy flicker red when damage is taken. To do this, I'll create a new class, PingPongSpriteColor, which works much like the PingPong movement script created for power-up objects in Chapter 4, except here the script will ping-pong between sprite material colors, allowing us to transition a sprite from one color to another over a specified time. Listing 7-3 lists that class in full.

Listing 7-3. PingPongSpriteColor.cs: Transitions Between Material Colors

```
01 //Sets color for all child sprite renderers in a gameobject
02 //-------------------------------------------------
03 using UnityEngine;
04 using System.Collections;
05 //-------------------------------------------------
06 public class PingPongSpriteColor : MonoBehaviour
07 {
08        //Source (from) color
09        public Color Source = Color.white;
10
11        //Destination (to) color
12        public Color Dest = Color.white;
13
14        //Custom ID for this animation
15        public int AnimationID = 0;
16
17        //Total time in seconds to transition from source to dest
18        public float TransitionTime = 1.0f;
19
20        //List of sprite renders whose color must be set
21        private SpriteRenderer[] SpriteRenderers = null;
22
23        //-------------------------------------------------
24        // Use this for initialization
25        void Start ()
26        {
27                //Get all child sprite renderers
28                SpriteRenderers = GetComponentsInChildren<SpriteRenderer>();
29        }
30        //-------------------------------------------------
31        public void PlayColorAnimation(int AnimID = 0)
32        {
33                //If Anim ID numbers do not match, then exit - should not play this animation
34                if(AnimationID != AnimID) return;
35
```

```
36          //Stop all running coroutines
37          StopAllCoroutines();
38
39          //Start new sequence
40          StartCoroutine(PlayLerpColors());
41      }
42      //------------------------------------------------
43      //Start animation
44      private IEnumerator PlayLerpColors()
45      {
46          //Lerp colors
47          yield return StartCoroutine(LerpColor(Source, Dest));
48          yield return StartCoroutine(LerpColor(Dest, Source));
49      }
50      //------------------------------------------------
51      //Function to lerp over time, from Color X to Color Y
52      private IEnumerator LerpColor(Color X, Color Y)
53      {
54          //Maintain elapsed time
55          float ElapsedTime = 0.0f;
56
57          //Loop for transition time
58          while(ElapsedTime <= TransitionTime)
59          {
60              //Update Elapsed time
61              ElapsedTime += Time.deltaTime;
62
63              //Set sprite renderer colors
64              foreach(SpriteRenderer SR in SpriteRenderers)
65                  SR.color = Color.Lerp(X, Y, Mathf.Clamp(ElapsedTime/TransitionTime,
                        0.0f, 1.0f));
66
67              //Wait until next frame
68              yield return null;
69          }
70
71          //Set dest color
72          foreach(SpriteRenderer SR in SpriteRenderers)
73              SR.color = Y;
74      }
75      //------------------------------------------------
76  }                       //Send enemy destroyed notification
```

> **Note** In Listing 7-3, coroutines have been used to create a ping-pong effect between color data structures.
> There are, however, other methods for achieving similar ping-ponging behavior. For example, see the online
> Unity documentation at `https://docs.unity3d.com/Documentation/ScriptReference/`
> `Mathf.PingPong.html`.

Go ahead and add this class as a component to the Enemy_Drone object in the scene. The PingPongSpriteColor class supports a range of public member variables, including Source and Dest colors, representing the color to blend with the sprite material using multiplicative blending. *Source* defines the default color to be blended with the sprite when it's *not* being attacked (this should be white to preserve the default colors defined in the sprite texture file), and *Dest* defines the blending color when the sprite is under attack (and this should be *red*). This is because the sprite should turn red when being attacked. The *transition* time defines the total time in seconds for the sprite to change color from its default (white) to red when being attacked. For the Drone character, I've specified a value of 0.3 seconds (see Figure 7-10).

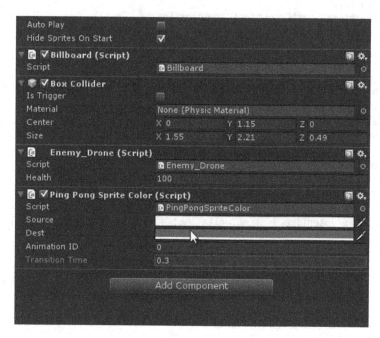

Figure 7-10. Configuring color animation for the sprite material

Just adding PingPongSpriteColor as a component to the game object isn't enough, however, for turning the Enemy red when attacked. We'll need some extra code in the Damage event for Enemy_Drone to initiate the red-flashing behavior at the appropriate time. Consider the amended Damage event in Listing 7-4. The Damage event now calls on the PingPongSpriteColor function PlayColorAnimation (as defined at line 31 in Listing 7-3).

Listing 7-4. Amending Enemy_Drone to Work with PingPongSpriteColor

```
01 using UnityEngine;
02 using System.Collections;
03
04 public class Enemy_Drone : Enemy
05 {
06     //------------------------------------------------
07     //Event called when damaged by an attack
08     public void Damage(int Damage = 0)
09     {
10         //Reduce health
11         Health -= Damage;
12
13         //Play damage animation
14         gameObject.SendMessage("PlayColorAnimation",0,SendMessageOptions.
            DontRequireReceiver);
15
16         //Check if dead
17         if(Health <= 0)
18         {
19             //Send enemy destroyed notification
20             GameManager.Notifications.PostNotification(this, "EnemyDestroyed");
21
22             //Remove object from scene
23             DestroyImmediate(gameObject);
24
25             //Clean up old listeners
26             GameManager.Notifications.RemoveRedundancies();
27         }
28     }
29     //------------------------------------------------
30 }
```

Let's see this code in action in the Unity Editor, as shown in Figure 7-11. The result: our Enemy now responds not only to attacks in terms of *health* reduction, but the gamer can actually see an indication that damage has been taken. Splendid work. Let's move on!

Figure 7-11. *The Enemy taking damage*

Enemies, Intelligence, and Philosophical Zombies

The problem with the enemy Drone created so far rests not so much in anything *he does*, but in what *he doesn't do*. Right now, he stands motionlessly on the spot wherever we put him, and he takes damage when delivered. But he doesn't move in any appropriate respect, he doesn't fight back, and he doesn't even try to avoid attacks. In short, he doesn't do anything we'd expect an "intelligent" person to do in the same or similar circumstances. As a result, the Enemy is technically functional but is practically unconvincing. And so to solve this issue, we enter naturally into the world of *artificial intelligence*. But what is that, really? What does it amount to in practice for CMOD? And more importantly, what does it mean for your games?

Artificial intelligence (AI) is a huge and controversial field. But a narrow part of it is worth considering here very briefly, pertaining to philosophy. Within this field, there are some who consider the word *artificial* in the term *artificial intelligence* to be highly misleading and incorrect. They say, when you really think about it, the only good basis you have for believing that other humans are intelligent is from what *you personally observe them doing*. Everybody could really be zombies, for all you know. After all, you can't open people's heads and see them thinking. You can't see their *thoughts* with your own eyes. All you can do is *observe how people behave* in particular contexts. And when you see them behaving in *specific ways* in *specific situations*, (like trying to avoid being attacked, and trying to retaliate against an aggressor), we call that kind of behavior *intelligent*. And that's all intelligence is: a behavior pattern.

The word *artificial* in artificial intelligence serves no purpose, because when a preprogrammed character in a video game (like our Enemy) responds in *intelligent-looking ways*, even in a virtual world, it's *not* demonstrating *fake* or *artificial* intelligence, it's demonstrating *real* intelligence. Its intelligence is fundamentally no different from human intelligence. After all, in *both* cases we identify the intelligence *by appearances alone*, and that's all we ever have to base our belief on. So, for these thinkers (I'll call them *Functionalists*), there's no point asking whether computers will *one day* be intelligent. They're intelligent *right now!* It's only common misunderstandings that prevent most people accepting it.

This Functionalist view runs against common sense today. Most people think there's a fundamental difference of *some kind* between a human and a computer regarding intelligence. We feel the Functionalist is missing an important piece of the puzzle. We feel that a computer, no matter how sophisticated, will never be "truly" intelligent because it lacks an important, conscious and inward ingredient that humans have. Now, whatever the case may be, there's something very useful in the Functionalist view for the game developer, and also something very hindering and troubling in the common-sense view. For this reason, whatever you personally think on the matter (I change my mind every time I think about it), I recommend a pragmatic approach: suspend your position temporarily and see intelligence from the perspective of the Functionalist. Why?

Often, when developers start creating a game with AI, they approach the matter believing their aim is to develop some kind of *super-intelligent* and *truly clever* enemy; one that calculates and figures out what to do just like a clever human would, and in just the same way. But because the common-sense view maintains an intuitive feeling of incompatibility between human and computer intelligence, it lures us into thinking that AI is something very difficult; into feeling as though we're "out of our depth." However, by taking the Functionalist view instead, and by seeing AI with *those* eyes, then new and exciting possibilities emerge. For game AI, the artistic rule applies: if it *looks* right, then *it is* right. If the enemy *appears* intelligent when the gamer is looking, then that's intelligence enough. It's the appearance that we recognize as intelligence, despite what philosophical debaters may have to say about "true intelligence." If it's good enough to fool the gamer and offer a believable experience, then it's "good enough" for us, and we needn't trouble ourselves unduly in creating something beyond.

> **Note**   There are some exceptional games that "go further" with AI and explore new boundaries and ideas, and approach the task from new perspectives. These are often experimental games, "serious" games, or simulators. But for CMOD and most other games, the Functionalist view will be our friend when coding AI in C# and Unity.

Finite State Machines (FSMs)

So let's start creating intelligent enemies (notice that I didn't say *artificially* intelligent)! The three Enemy types for CMOD (the Drone, the Tough Guy, and Mr. Big Cheese) will all *share* the same behavior; and so the intelligence will be coded into the Enemy base class, and not into any of the derivatives—allowing all the derived classes to inherit the functionality. For CMOD, the three Enemies will work as follows in terms of intelligence:

1. When the level begins, *all* Enemies will wander or *patrol* around the environment. They will continue doing this until they come close to the Player and the Player enters their line of sight. That is, when the Player enters an Enemy's *observation radius*.

2. When the Player enters an Enemy's observation radius, the Enemy will change its behavior. Specifically, it will stop patrolling, and will start pursuing or *chasing* the Player.

3. The Enemy will continue to chase the Player until *either* the Player leaves the Enemy's observation radius (the Player outruns the Enemy), or when the Enemy comes within *attacking distance* to the Player.

4. If the Player leaves the Enemy's observation radius, the Enemy returns back to a Patrol state, wandering the level repeatedly.

5. If the Enemy enters attacking distance to the Player, the Enemy will change behavior again. Specifically, he will change from chasing to attacking.

6. When an Enemy is attacking the Player, he will continue to deal damage using his weapon, until either the Player dies, or the Player is no longer within attacking distance.

Together these conditions and this logic define the general intelligence pattern for the Enemy. This kind of system is called a *finite state machine*, *because* the Enemy can be in only one state at any one time (Patrol, Chase, or Attack), and all of these states are known in advance and are connected to one another by relationships in a complete system. That is, the Enemy can change from any one state to another, only when certain conditions happen. We may start to define the states for this machine in the Enemy class using C# code with an *enum*, as shown in Listing 7-5.

Listing 7-5. Defining the States for an FSM

```
01 using UnityEngine;
02 using System.Collections;
03
04 public class Enemy : MonoBehaviour
05 {
06     //Enum of states for FSM
07     public enum ENEMY_STATE {PATROL = 0, CHASE = 1, ATTACK=2};
08
```

```
09      //Current state of enemy - default is patrol
10      public ENEMY_STATE ActiveState = ENEMY_STATE.PATROL;
11
12      //Current health of this enemy
13      public int Health = 100;
14 }
```

Changing Between States

Each of the three states for the Enemy will be implemented as separate coroutines, with each respective coroutine repeating every frame for as long as the state is active. To achieve this, we'll need three coroutines, one for each state, and a function to manage and change between states. The Enemy class be updated as shown in Listing 7-6; comments follow.

Listing 7-6. Moving Further with FSMs: Defining State Relationships with Coroutines

```
001 using UnityEngine;
002 using System.Collections;
003
004 public class Enemy : MonoBehaviour
005 {
006      //Enum of states for FSM
007      public enum ENEMY_STATE {PATROL = 0, CHASE = 1, ATTACK=2};
008
009      //Current state of enemy - default is patrol
010      public ENEMY_STATE ActiveState = ENEMY_STATE.PATROL;
011
012      //Current health of this enemy
013      public int Health = 100;
014
015      //Reference to active PlayerController component for player
016      protected PlayerController PC = null;
017
018      //Enemy cached transform
019      protected Transform ThisTransform = null;
020
021      //Reference to Player Transform
022      protected Transform PlayerTransform = null;
023
024      //Total distance enemy must be from player, in Unity Units, before chasing them
              (entering chase state)
025      public float ChaseDistance = 10.0f;
026
027      //Total distance enemy must be from player before attacking them
028      public float AttackDistance = 0.1f;
029
030      //------------------------------------------------
```

```
031        void Start()
032        {
033                //Get Player Controller Component
034                GameObject PlayerObject = GameObject.Find("Player");
035                PC = PlayerObject.GetComponentInChildren<PlayerController>();
036
037                //Get Player Transform
038                PlayerTransform = PC.transform;
039
040                //Get Enemy Transform
041                ThisTransform = transform;
042
043                //Set default state
044                ChangeState(ActiveState);
045        }
046        //-------------------------------------------------
047        //Change AI State
048        public void ChangeState(ENEMY_STATE State)
049        {
050                //Stops all AI Processing
051                StopAllCoroutines();
052
053                //Set new state
054                ActiveState = State;
055
056                //Activates new state
057                switch(ActiveState)
058                {
059                case ENEMY_STATE.ATTACK:
060                        StartCoroutine(AI_Attack());
061
062                        //Notify Game Object - in case we want to handle state change
063                        SendMessage("Attack", SendMessageOptions.DontRequireReceiver);
064                        return;
065
066                case ENEMY_STATE.CHASE:
067                        StartCoroutine(AI_Chase());
068
069                        //Notify Game Object - in case we want to handle state change
070                        SendMessage("Chase", SendMessageOptions.DontRequireReceiver);
071                        return;
072
073                case ENEMY_STATE.PATROL:
074                        StartCoroutine(AI_Patrol());
075
076                        //Notify Game Object - in case we want to handle state change
077                        SendMessage("Patrol", SendMessageOptions.DontRequireReceiver);
078                        return;
079                }
080        }
081        //-------------------------------------------------
```

```
082        //AI Function to handle patrol behaviour for enemy
083        //Can exit this state and enter chase
084        IEnumerator AI_Patrol()
085        {
086                //Loop forever while in patrol state
087                while(ActiveState == ENEMY_STATE.PATROL)
088                {
089                        //Check if should enter chase state
090                        if(Vector3.Distance(ThisTransform.position, PlayerTransform.position) <
                           ChaseDistance)
091                        {
092                                //Exit patrol and enter chase state
093                                ChangeState(ENEMY_STATE.CHASE);
094                                yield break;
095                        }
096
097                        yield return null;
098                }
099        }
100        //-------------------------------------------------
101        //AI Function to handle patrol behaviour for enemy
102        //Can exit this state and enter chase
103        IEnumerator AI_Chase()
104        {
105                //Loop forever while in chase state
106                while(ActiveState == ENEMY_STATE.CHASE)
107                {
108                        //Check distances and state exit conditions
109                        float DistanceFromPlayer = Vector3.Distance(ThisTransform.position,
                           PlayerTransform.position);
110
111                        //If within attack range, then change to attack state
112                        if(DistanceFromPlayer < AttackDistance) {ChangeState(ENEMY_STATE.ATTACK);
                           yield break;}
113
114                        //If outside chase range, then revert to patrol state
115                        if(DistanceFromPlayer > ChaseDistance) {ChangeState(ENEMY_STATE.PATROL);
                           yield break;}
116
117                        //Wait until next frame
118                        yield return null;
119                }
120        }
121        //-------------------------------------------------
122        //AI Function to handle attack behaviour for enemy
123        //Can exit this state and enter either patrol or chase
124        IEnumerator AI_Attack()
125        {
126                //Loop forever while in chase state
127                while(ActiveState == ENEMY_STATE.ATTACK)
128                {
129                        //Check distances and state exit conditions
```

```
130                  float DistanceFromPlayer = Vector3.Distance(ThisTransform.position,
                     PlayerTransform.position);
131
132                  //If outside chase range, then revert to patrol state
133                  if(DistanceFromPlayer > ChaseDistance) {ChangeState(ENEMY_STATE.PATROL);
                     yield break;}
134
135                  //If outsideattack range, then change to chase state
136                  if(DistanceFromPlayer > AttackDistance) {ChangeState(ENEMY_STATE.CHASE);
                     yield break;}
137
138                  yield return null;
139              }
140          }
141      //-------------------------------------------------
142 }
```

- **Lines 25 and 28**. Here we defined some distances (measured in *Unity units*) for the *Chase* and *Attack* behaviors. When chasing, the ChaseDistance is critical in determining whether the Enemy should switch to the patrolling or attacking state. When attacking, the AttackDistance determines whether the Enemy should switch back to the Chase state.

- **Line 48**. The ChangeState function is responsible for switching or moving the state machine from one state to another. When a state-changing condition in the system is detected (such as when the Enemy enters the AttackDistance from the Player), the ChangeState function must be called to change states.

- **Lines 56, 84, and 103**. The coroutines AI_Patrol, AI_Chase, and AI_Attack are looping routines that repeat *for as long as* the enemy is in the respective state. In essence, these functions handle all frame-based functionality for a state.

Note   Right now the states do not perform all the needed behavior. For example, the Chase state will not (yet) make the Enemy actually chase the Player. This will be implemented in coming sections.

Preparing for State Implementation

In the previous section, we coded the main logic governing the enemy FSM. This included all its states (Patrol, Chase, and Attack), all of which are controlled through specific coroutines in the class. And finally, we implemented a function (ChangeState) to switch between states whenever the appropriate conditions arise during gameplay; and generally, these conditions relate to the amount of distance between the Enemy and the Player at any time. Together, this functionality represents the core of the enemy FSM, but so far the states are not "fleshed out." The various states can handle state switching, allowing us to immediately change from one state to another, but none of them actually make the Enemy *do anything* else. The Chase state doesn't make the Enemy chase the Player, the Patrol state doesn't make the Enemy patrol, and the Attack state doesn't make the Enemy attack. So now it's time to implement these.

Let's consider the Patrol state. In the Patrol state, the Enemy should *appear* to be moving around and to be "up to something." In practice, this means the Enemy class should internally *generate a random location inside the level*, and then move there. And when the destination is reached, the Enemy should generate a new location elsewhere, and then move there, and so on for as long as the Patrol state is active. Now, to achieve this, we'll need to make use of *pathfinding* and *navigation*. Before considering this, let's add a *NavMeshAgent* component to the Enemy character. Doing this *signifies* that our Enemy will be the kind of thing that can move intelligently around the level. To add a NavMeshAgent component, select the Enemy_Drone in the scene, and choose **Component ➤ Navigation ➤ Nav Mesh Agent** from the application menu (see Figure 7-12). The Component settings can be left at their defaults *for now*.

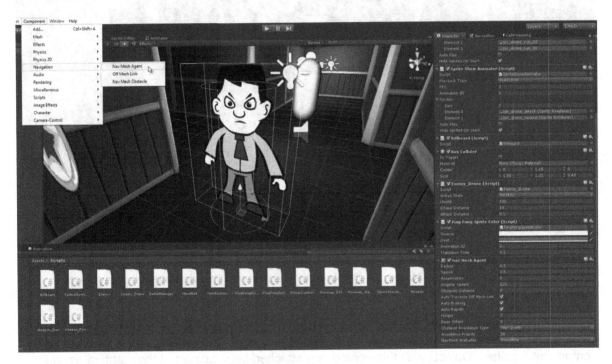

Figure 7-12. Adding a NavMeshAgent component to the enemy Drone

The NavMeshAgent component will be necessary because, for the Enemy to move around the level, pathfinding and navigation will be used. Why is this? Consider Figure 7-13. Suppose the Enemy (standing in position A), in a Patrol state, decides to move to a new destination (position B). The blue arrows in Figure 7-13 indicate the route he should take to travel from A to B. We, as humans, can clearly see and plan the route as shown, because we know certain things about the world: we know we can't walk through walls, for example. To accommodate this, we therefore create a route that conforms to the environment, ensuring we only travel along possible routes. But the problem is that the enemy Drone doesn't know any of this! He would quite happily take the direct route, passing ethereally through all walls and obstacles to reach the destination. And Unity will do absolutely nothing to stop him. Thus, we need the Enemy to act smart and consider *obstacle avoidance* when traveling. To solve this, we'll use the Unity NavMesh system.

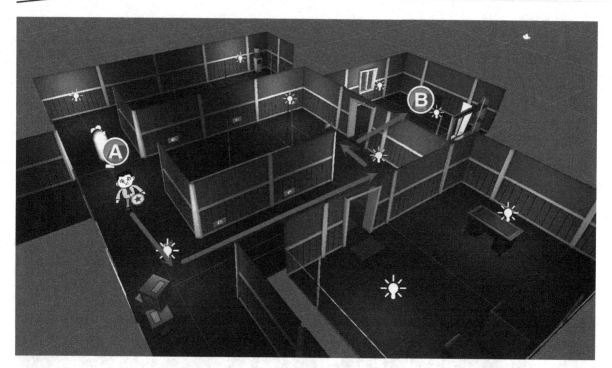

Figure 7-13. A sample route for an Enemy character requires obstacle avoidance

In Chapter 2 we constructed the main environment for CMOD, and this included generating an internal mesh structure, known as a *NavMesh*. To do this, we used the Navigation window (available from the menu at **Window ➤ Navigation**). When this window is active *and* the Show NavMesh check box is enabled from the NavMesh Display utility window in the viewport, the NavMesh for the scene will be displayed at the floor level, as shown in Figure 7-14. The NavMesh is highlighted in blue and represents the total surface area in the scene that Unity regards as walkable. That is, the blue area marks out the region inside which travel and movement can occur. Now for most objects in the scene, the NavMesh is completely ineffectual. It only applies to objects with a NavMeshAgent component attached. Objects with this component attached become part of the pathfinding and navigation system; these objects become linked to the navigation meshes and respond to intelligent navigation. Let's see how by implementing each of the states for the FSM, in turn.

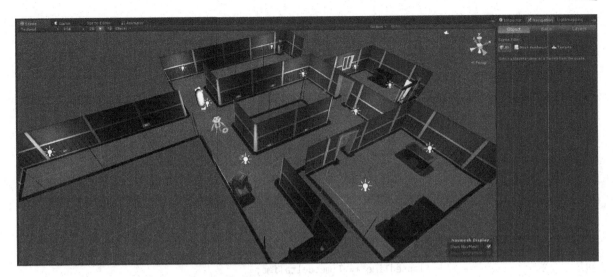

Figure 7-14. The navigation mesh marks out walkable space in the level

The Patrol State

In the Patrol state, the Enemy will wander the scene, traveling from its current position to a randomly selected destination elsewhere in the level. Achieving this requires some amendment to the Enemy class. Let's see some of the changes to the AI_Patrol coroutine, as shown in Listing 7-7. In-depth comments follow.

Listing 7-7. Updating the Patrol State Coroutine

```
01      //-------------------------------------------------
02      //AI Function to handle patrol behaviour for enemy
03      //Can exit this state and enter chase
04      IEnumerator AI_Patrol()
05      {
06              //Stop Agent - NavMeshAgent - declared as a member of the class. See Code 7-9
07              Agent.Stop();
08
09              //Loop forever while in patrol state
10              while(ActiveState == ENEMY_STATE.PATROL)
11              {
12                      //Get random destination on map
13                      Vector3 randomPosition = Random.insideUnitSphere * PatrolDistance;
14
15                      //Add as offset from current position
16                      randomPosition += ThisTransform.position;
17
18                      //Get nearest valid position
19                      NavMeshHit hit;
20                      NavMesh.SamplePosition(randomPosition, out hit, PatrolDistance, 1);
21
```

```
22                    //Set destination
23                    Agent.SetDestination(hit.position);
24
25                    //Set distance range between object and destination to classify as 'arrived'
26                    float ArrivalDistance = 2.0f;
27
28                    //Set timeout before new path is generated (5 seconds)
29                    float TimeOut = 5.0f;
30
31                    //Elapsed Time
32                    float ElapsedTime = 0;
33
34                    //Wait until enemy reaches destination or times-out, and then get new position
35                    while(Vector3.Distance(ThisTransform.position, hit.position) >
                      ArrivalDistance && ElapsedTime < TimeOut)
36                    {
37                            //Update ElapsedTime
38                            ElapsedTime += Time.deltaTime;
39
40                            //Check if should enter chase state
41                            if(Vector3.Distance(ThisTransform.position, PlayerTransform.position) <
                          ChaseDistance)
42                            {
43                                    //Exit patrol and enter chase state
44                                    //ChangeState(ENEMY_STATE.CHASE);
45                                    //yield break;
46                            }
47
48                            yield return null;
49                    }
50            }
51    }
52    //------------------------------------------------
```

■ **Line 07**. This coroutine begins by calling the Stop function in the member agent.
   The member agent is newly added to the class as a *protected* NavMeshAgent
   agent. It is a reference to the NavMeshAgent component attached to the game
   object. An instance to this component is retrieved in the Start event for the
   class. The Stop function of NavMeshAgent simply terminates any outstanding
   navigation and movement operations, if they were any.

Note   More information on the NavMeshAgent component can be found at the online Unity documentation at
https://docs.unity3d.com/Documentation/ScriptReference/NavMeshAgent.html.

- **Line 13**. Here we draw an imaginary circle or area around the Enemy character, and randomly pick a point inside it within the scene. This process is about choosing a random new location to act as the destination for traveling.

- **Lines 19 and 20**. The problem with picking a random location inside the level is that we don't know where the location will be. This entails risk. For example, it's possible the Enemy could be standing close to a wall and that we randomly pick a point *behind the wall*, perhaps a location that's *impossible* to ever reach because it's outside the navigation mesh and area of the level in general. In this case, the destination is indeed *random*, but it's unreachable in all possible scenarios. To avoid this problem, we can use the function NavMesh.SamplePosition to validate our random destination before traveling there. This function will give us the *nearest valid position* on the navigation mesh to our specified destination, if the original destination is not valid.

- **Line 23**. Here we set the agent destination in script. When we do this, the NavMeshAgent will automatically travel there, avoiding obstacles and observing the topology of the NavMesh.

- **Lines 26–51**. Being able to send the NavMeshAgent toward a destination is great. But, how do we know when it's arrived there? It's important to know this because, when it arrives, we'll need to pick a new and random destination elsewhere to travel toward. Currently in Unity, there's no function to answer this query directly; we must code our own functionality to determine destination arrival. We do this at line 35. You might wonder why we can't simply compare the Enemy position directly to the destination to see whether he's arrived, such as *enemy.position == destination.position*. The reason relates to floating-point precision on computers due to rounding issues and large number storage. In practice, it may be that two objects are (to the eye) at the same location in the scene, even though their world positions (expressed in floating-point numbers) are fractionally different, mathematically speaking. This makes direct comparison troublesome when attempting to assess equality, and so often, two objects that appear to be in the same position actually have slightly different positional values. So, instead we can use an *Epsilon* and a *Timeout*. The Epsilon means that if the Enemy arrives within a *certain distance* of the destination (ArrivalDistance), then we'll classify the destination as reached. The *Timeout* technique is used as a *fail-safe* feature, in case any inaccuracies or slip-ups occur during the pathfinding process (which is possible, in practice). This means that, if a specified *time has elapsed* since travel began (TimeOut), then pick a new destination, as though the Enemy had arrived (see Figure 7-15).

Figure 7-15. The Patrol state in action!

> **Note**   If you're interested in some of the reasons why pathfinding can fail in practice, and you like math,
> I recommend searching the web for *under-constrained problems*.

- ■ **Line 43–45**. Notice that, for this sample, I've commented out all lines relating
  to state-changing functionality. This is simply for testing purposes so that
  when unit testing the code in Listing 7-7, no confusion arises because of any
  state changes. The Enemy will begin *and remain* in the Patrol state, allowing
  us to observe and test that state alone. We'll reactivate these lines later, when
  completing the whole FSM.

> **Note**   Give the Patrol state a try in-game. Remember, the associated script files for this functionality (should
> you require them) are included in the book companion files in the Chapter07 folder, in the files Enemy.cs
> and Enemy_Drone.cs.

Refining the Patrol State

The Patrol state is now operational in the sense that our Enemy character moves around the scene,
traveling intelligently to a random destination using the navigation mesh feature. But there's a problem:
he doesn't animate while moving. The character moves, in terms of *position and rotation* within the

scene, but the run animation never plays back during the move, and so the Enemy simply looks like he's hovering or sliding around the level. Creepy! So let's change that now. To do this, we'll return to the Enemy_Drone class and make use of the SendMessage functionality, coded earlier in Listing 7-6, where the ChangeState function sends a change state message to the enemy object. We'll use this message to initiate playback of the relevant animation (see the amended Enemy_Drone script in Listing 7-8).

Listing 7-8. Enemy_Drone.cs: Integrating with Navigation

```
01 //-----------------------------------------------
02 using UnityEngine;
03 using System.Collections;
04 //-----------------------------------------------
05 public class Enemy_Drone : Enemy
06 {
07        //-------------------------------------------
08        //Sprites for walk animation
09        public SpriteRenderer[] WalkSprites = null;
10
11        //Sprites for attack animation
12        public SpriteRenderer[] AttackSprites = null;
13
14        //Default Sprite (neutral state)
15        public SpriteRenderer DefaultSprite = null;
16
17        //-------------------------------------------
18        //Event called when damaged by an attack
19        public void Damage(int Damage = 0)
20        {
21                //Reduce health
22                Health -= Damage;
23
24                //Play damage animation
25                gameObject.SendMessage("PlayColorAnimation",0,SendMessageOptions.
                   DontRequireReceiver);
26
27                //Check if dead
28                if(Health <= 0)
29                {
30                        //Send enemy destroyed notification
31                        GameManager.Notifications.PostNotification(this, "EnemyDestroyed");
32
33                        //Remove object from scene
34                        DestroyImmediate(gameObject);
35
36                        //Clean up old listeners
37                        GameManager.Notifications.RemoveRedundancies();
38                }
39        }
```

```
40      //---------------------------------------------
41      //Handle patrol state
42      public void Patrol()
43      {
44              //Hide default and attack sprites
45              foreach(SpriteRenderer SR in AttackSprites)
46                      SR.enabled=false;
47
48              //Hide default sprite
49              DefaultSprite.enabled = false;
50
51              //Entered patrol state
52              SendMessage ("StopSpriteAnimation", ((int)ENEMY_STATE.PATROL),
                SendMessageOptions.DontRequireReceiver);
53              SendMessage ("StopSpriteAnimation", ((int)ENEMY_STATE.ATTACK),
                SendMessageOptions.DontRequireReceiver);
54              SendMessage("PlaySpriteAnimation", ((int)ENEMY_STATE.PATROL),
                SendMessageOptions.DontRequireReceiver);
55      }
56      //---------------------------------------------
57 }
58 //---------------------------------------------
```

Now the Enemy_Drone integrates with the pathfinding functionality coded into its base, at least for the *Patrol state*. Take it for a test run and see the Enemy run along, his legs in motion (also see Figure 7-16).

Figure 7-16. Enemy in motion!

In observing the motion and movement of the Enemy in general, you may want to tweak his speed and pathfinding size. Perhaps when moving, the Enemy's arms or legs, or the fringes of his body, sometimes penetrate through the wall and other obstacles. This is because pathfinding calculates object position and motion using an invisible cylinder object. The idea is to size and position the cylinder to act as a bounding volume. These settings can be controlled by the NavMeshAgent component (see Figure 7-17). Here, I've set the agent Speed to *2* (units per second), the Stopping Distance to *1.5*, the cylinder Radius to *0.69*, and the cylinder Height to *2.3*.

Figure 7-17. Sizing the Enemy pathfinding cylinder: this can improve agent navigation and behavior

The Chase and Attack States

Having seen the fundamentals of creating an FSM through previous sections, let's now put it all together. Here we'll finalize the enemy Drone character, complete with Patrol, Chase, and Attack states. Consider Listings 7-9 and 7-10 for the complete Enemy class and the relevant changes to the Enemy_Drone classes. Get ready for some longer code listings! Comments on critical code additions and changes follow.

Listing 7-9. Final Enemy.cs Class with a Completed FSM

```
001 //Sets up FSM for enemy AI
002 //-----------------------------------------------
003 using UnityEngine;
004 using System.Collections;
005 using System.Collections.Generic;
006 //-----------------------------------------------
007 public class Enemy : MonoBehaviour
008 {
009       //Enemy types
010       public enum ENEMY_TYPE {Drone = 0, ToughGuy = 1, Boss=2};
011
012       //Type of this enemy
013       public ENEMY_TYPE Type = ENEMY_TYPE.Drone;
014
015       //Custom ID of this enemy
016       public int EnemyID = 0;
017
018       //Current health of this enemy
019       public int Health = 100;
020
021       //Attack Damage - amount of damage this enemy deals to player when attacking
022       public int AttackDamage = 10;
023
024       //Recovery delay in seconds after launching an attack
025       public float RecoveryDelay = 1.0f;
026
027       //Enemy cached transform
028       protected Transform ThisTransform = null;
029
030       //-----------------------------------------------
031       //AI Properties
032
033       //Reference to NavMesh Agent component
034       protected NavMeshAgent Agent = null;
035
036       //Reference to active PlayerController component for player
037       protected PlayerController PC = null;
038
039       //Reference to Player Transform
040       protected Transform PlayerTransform = null;
041
```

```
042        //Total distance in Unity Units from current position that agent can wander when patrolling
043        public float PatrolDistance = 10.0f;
044
045        //Total distance enemy must be from player, in Unity Units, before chasing them
           (entering chase state)
046        public float ChaseDistance = 10.0f;
047
048        //Total distance enemy must be from player before attacking them
049        public float AttackDistance = 0.1f;
050
051        //Enum of states for FSM
052        public enum ENEMY_STATE {PATROL = 0, CHASE = 1, ATTACK=2};
053
054        //Current state of enemy - default is patrol
055        public ENEMY_STATE ActiveState = ENEMY_STATE.PATROL;
056
057        //------------------------------------------------
058        //Called on object start
059        protected virtual void Start()
060        {
061                //Get NavAgent Component
062                Agent = GetComponent<NavMeshAgent>();
063
064                //Get Player Controller Component
065                GameObject PlayerObject = GameObject.Find("Player");
066                PC = PlayerObject.GetComponentInChildren<PlayerController>();
067
068                //Get Player Transform
069                PlayerTransform = PC.transform;
070
071                //Get Enemy Transform
072                ThisTransform = transform;
073
074                //Set default state
075                ChangeState(ActiveState);
076        }
077        //------------------------------------------------
078        //Change AI State
079        public void ChangeState(ENEMY_STATE State)
080        {
081                //Stops all AI Processing
082                StopAllCoroutines();
083
084                //Set new state
085                ActiveState = State;
086
```

```
087                //Activates new state
088                switch(ActiveState)
089                {
090                case ENEMY_STATE.ATTACK:
091                        StartCoroutine(AI_Attack());
092                        SendMessage("Attack", SendMessageOptions.DontRequireReceiver);
                           //Notify Game Object
093                        return;
094
095                case ENEMY_STATE.CHASE:
096                        StartCoroutine(AI_Chase());
097                        SendMessage("Chase", SendMessageOptions.DontRequireReceiver);
                           //Notify Game Object
098                        return;
099
100                case ENEMY_STATE.PATROL:
101                        StartCoroutine(AI_Patrol());
102                        SendMessage("Patrol", SendMessageOptions.DontRequireReceiver);
                           //Notify Game Object
103                        return;
104                }
105        }
106        //-------------------------------------------------
107        //AI Function to handle patrol behaviour for enemy
108        //Can exit this state and enter chase
109        IEnumerator AI_Patrol()
110        {
111                //Stop Agent
112                Agent.Stop();
113
114                //Loop forever while in patrol state
115                while(ActiveState == ENEMY_STATE.PATROL)
116                {
117                        //Get random destination on map
118                        Vector3 randomPosition = Random.insideUnitSphere * PatrolDistance;
119
120                        //Add as offset from current position
121                        randomPosition += ThisTransform.position;
122
123                        //Get nearest valid position
124                        NavMeshHit hit;
125                        NavMesh.SamplePosition(randomPosition, out hit, PatrolDistance, 1);
126
127                        //Set destination
128                        Agent.SetDestination(hit.position);
129
130                        //Set distance range between object and destination to classify as 'arrived'
131                        float ArrivalDistance = 2.0f;
132
133                        //Set timeout before new path is generated (5 seconds)
134                        float TimeOut = 5.0f;
135
```

```
136              //Elapsed Time
137              float ElapsedTime = 0;
138
139              //Wait until enemy reaches destination or times-out, and then get new
                 position
140              while(Vector3.Distance(ThisTransform.position, hit.position) >
                 ArrivalDistance && ElapsedTime < TimeOut)
141              {
142                      //Update ElapsedTime
143                      ElapsedTime += Time.deltaTime;
144
145                      //Check if should enter chase state
146                      if(Vector3.Distance(ThisTransform.position, PlayerTransform.position)
                         < ChaseDistance)
147                      {
148                              //Exit patrol and enter chase state
149                              ChangeState(ENEMY_STATE.CHASE);
150                              yield break;
151                      }
152
153                      yield return null;
154              }
155          }
156      }
157  //-------------------------------------------------
158  //AI Function to handle chase behaviour for enemy
159  //Can exit this state and enter either patrol or attack
160  IEnumerator AI_Chase()
161  {
162      //Stop Agent
163      Agent.Stop();
164
165      //Loop forever while in chase state
166      while(ActiveState == ENEMY_STATE.CHASE)
167      {
168              //Set destination to player
169              Agent.SetDestination(PlayerTransform.position);
170
171              //Check distances and state exit conditions
172              float DistanceFromPlayer = Vector3.Distance(ThisTransform.position,
                 PlayerTransform.position);
173
174              //If within attack range, then change to attack state
175              if(DistanceFromPlayer < AttackDistance) {ChangeState(ENEMY_STATE.ATTACK);
                 yield break;}
176
177              //If outside chase range, then revert to patrol state
178              if(DistanceFromPlayer > ChaseDistance) {ChangeState(ENEMY_STATE.PATROL);
                 yield break;}
179
```

```
180                        //Wait until next frame
181                        yield return null;
182                }
183        }
184        //-----------------------------------------------
185        //AI Function to handle attack behaviour for enemy
186        //Can exit this state and enter either patrol or chase
187        IEnumerator AI_Attack()
188        {
189                //Stop Agent
190                Agent.Stop();
191
192                //Elapsed time - to calculate strike intervals
193                float ElapsedTime = RecoveryDelay;
194
195                //Loop forever while in chase state
196                while(ActiveState == ENEMY_STATE.ATTACK)
197                {
198                        //Update elapsed time
199                        ElapsedTime += Time.deltaTime;
200
201                        //Check distances and state exit conditions
202                        float DistanceFromPlayer = Vector3.Distance(ThisTransform.position,
                           PlayerTransform.position);
203
204                        //If outside chase range, then revert to patrol state
205                        if(DistanceFromPlayer > ChaseDistance) {ChangeState(ENEMY_STATE.PATROL);
                           yield break;}
206
207                        //If within attack range, then change to attack state
208                        if(DistanceFromPlayer > AttackDistance) {ChangeState(ENEMY_STATE.CHASE);
                           yield break;}
209
210                        //Make strike
211                        if(ElapsedTime >= RecoveryDelay)
212                        {
213                                //Reset elapsed time
214                                ElapsedTime = 0;
215                                SendMessage("Strike",SendMessageOptions.DontRequireReceiver);
216                        }
217
218                        //Wait until next frame
219                        yield return null;
220                }
221        }
222 }
223 //-----------------------------------------------
```

- **Lines 34 and 43**. Notice the additional member variable declarations that were used in previously coded listings for accessing the NavMeshAgent component and generating random destinations within the scene, for use with the Patrol state.

- **Lines 160–183**. The AI_Chase coroutine defines the Chase state behavior. In short, this function uses the Agent.SetDestination function to specify the Player as the travel destination for the Enemy, since the Enemy must *follow* the Player. The state will transition to another when the Player leaves the chase distance, or when the Enemy is close enough to attack. The exact attack range for an Enemy will vary, depending on the Enemy type. For example, Enemies with gun weapons will feature a longer attack range.

- **Lines 187–221**. The AI_Attack coroutine handles the attack behavior for the Enemy. From lines 211–219, the Enemy loops in an attack mode, and issues a strike (or an attack), allowing for an intervening recovery or reload delay for its weapon, for each strike. Each attack will invoke a Strike function call on the object (in line 215), allowing each unique Enemy type to handle its own attack differently, if required. It's generally good practice to make base classes as abstract as possible, allowing derived classes to customize functionality as far as needed.

Listing 7-10. Relevant Additions to the Enemy Drone Class

```
01 //--------------------------------------------------
02 //Handle Chase State
03 public void Chase()
04 {
05      //Same animations as patrol
06      Patrol();
07 }
08 //--------------------------------------------------
09 //Entered Attack State
10 public void Attack()
11 {
12      //Hide default and walk sprites
13      foreach(SpriteRenderer SR in WalkSprites)
14          SR.enabled=false;
15
16      //Hide default sprite
17      DefaultSprite.enabled = false;
18
19      //Entered attack state
20      SendMessage ("StopSpriteAnimation", ((int)ENEMY_STATE.PATROL),
         SendMessageOptions.DontRequireReceiver);
21      SendMessage ("StopSpriteAnimation", ((int)ENEMY_STATE.ATTACK),
         SendMessageOptions.DontRequireReceiver);
22      SendMessage("PlaySpriteAnimation", ((int)ENEMY_STATE.ATTACK),
         SendMessageOptions.DontRequireReceiver);
23 }
24 //--------------------------------------------------
```

```
25 //Strike - called each time the enemy makes a strike against the player (deal damage)
26 public void Strike()
27 {
28     //Damage player
29     PC.gameObject.SendMessage("ApplyDamage", AttackDamage,
       SendMessageOptions.DontRequireReceiver);
30 }
31 //-------------------------------------------------
```

- **Lines 26–30**. The most noteworthy functionality for the Enemy_Drone here concerns the attacking functionality. Here, the Strike function is called from the base class Enemy to implement damage-dealing to the Player. To achieve this, the Enemy invokes the ApplyDamage function on the Player, which both deals damage and plays the red-flash animation (created in Chapter 5 using procedural textures).

Let's now apply these code changes and take CMOD for a test run to see the complete FSM for the enemy Drone character in action. On pressing Play, you'll have an Enemy that patrols, chases, and attacks! As a gamer, it can be difficult to observe the Patrol state fully with the complete FSM. This is because, typically, the Enemy will see and chase the Player whenever the Player enters the Enemy's line of sight. So, if you can see the Enemy in-game, he's probably already in the Chase or Attack state—coming to get you. But Unity makes it easy to test functionality for all states, by observing out-of-sight enemy movements in the *Scene* viewport, as opposed to the Game viewport. You can align the viewports side by side and debug as much as you need (see Figure 7-18).

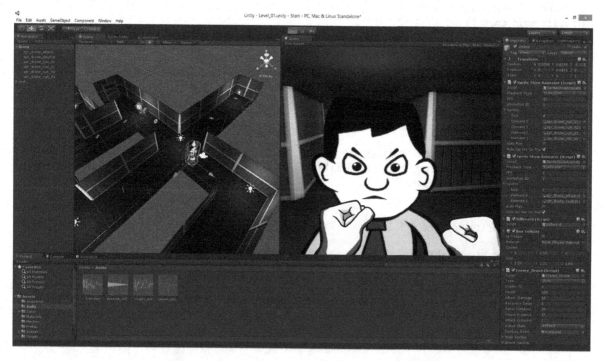

Figure 7-18. Testing Enemy AI. Using a split screen view, between the Scene and Game viewports, to observe enemy movement in all three states

> **Note**   Be sure to configure the attack, patrol, and chase distances for the Enemy component in the Object Inspector. For the Drone, I've used a Chase of 10, a Patrol of 30, and an Attack of 2. Also be sure to set the Stopping Distance of the NavMeshAgent component to 1.5 or less, to stop the Enemy from walking through the Player, but to allow enough "closeness" to make an attack possible.

Adding More Enemy Types

Implementation of the Drone enemy is now completed, which means we can "Prefab" him! That is, we can now create a Prefab for this enemy, ready to duplicate and position him in the level wherever we need additional Drone enemies. But, of course, CMOD will feature more than simply the Drone enemies; there's the Tough Guy and Mr. Big Cheese, too. They are tougher and meaner Enemies. However, their implementation requires only two additional classes, one for each Enemy type: Enemy_ToughGuy and Enemy_Boss. Both of these classes will derive from the base Enemy class. This means that all the core AI functionality and behavior inherited by the *Drone* will also be inherited by the Tough Guy and Mr. Big Cheese.

In fact, the only critical ways in which the Tough Guy and Mr. Big Cheese differ from the Drone, and from each other, is in terms of their *damage strength*, their *health*, and their *attack range*. In all other respects, all of the Enemies are identical—even though they may seem very different to the gamer. This is significant because it shows that, through class inheritance and by using varied assets, it's possible to create the appearance of great variety and divergence atop a common and shared codebase.

Given the similarities between the Enemy types, the source code for the Tough Guy and Mr. Big Cheese will not be listed here, although it can be found in the book companion files for Chapter 7, should you need further guidance on how to implement additional enemies. Take a look at Figure 7-19 for a level full of dangerous Enemies. Congratulations! You've now implemented another critical and core mechanic into the FPS game CMOD.

Figure 7-19. CMOD, up and running with multiple Enemy types

Summary

By now, CMOD is really looking good! We have almost everything we need for an enjoyable game: a Player character, an environment to explore, power-ups, weapons, interesting enemies, and—in addition—the enemies are intelligent. Next up, we'll consider the issue of graphical user interfaces (GUIs) to add further polish to the game. Specifically, we'll create a main menu for the game, allowing the gamer to restart, exit, and load and save the game. At this point, you should be able to do the following:

- Create an Enemy prefab
- Create a Drone, Tough Guy, and Mr. Big Cheese enemy
- Understand how to deal and receive damage to and from the Player
- Understand what AI is and its purpose in games
- Understand what an FSM is and how it works
- Create an FSM for the Enemy character AI
- Understand the NavMeshAgent component and how it works with NavMeshes
- Understand what pathfinding and navigation is
- Create C# script files that use the navigation system
- Create agents that can move around the scene intelligently
- Create different Enemy types through class inheritance

Chapter 8

Graphical User Interfaces

In this chapter we'll create a basic graphical user interface (GUI) system for CMOD. This includes a main menu and a HUD (head-up display). The main menu will appear when the user presses the Escape key on the keyboard, allowing him to restart, load, save, and exit the game. And the head-up display will continually show Player health, as well as the ammo status for the active weapon. In creating the GUI, we'll explore a range of subjects, including screen dimensions, the aspect ratio, widgets, anchoring, GUI scaling, and resolution independence. As always, these subjects apply practically, not just for CMOD or Unity specifically, but for game engines and games, as well as software and web sites in general. So, let's get started with creating GUIs.

GUIs in Games

Graphical user interfaces refer to, in sum, all 2D graphics rendered in screen space, such as menus, health bars, and buttons. These let the gamer interact with the game, performing critical functions. Using GUIs, gamers can load and save their game states, monitor their health status, consult minimaps and radar displays, see the ammo status of their weapons, and lots more besides, depending on the types of games they're playing.

GUIs are, in many respects, unique among all other assets and objects in a video game. Specifically, they're *not* supposed to exist *within* the game world itself. Enemies, like the drone and boss characters for CMOD, live within the game world and interact directly with the Player, attacking or chasing. Weapons and props also exist in game space; they can be collected and used by the Player to attack Enemies. With these objects and more, the Player can *do* things, and the presence of these objects makes a substantive difference on the course of events *in-game*. But GUIs are different. They work at a different level; existing outside the game space, and working at a level of abstraction from the game. Their purpose is either to *provide information* in an *augmented reality* sense, such as displaying the health status of the Player, or to provide access to fundamental game functionality at a system level, such as *exiting*, *restarting*, or *pausing* the game.

It's perhaps this logistical distinctiveness of GUIs that have historically made them an uneasy and awkward fit in the feature-set of most 3D engines. Most engines have legacy features and editor quirks for GUIs, which are the direct result of attempts over time by engine developers to rethink and reinvent how GUI development could optimally work with the rest of the 3D development tools. The hope of most game developers is to have a fully functional 2D GUI editor, complete with GUI widgets and controls like those in popular GUI IDEs (integrated development environments), such as the Qt framework, the Embarcadero C++Builder, or the .NET Framework. But this dream has still not been realized in most engines, at the time of writing. This has made GUI development for games a comparatively laborious and messy affair. One common solution in engines today is to simply disregard support for any native GUI development. With this solution, GUI development is typically delegated entirely to third-party tools, like Adobe Flash. From here, the engine offers support by allowing a compiled Flash presentation to be embedded into and connected to the game through add-ons and plug-ins like Autodesk Scaleform.

Unity, however, doesn't take the Scaleform approach natively. Instead, it makes an attempt to offer native GUI development features. Until Unity 4.3, it offered these almost exclusively through the GUI class. More information on this class can be found at `https://docs.unity3d.com/Documentation/Components/GUIScriptingGuide.html`. However, this class became unpopular among many developers for performance reasons. And many developers even abandoned the GUI class entirely, coding their own custom GUI solutions from the ground upward, or else they used a range of third-party GUI frameworks from the Unity Asset Store.

But since version 4.3, newer and easier possibilities beyond the GUI class have emerged through the added 2D functionality and sprite features; and (as I write this) it is expected that there will be even more GUI functionality and further developments in an upcoming Unity 4.6 release. This release is not available to me at the time of writing this chapter, but it may be available to you when you are reading this chapter.

In short, this chapter will explore GUI development *almost* entirely with the Unity 4.3 sprite functionality, along with orthographic cameras (as explained in Chapter 6 when creating weapons). It may be that upcoming GUI features—whatever they are—will make GUI development even easier than the methods I've outlined here, but nonetheless, the methods here should remain valid and applicable to later versions, too, and even apply in principle to other engines supporting similar 2D sprite functionality.

Getting Started with GUIs

Since we'll be using the Unity 4.3 2D sprite functionality to create a GUI for CMOD, our first steps in GUI development will resemble the first steps for creating weapons. Specifically, we'll create an *orthographic camera* in the scene (to render graphics in 2D), with a *Depth Only* value set for the *Clear Flag* field in the Object Inspector. And we'll also restrict camera rendering to only a designated GUI layer using the *Culling Mask* field. More in-depth instructions on how to configure a dedicated 2D camera in Unity is covered in Chapter 6. You can also see the GUI camera setup and object arrangement I've used in Figure 8-1 (and this project is included in the book companion files `/Chapter08/`).

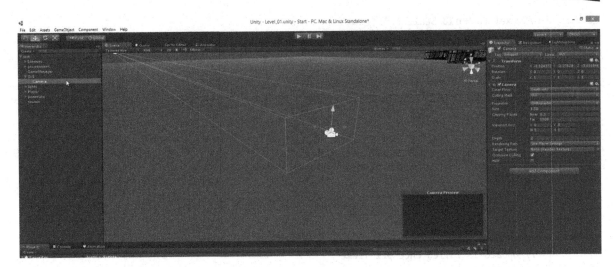

Figure 8-1. Configuring a dedicated UI camera

Notice that I've grouped the GUI camera as a child object beneath an empty game object named *GUI* to organize and group together all GUI elements in the scene. This is not essential, but recommended. Take care to assign the GUI camera a unique and highest value for *Depth* (I've used two here) to ensure it renders *on top* or *in front* of all other scene objects. This is important because GUI objects should appear in front of everything else in-game, except for a mouse cursor graphic and other input helpers (like gizmos), if your game supports them.

We've now created an orthographic camera in the scene for displaying a GUI. One of the most notable features of a GUI camera is that all GUI graphics will be rendered in *screen space* in pixels. To make this kind of GUI-rendering easier and more intuitive, it'll be useful to customize the camera further through a C# script, in a GUICam class. First, since it's possible for the game window to change size *during gameplay* (such as when the user resizes the window), we'll want to update the *Orthographic Size* field of the camera *on each frame*, to ensure that its orthographic size will always render world units to pixels at a 1:1 ratio. Second, because all GUI elements (such as buttons and windows) will render together in a single orthographic coordinate system, it'll be useful to set the origin of the coordinate space (0,0) at the top-left corner of the screen, as opposed to the center. This means the bottom-right corner will always be *screen width, screen height* (whatever the screen width and height is). To achieve this behavior, consider Listing 8-1 for GUICam.cs, which is attached as a component to the GUI camera.

Listing 8-1. GUICam.cs: Customizing a GUI Camera

```
01 //-------------------------------------------------------------
02 using UnityEngine;
03 using System.Collections;
04 [ExecuteInEditMode]
05 //-------------------------------------------------------------
06 public class GUICam : MonoBehaviour
07 {
08        //Camera Component
09        private Camera Cam = null;
10
```

```
11          //Pixel to World Scale
12          public float PixelToWorldScale = 200.0f;
13
14          //Cached transform for camera
15          private Transform ThisTransform = null;
16          //-----------------------------------------------------------
17          // Use this for initialization
18          void Start ()
19          {
20                  //Get camera component for GUI
21                  Cam = GetComponent<Camera>();
22
23                  //Get camera transform
24                  ThisTransform = transform;
25          }
26          //-----------------------------------------------------------
27          // Update is called once per frame
28          void Update ()
29          {
30                  //Update camera size
31                  Cam.orthographicSize = Screen.height/2/PixelToWorldScale;
32
33                  //Offset camera so top-left of screen is position (0,0) for game objects
34                  ThisTransform.localPosition = new Vector3(Screen.width/2/PixelToWorldScale, -
                    (Screen.height/2/PixelToWorldScale), ThisTransform.localPosition.z);
35          }
36          //-----------------------------------------------------------
37 }
38 //-----------------------------------------------------------
```

- **Line 04.** The [ExecuteInEditMode] directive allows all instances of the class in the scene to run in Edit mode, *as well as* Play mode. Doing this for GUI classes allows you to get real-time previews of your GUIs and arrangements from the Game tab in the Editor, as we'll see later.

- **Line 34.** The position of the camera in the scene is offset away from the local origin (the origin of the parent object) so that any other sibling objects will be rendered as though they were offset from the top-left corner of the screen.

Resolution Dependence and Independence

Now that we have a GUI camera in place in the scene, we can start thinking carefully about adding GUI widgets to the mixture—that is, visual controls (such as buttons and images) constituting the GUI. When considering this (specifically, considering how to position and draw GUI graphics on-screen), a very significant problem arises relating to screen sizes. The problem is that different devices, hardware, and systems support *different* resolutions (pixel dimensions), and so your game may not always appear at single, default resolution. You can, of course, configure your game in Unity (through *Player Settings*) to run at only *one* resolution, rejecting all other resolutions, but this exclusionary tactic will severely limit the kinds of devices your game can support, and will also frustrate users who like more control over how their games are displayed. Furthermore, some mobile devices (in their default state) don't allow users to change the resolution.

So, a more positive response from game developers is to create a *single* GUI with the intention of supporting *as many different screen sizes as possible*. But this has troublesome implications for GUIs, which are rendered in screen space and are intimately linked to pixels and to pixel positions. In particular, if you can't *know in advance* which screen size a gamer will use for your game, then you can't reliably position GUI elements on screen in terms of pixels and expect a consistent experience and look for all users. While 512 pixels is the horizontal center for a 1024 pixels–wide display, it will not be so for a 2048 pixels–wide display (there, it'll be a quarter width). And this problem applies for *any* screen sizes and for *both* dimensions (X and Y), across *all* devices and *all* pixel values. This tells us that specifying the positions of GUI elements in absolute pixel values can't help much, if we want to create multiresolution compliant GUIs—that is, a single GUI system that works across all resolutions (*resolution independence*). One solution to this problem (chosen here) is to develop a *relative* positioning scheme, known as *anchoring*. Consider Figure 8-2.

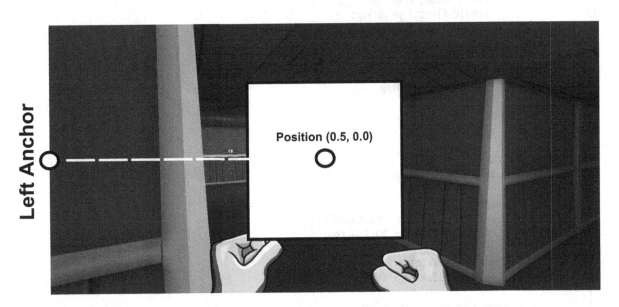

Figure 8-2. Configuring a dedicated UI camera

Using anchoring, positions are specified not in terms of absolute pixels, but as normalized offsets from a fixed and static screen position known to remain constant across all possible resolutions. In Figure 8-2, the screen center is specified as (0.5, 0.0) from a left-center anchor on screen. Thus, the left-center anchor is positioned at (0.0, 0.5), and is *always* half the vertical height of the screen. And the anchored square at the screen center is offset from *that* point by (0.5, 0.0), meaning half the horizontal width of the screen. This form of relative positioning is powerful because it lets you to resolve screen positions across multiple resolutions, simply by expressing positions as proportions rather than absolute pixels. With this technique in mind, let's create a GUIObject class, which will act as a relative-positioning component for any GUI objects we create. This component will be a "base" component in that all GUI game objects (at least, those wanting to be positioned relatively) should have the *GUIObject* component attached (see Listing 8-2 for the full GUIObject source code). Comments follow.

Listing 8-2. GUIObject.cs: A GUI Positioning Component

```
01 //-----------------------------------------------
02 using UnityEngine;
03 using System.Collections;
04 [ExecuteInEditMode]
05 //-----------------------------------------------
06 public class GUIObject : MonoBehaviour
07 {
08          [System.Serializable]
09          public class PixelPadding
10          {
11                  public float LeftPadding;
12                  public float RightPadding;
13                  public float TopPadding;
14                  public float BottomPadding;
15          }
16
17          //Pixel Padding
18          public PixelPadding Padding;
19
20          //HALIGN
21          public enum HALIGN {left=0, right=1};
22
23          //VALIGN
24          public enum VALIGN {top=0, bottom=1};
25
26          //Alignment
27          public HALIGN HorzAlign = HALIGN.left;
28          public VALIGN VertAlign = VALIGN.top;
29
30          //Reference to GUICamera for this object
31          public GUICam GUICamera = null;
32
33          //Reference to cached transform
34          private Transform ThisTransform = null;
35
36          //-----------------------------------------------
37          // Use this for initialization
38          void Start ()
39          {
40                  //Get cached transform
41                  ThisTransform = transform;
42          }
43          //-----------------------------------------------
```

```
44        // Update is called once per frame
45        void Update ()
46        {
47                //Calculate position on-screen
48                Vector3 FinalPosition = new Vector3(HorzAlign == HALIGN.left ? 0.0f : Screen.width,
49                                                   VertAlign == VALIGN.top ? 0.0f : -Screen.height,
50                                                   ThisTransform.localPosition.z);
51
52                //Offset with padding
53                FinalPosition = new Vector3(FinalPosition.x + (Padding.LeftPadding *
                  Screen.width) - (Padding.RightPadding * Screen.width), FinalPosition.y -
                  (Padding.TopPadding * Screen.height) + (Padding.BottomPadding * Screen.height),
                  FinalPosition.z);
54
55                //Convert to pixel scale
56                FinalPosition = new Vector3(FinalPosition.x / GUICamera.PixelToWorldScale,
                  FinalPosition.y / GUICamera.PixelToWorldScale, FinalPosition.z);
57
58                //Update position
59                ThisTransform.localPosition = FinalPosition;
60        }
61        //-------------------------------------------------
62 }
63 //-------------------------------------------------
```

- **Line 08.** Here, the [System.Serializable] directive is used to declare the class PixelPadding to be a serializable class. This means that any instances of the class, and its members, will be accessible and editable via the Object Inspector in the Unity Editor. This directive is significant for member variable Padding, declared at line 18. This member is viewable and editable in the Object Inspector (see Figure 8-3).

Figure 8-3. Starting to create a menu object . . .

- ■ **Lines 9–15.** The pixel padding class specifies the amount of padding to be added onto an anchor to offset the GUI onto the screen into its desired position. Though the member is called *pixel padding*, the value is specified in relative terms (using normalized values, between 0 and 1), as shown in Figure 8-2. The word *pixel* in the title emphasizes that, whatever relative values are used, the values ultimately resolve to pixel values, depending on the screen resolution.

- ■ **Lines 27 and 28.** Here, two member variables are added to indicate the anchoring for the GUI control on both the horizontal and vertical axes. *Left* or *Right*, and *Top* and *Bottom*. Thus, to anchor this GUI object to the screen's top-left, *HorzAlign* should be *Left*, and *VertAlign* should be *Top*.

- ■ **Lines 45–60.** The Update function calculates the position of the control, based on its anchoring and padding values, as well as the orthographic size of the GUI camera, ensuring the object is positioned and scaled correctly on screen.

To put our newly coded GUI object into practice, let's begin work on creating the game's main menu. Right now, we don't have all the code we need—after all, we'll need additional code to actually render the menu on-screen using sprites. But, right now, we have some core relative-positioning functionality to get us started. For the menu, create a new object in the scene, taking care to add it to a GUI layer and to assign the GUICamera field to the GUICamera object in the scene. And then add a GUIObject component to it. For CMOD, the menu graphic should be centered on-screen. Therefore, *HorzAlign* should be *Left*, *VertAlign* should be *Top. Left Padding* should be *0.5*, and *Top Padding* should be *0.5* (see Figure 8-3). In the next section, Figure 8-4 displays the complete menu graphic.

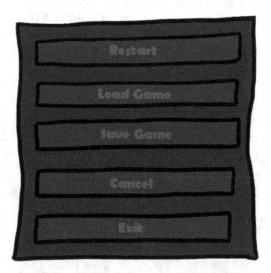

Figure 8-4. The main menu background graphic (559×549 pixels), to be positioned at screen center (0.5, 0.5)

Main Menu and Aspect Ratio

The relative *anchoring system* created in the previous section works insofar as it will *position* graphical elements on the screen consistently across multiple resolutions, as we'll see shortly. The system could, of course, be taken even further to support hierarchical anchoring with multiple local spaces and embedded offsets. But this kind of elaboration and additional complexity will not be required for CMOD. Here, the system will be used to position a menu and its buttons on the screen. The menu is shown in Figure 8-4.

When considering the main menu graphic, as well as any other GUI graphic, a new problem presents itself. Even though the menu will always be positioned at screen center (0.5, 0.5), there are still questions: What should the *size* and the *dimensions* of the menu be? Should we simply render the menu at its default size (559×549 pixels) for every resolution? Or should we *scale* the graphic up or down to always encompass the same screen *proportions* for every resolution (a relative size)? If we accept the first solution (an absolute size), then (like absolute positioning) we place concrete limits on the number of resolutions we can practically support: specifically, we cannot support resolutions smaller than the menu graphic, otherwise the menu will not fit entirely on the screen (the edges will be cut off). Additionally, if the screen resolution is much larger than expected, the menu may appear much smaller than desired at the screen's center. Now, the second option is to use *scaling*. This is one route we could take to support every possible resolution, but it entails complications due to aspect ratio. What are those complications? How do we overcome them? And what is *aspect ratio* anyway?

Aspect ratio is the *relationship* between the screen width and the screen height in pixels. Aspect ratio can be calculated using the formula *AR = Screen Width/Screen Height*. This decimal can resolve to a simplified ratio. The most common ratios are: 4:3, 5:4, 16:10, and 16:9 (widescreen). The problem with aspect ratio regarding image scaling is that an image (like the menu) made at one resolution and aspect ratio cannot be up- or downscaled to a different size and aspect ratio without distortion. Specifically, an image scaled across multiple aspect ratios will scale nonuniformly: it'll either appear more squashed or more expanded in one dimension only. This can lead to ugly graphics. So, the solution that developers have traditionally sought has been to either create multiple versions of GUI graphics at different aspect ratios, switching between the versions at runtime to accommodate the active resolution, *or* to scale the graphics uniformly (in both dimensions) within certain constraints to accommodate the active resolution to an extent, but avoiding graphical distortions at the same time.

For CMOD, however, we'll take the former approach of avoiding the scaling issue altogether. We'll use a fixed size for the menu, setting the minimum resolution at 1024×768, meaning that the menu will show at this resolution and higher. With this solution in mind, we can create the following new GUI class for rendering the menu graphic (see Listing 8-3).

Listing 8-3. GUIOptions.cs: A Class for the Main Menu

```
01 //---------------------------------------------------------------
02 //Class for menu functionality
03 using UnityEngine;
04 using System.Collections;
05 //---------------------------------------------------------------
06 public class GUIOptions : MonoBehaviour
07 {
08         //Sprite Renderer for menu
09         private SpriteRenderer SR = null;
10
11         //Collision objects for buttons
12         private BoxCollider[] Colliders = null;
13
14         //---------------------------------------------------------
15         // Use this for initialization
16         void Start ()
17         {
18                 //Get sprite renderer
19                 SR = GetComponent<SpriteRenderer>();
20
21                 //Get button colliders
22                 Colliders = GetComponentsInChildren<BoxCollider>();
23
24                 //Add listeners
25                 GameManager.Notifications.AddListener(this, "ShowOptions");
26                 GameManager.Notifications.AddListener(this, "HideOptions");
27
28                 //Hide menu on startup
29                 HideOptions(null);
30         }
31         //---------------------------------------------------------
32         //Hide options event
33         public void HideOptions(Component Sender)
34         {
35                 SetOptionsVisible(false);
36         }
37         //---------------------------------------------------------
38         //Show options event
39         public void ShowOptions(Component Sender)
40         {
41                 SetOptionsVisible();
42         }
43         //---------------------------------------------------------
44         //Function to show/hide options
45         private void SetOptionsVisible(bool bShow = true)
46         {
47                 //If enabling, then pause game - else resume
48                 Time.timeScale = (bShow) ? 0.0f : 1.0f;
49
```

```
50              //Enable/Disable input
51              GameManager.Instance.InputAllowed = !bShow;
52
53              //Show/Hide menu graphics
54              SR.enabled = bShow;
55
56              //Enable/Disable button colliders
57              foreach(BoxCollider B in Colliders)
58                      B.enabled = bShow;
59      }
60      //-------------------------------------------------------------
61      //Watch escape key input
62      void Update()
63      {
64              //If escape key pressed
65              if(Input.GetKeyDown(KeyCode.Escape))
66                      SetOptionsVisible(!SR.enabled);
67      }
68      //-------------------------------------------------------------
69 }
```

- **Line 09.** Features the main reference to a Sprite Renderer component for drawing the main menu graphic to the screen. This will refer to a sprite from the project atlas texture. The object reference is retrieved during the Start function, at line 19.

- **Line 12.** Features an array of collider objects, which will be used later in the chapter to represent clickable areas for the menu buttons. A reference to a collider array is required to disable the colliders when the menu is hidden, to prevent the gamer from clicking buttons when the menu is off-screen.

- **Lines 45–59.** The SetOptionsVisible function toggles the visibility of the menu. Line 48 uses the TimeScale member of the native Time class to pause the game when the menu is displayed. A TimeScale value of 1 represents normal speed, a value of 0.5 represents half speed, and 0 means paused.

> **Note** More information on the Time class and its TimeScale member can be found in the online Unity documentation at http://docs.unity3d.com/Documentation/ScriptReference/Time-timeScale.html.

Let's give this class a test, along with the GUIObject class coded in the previous section. By adding both components to a single menu object, we can create a menu that displays and hides on the screen by pressing the Escape key. Be sure to add a sprite component to the object, too, referencing the menu object (spr_Menu) in the atlas texture. You can add a sprite component to an object manually by choosing **Component ➤ Rendering ➤ Sprite Renderer** from the application menu. Then from the Object Inspector, set the *Sprite* field to *spr_Menu* (see Figure 8-5).

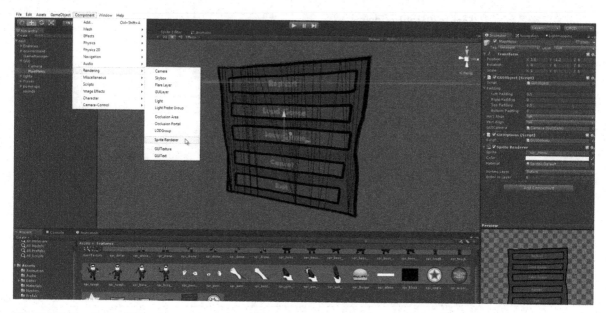

Figure 8-5. Creating a main menu object from a combination of GUIObject, GUIOptions and a sprite renderer component

Notice in Figure 8-5 that the viewport texture-wire display shows the general sprite topology for the menu object. Unity has autotopologized the mesh with multiple edges running downward through the length of the sprite. This is more topology than really required for such a GUI sprite. In this case, a *quad mesh* would be more suitable. You can change this, if you want, by selecting the atlas texture in the Project panel, and from the Object Inspector, changing the *Mesh Type* from *Tight* to *Full Rect*. This ensures all sprites in the atlas will use quad meshes rather than tightly generated meshes. However, tightly generated meshes, conforming more closely to the sprite pixel data, can result in more accurate collisions. You'll need to make careful judgments about the mesh type most appropriate for your sprites (see Figure 8-6).

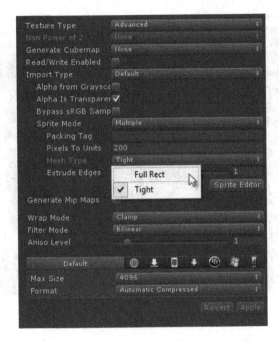

Figure 8-6. Changing the sprite Mesh Type from Tight to Full Rect

Testing the Main Menu

The GUI classes created so far all make use of the [ExecuteInEditMode] directive, meaning they run and operate in the background, even when the Unity Editor is not in Play mode. This feature allows us to preview and see the effects of our GUI in real time; but this comes with important limitations. Specifically, we'll need to use the *Game* tab (not the Scene tab) to preview our GUI, since this view shows us the complete consolidation of scene cameras. So let's switch to the Game tab; the GUI menu is then displayed in the viewport (see Figure 8-7).

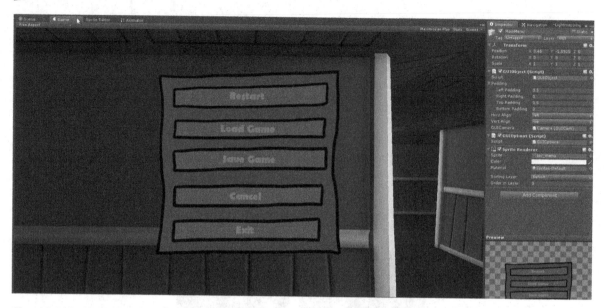

Figure 8-7. Previewing the GUI menu in the Game tab

Go ahead and tweak any GUI values in the Object Inspector, if required, and see the changes update in real time in the Game tab. Further, change the game resolution, too, and see the menu adjust its position to reflect the change, centering itself in the view regardless of the resolution. See Figure 8-8.

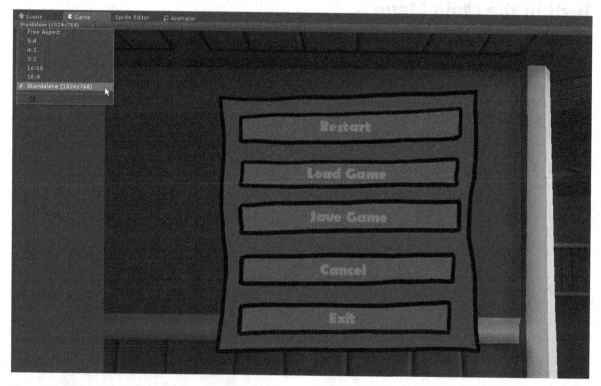

Figure 8-8. Testing real-time changes to the GUI

Adding Buttons to the Main Menu

The main menu graphic in Figure 8-4 already features the button graphics "built-in"—that is, the image already features the button objects. In most games, this will not be the case. Typically, GUI button graphics are isolated as separate sprites and are overlaid atop the menu background to support additional functionality, such as animations and hover states when the cursor moves over the buttons. But here, the buttons are built into the menu, and this will still serve our needs. Now, there are many ways the button functionality could be handled in CMOD; for example, each button could detect presses as they happen, and then internally handle the responses, performing appropriate on-click functionality. But for CMOD, our buttons will be "hollow" in the sense that they'll exist only to *detect button presses*, and then they'll trigger a system-wide event using the NotificationsManager, allowing any other listening processes to respond as needed when clicks happen. Other processes, if any, will essentially handle button presses. To get started on creating clickable buttons, create five new game objects, one for each button, as children of the menu, resetting their transforms to (0, 0, 0). The buttons are named *button_Cancel*, *button_Exit*, *button_Load*, *button_Restart*, and *button_Save* (see Figure 8-9).

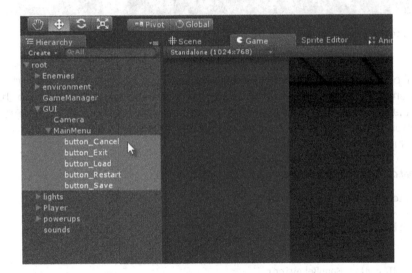

Figure 8-9. Adding button objects to the scene as children of the menu object

Next, add a *Box Collider* component to each button object (**Component ➤ Physics ➤ Box Collider**) to approximate the button volume on-screen to allow click detection. Use the Game tab to align the colliders with the button graphics on the menu in the viewport. Remember, if you don't see the collider gizmo outline in the Game view, then click the Gizmos drop-down box to enable the Colliders option (see Figure 8-10).

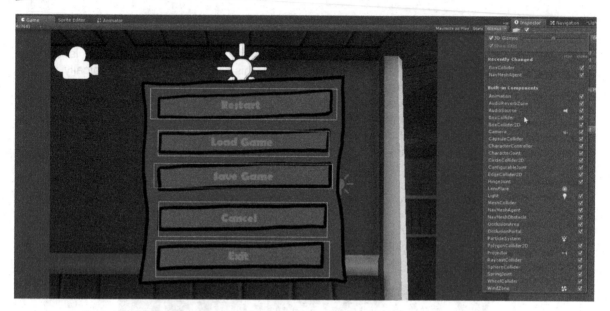

Figure 8-10. Adding colliders for button objects on the menu

Each button will post a unique notification to the NotificationsManager when clicked, invoking the kind of response required for the button, if any valid listeners are registered with the NotificationsManager. To achieve this behavior, a new script should be created and added to each button as a component—specifically a new class, called GUIEvent. Let's create this script file now, as shown in Listing 8-4.

Listing 8-4. GUIEvent.cs: Click Detection Functionality for the Button Objects

```
01 //Posts notification when gui element is clicked
02 //------------------------------------------------
03 using UnityEngine;
04 using System.Collections;
05 //------------------------------------------------
06 public class GUIEvent : MonoBehaviour
07 {
08        //Notification to send when activated
09        public string Notification = null;
10
11        //Check for input
12        void OnMouseDown()
13        {
14                GameManager.Notifications.PostNotification(this, Notification);
15        }
16 }
17 //------------------------------------------------
```

Listing 8-4 and its general mechanics should look familiar now. If not, then jump back to Chapter 3 to consider the NotificationsManager, as a refresher. Add an instance of this class to each button object, assigning the Notification member to a unique string describing the event to be generated for that button instance. I've used the strings: HideOptions, ExitGame, LoadGame, RestartGame, and SaveGame. You don't need to use these names exactly for your own functions; but remember, these names (whatever they are) should match the names of functions elsewhere that are intended to handle the events when they happen through the NotificationsManager (see Figure 8-11 where the GUIEvent component is assigned to button objects).

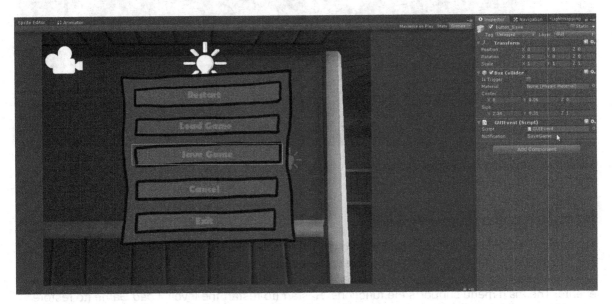

Figure 8-11. GUIEvent components are added to button objects in preparation for click detection and response

Before proceeding further to handle button clicks, I recommend testing the click-detection code for your buttons to make sure they do actually detect clicks when they happen, as they should do. You can achieve this easily by inserting a Debug.Log statement inside the OnMouseDown function of GUIEvent, for example. If you've added a GUIEvent component but find that no button press is detected, make sure your button has a collider component with depth in all three axes (not just two), and also that your buttons and colliders are completely *in front* of the GUI camera. That is, no part of the colliders should appear behind the camera. Otherwise, the click will probably not be detected (see Figure 8-12).

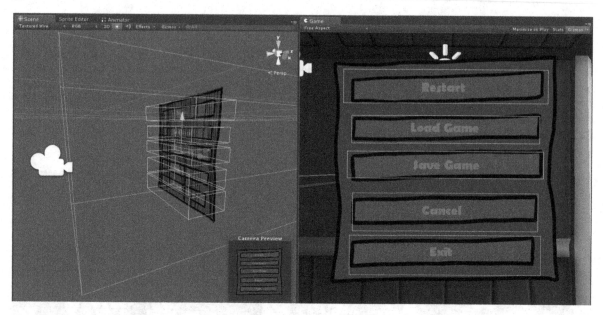

Figure 8-12. Configuring colliders to detect mouse down events

Handling Button Presses

The buttons for the main menu GUI are almost empty shells. Their task is simply to post notifications into the event system when clicks are made and the menu is visible. The real "core" functionality to be invoked from button presses will actually occur in other classes listening for the button-press events. The main menu supports the functions: *Restart* (to restart the level), *Load Game* (to restore a previously saved game), *Save Game* (to save the current game state to persistent storage), *Cancel* (to close the menu and resume the game), and *Exit* (to terminate the game). The next chapter will consider the implementation of loading and saving games. In this section, we'll perform the Restart, Cancel, and Exit feature set. Actually, considering Listing 8-3, the GUIOptions class already features the code we need to respond to menu cancelling. At line 26, the menu registers for the HideOptions event, which is invoked when the Cancel button is pressed. The remaining two features, Restart and Exit can be added into the GameManager (see Listing 8-5 for a revised Start function for GameManager class, as well as the relevant methods; this class is also included in the book companion files for /Chapter08/).

Listing 8-5. Revised GameManager class to respond to menu button presses

```
01 //GameManager
02 //For high level control over game
03 //----------------------------------------------------------------
04 using UnityEngine;
05 using System.Collections;
06 //Game Manager requires other manager components
07 [RequireComponent (typeof (NotificationsManager))] //Component for sending and receiving notifications
08 //----------------------------------------------------------------
09 public class GameManager : MonoBehaviour
10 {
11         //----------------------------------------------------------
12         //[Other GameManager code here...]
13         //----------------------------------------------------------
14         // Use this for initialization
15         void Start ()
16         {
17                 //Add cash collected listener to listen for win condition
18                 Notifications.AddListener(this, "CashCollected");
19
20                 //Add listeners for main menu
21                 Notifications.AddListener(this, "RestartGame");
22                 Notifications.AddListener(this, "ExitGame");
23         }
24         //----------------------------------------------------------
25         //[Other GameManager code here...]
26         //----------------------------------------------------------
27         //Restart Game
28         public void RestartGame()
29         {
30                 //Load first level
31                 Application.LoadLevel(0);
32         }
33         //----------------------------------------------------------
34         //Exit Game
35         public void ExitGame()
36         {
37                 Application.Quit();
38         }
39         //----------------------------------------------------------
40 }
```

- **Line 31.** The Application.LoadLevel method is used to reload the active level, effectively restarting the game.

- **Line 37.** Application.Quit is called to terminate the game. The code, as given in line 37, only works when the game is running as a stand-alone application, and not in the editor. For more information, see the following note.

> **Note**   Line 37 of Listing 8-5 will terminate game execution using the `Application.Quit` function. You could adapt this code as follows to support application quitting from the editor, too:
>
> ```
> #if UNITY_EDITOR
>         UnityEditor.EditorApplication.isPlaying = false;
> #else
>         Application.Quit();
> #endif
> ```
>
> More information on the high-level `Application` class can be found in the Unity documentation at `https://docs.unity3d.com/Documentation/ScriptReference/Application.html`.

HUD: Ammo and Health Statuses

CMOD now has a complete and working main menu for the GUI, except for load and save game functionality, which are covered in the next chapter. Here, we'll focus our attention on some basic text displays for a head-up display using the font rendering features provided by the `GUI` class and its associated structures. The text created will display the Player health and any remaining ammo for the active weapon. To achieve this, two C# classes will be coded, namely a label class (`GUILabel`) for displaying text, and a `GUIUpdate` class, which relies on the label classes to display text on the screen, describing health and ammo. Let's start with the label class, as shown in Listing 8-6.

> **Note**   A head-up display (or HUD) refers to all on-screen graphical displays that appear while the game is being played (such as health bar and score).
>
> Often, game developers avoid dynamic font rendering, as used here, for performance reasons. Instead, they typically use a *font atlas texture*—that is, a texture file containing each alphanumeric character in a font set. Text is then shown on-screen in-game like a regular sprite or texture, with various letters in the text combined like sprites to form complete text statements and sentences. There are many programs available to produce font atlas textures. One includes BMFont (`www.angelcode.com/products/bmfont/`). Dynamic fonts are used here, however, to demonstrate basic GUI functionality and how to quickly render text on-screen. One exceptional case to using atlas font textures might be rendering text from Asian-based languages, in which the full character set is often too large to store inside a texture that performs well across multiple platforms.

Listing 8-6. GUILabel.cs: Class for Rendering Text on Screen Using the GUI Framework

```
01 using UnityEngine;
02 using System.Collections;
03 [ExecuteInEditMode]
04 public class GUILabel : MonoBehaviour
05 {
06        //Content for label
07        public GUIContent LabelData;
08
09        //Style for label
10        public GUIStyle LabelStyle;
11
12        //Rect for label
13        public Rect LabelRegion;
14
15        //Draw label
16        void OnGUI()
17        {
18            Rect FinalRect = new Rect(LabelRegion.x * Screen.width, LabelRegion.y *
                  Screen.height, LabelRegion.width * Screen.width, LabelRegion.height * Screen.height);
19
20            GUI.Label(FinalRect, LabelData, LabelStyle);
21        }
22 }
```

- **Lines 07, 10, and 13.** The public members LabelData, LabelStyle, and LabelRegion have been added to define the contents of a label (what it will say), its style (how it will look), and its positional data (where it will appear on the screen). These properties will all be accessible and customizable through the Object Inspector when a Label component is added to an object.

- **Line 20.** The GUI.Label function is called on the OnGUI event to render the label text to the screen with specified content, style, and size.

> **Note**   More information on the GUI classes can be found in the online Unity documentation at http://docs.unity3d.com/Documentation/Components/gui-Basics.html.

We'll need the label class to display the ammo count and Player health status. For this reason, let's add two label components to the root GUI object in the scene, by dragging and dropping the GUILabel class onto the GUI object. Once added, configure each label through its *Label Data*, *Label Style* and *Label Region* values in the Object Inspector (see Figure 8-13). For Label Data, the text should be set to *Health* for the health label and to *Ammo* for the ammo label. For both labels, the text color should be *White*. For the Label Style object, the Font Size should be *20*. And for the Label Region, the position of the health label is rendered at *(0.01, 0.01)*, and the ammo label at *(0.9, 0.01)*. Notice the positions for each label are specified in *screen relative coordinates*.

Figure 8-13. Configuring GUI labels for Player health and ammo

Further, as you configure each label's content, style, and position data from the Object Inspector, you'll also see a real-time preview in the Game tab. This will appear after setting the font color, size, text, and position (see Figure 8-14).

Figure 8-14. Previewing a GUI label in real time

Right now, the root GUI object features two label components that each display default static text for both the ammo status and health status. This text currently never changes throughout gameplay, as it is. So we'll need to code extra functionality in the GUIUpdateStats class to update the label text on each frame, displaying the latest Player health and ammo status as the game unfolds. The C# code for this class is given in Listing 8-7. This class should also be added as a component to the root GUI object, alongside the labels.

Listing 8-7. GUIUpdateStats.cs: Class for Updating GUI Text with Health and Ammo Status

```
01 //-----------------------------------------------------------------
02 using UnityEngine;
03 using System.Collections;
04 //-----------------------------------------------------------------
05 public class GUIUpdateStats : MonoBehaviour
06 {
07        //Player reference
08        private PlayerController PC = null;
09
10        //Health Label Component
11        public GUILabel HealthLabel = null;
12
13        //Ammo Label Component
14        public GUILabel AmmoLabel = null;
15
```

```
16          //------------------------------------------------------------------
17          void Start()
18          {
19                  //Get Player Controller Component
20                  GameObject PlayerObject = GameObject.Find("Player");
21                  PC = PlayerObject.GetComponentInChildren<PlayerController>();
22          }
23          //------------------------------------------------------------------
24          // Update is called once per frame
25          void Update ()
26          {
27                  //Update health and ammo strings
28                  AmmoLabel.LabelData.text = "Ammo: " + ((PC.ActiveWeapon.Ammo < 0) ? "None" :
                    PC.ActiveWeapon.Ammo.ToString());
29                  HealthLabel.LabelData.text = "Health: " + Mathf.Clamp(PC.Health,0,100).ToString();
30          }
31          //------------------------------------------------------------------
32 }
```

- **Line 29.** The `Mathf.Clamp` utility function is used while constructing an ammo string for the active weapon. `Clamp` ensures a numerical argument is always within a specified minimum and maximum range, rounding the value to the nearest number at the minimum or maximum extreme, if required.

Add the `GUIUpdateStats` class to the root GUI object in the scene, and then use the Object Inspector to specify the two label controls for the text data. To do this, simply drag and drop the existing GUILabel components in the Objector Inspector into the GUILabel fields of the GUIUpdateStats component (see Figure 8-15).

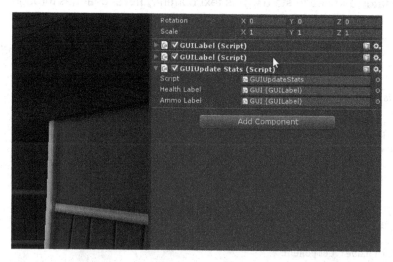

Figure 8-15. Referencing label widgets in the GUIUpdateStats class, for rendering status text on the screen

Finally, give the game a test run to see the labels and status fields in action! Good work! You've got a game up and running with live status indicators. If you take damage, your health indicator will be reduced to reflect your current health. And your ammo indicator will also reflect the current ammo status for your weapon. If your weapon is fists/punch (having no ammo), then the ammo indicator will simply say "None" (see Figure 8-16).

Health: 90

Ammo: 9

Figure 8-16. Test-run the game with HUD health and ammo indicators

Summary

Splendid. CMOD is now looking really great. We have almost everything we need to complete the game, and to think about taking it further by adding extra levels, characters, weapons, power-ups, and more. In this chapter, we added further polish by creating a basic but functional GUI interface, relying partially on the older GUI class, but also taking into consideration some of Unity's newer features, such as 2D sprites, seeing how they can be creatively applied to create GUI graphics that will perform better overall than the standard GUI functionality. At this point, you should be able to do the following:

- ▪ Understand what a GUI is
- ▪ Understand what a HUD is
- ▪ Render text on-screen using labels and the GUI class
- ▪ Understand concepts such as resolution and aspect ratio
- ▪ Appreciate the benefits of relative positioning through anchoring

- Create a relative position framework for your own GUIs
- Understand the size and scale issues involved with aspect ratio
- Use 2D sprites and orthographic cameras to create a main menu
- Use colliders to create hollow button objects
- Integrate your GUI system with the NotificationsManager
- Understand the GUIStyle and GUIContent class related to the GUI class

Chapter 9

Handling Persistent Data

CMOD is looking good now, and we could improve it even further by adding more levels and environments, such as rooftop levels, basements levels, and even exterior levels. If we did that, however, it'd be useful for gamers to be able to save their games so that the next time they played, they could resume from where they left off, preventing them from repeating their actions every time. In other words, if we're to expand the game, it'd be helpful for the gamer to have save-game functionality. Achieving this effectively means we'll need to store game data *persistently* on the local computer, between playing sessions, so that even between powering the computer off and on, the save-game data persists to be restored. Thankfully, Unity and Mono offer a range of handy features and classes for handling persistent data, and these will constitute the focus of this chapter as we implement load-and-save game functionality for CMOD. So let's go!

Persistent Data: PlayerPrefs, Binary Data, and More

Persistent data is a catch-all term for any game data that should remain across playing sessions. Unlike most game data, which is volatile and terminates when the game ends, persistent data is stored locally on the hard drive or other storage, and can be retrieved again for later playing sessions, even if the computer has been turned off or restarted in the interim. Hence, such data is said to *persist*. The most common use of persistent data is for storing game states, allowing gamers to resume from where they left off. Other uses include storing character profiles, screenshots, voice recordings, preferences and settings, network information, and also game licensing data. For CMOD, we'll be creating save-game functionality only.

Unity offers two main ways to create persistent data: one is to use the Player Preferences class, which acts like a cross-platform database with key values, and the other is to use system files (such as binary files and XML files). Before proceeding with our work on CMOD, I want to briefly consider the options that we *won't* be using throughout the rest of this chapter to give you an overview and appraisal of those features, and to explain why we won't be using them here.

Player Preferences Class

Perhaps the easiest and quickest way to save persistent data with Unity on all platforms is to use the PlayerPrefs class. This class abstracts itself from the local file system so that we don't have to worry about file names or specific file system paths. Instead, we can treat it like a key-value database. We write values to the database using integer, float, and string values, and data such as the game's brightness, whether the game should run in full-screen mode, the name of the gamer, and more. And we then read back those values, across playing sessions, by simply querying the appropriately named keys. As we do this, Unity internally handles all specifics about how data is written to and read from persistent storage. More information on PlayerPrefs can be found in the online Unity documentation at https://docs.unity3d.com/Documentation/ScriptReference/PlayerPrefs.html. Consider Listing 9-1, where some sample data is written to persistent storage with the PlayerPrefs class.

Listing 9-1. Saving Data with the PlayerPrefs Class

```
PlayerPrefs.SetString("PlayerName", "John Smith");
PlayerPrefs.SetInt("LastLevel", 10);
PlayerPrefs.SetFloat("Brightness", 0.7f);
PlayerPrefs.Save();
```

- The PlayerPrefs is a static class, meaning it can be accessed anywhere in a C# script file; its scope is global.

- The PlayerPrefs class automatically saves and commits all changes on a clean application exit, and so in theory, the final call to the Save method is optional. However, the Save function will not be called automatically if the application terminates prematurely, such as an unexpected crash. So it's often good practice to call the Save method after making PlayerPrefs changes.

Saved data can also be retrieved through the PlayerPrefs class at any time across all playing sessions using the GetString, GetInt, and GetFloat methods (see Listing 9-2).

Listing 9-2. Loading Data with the PlayerPrefs Class

```
string Name = PlayerPrefs.GetString("PlayerName");
int LastLevel = PlayerPrefs.SetInt("LastLevel");
float Brightness = PlayerPrefs.SetFloat("Brightness");
```

Saving and loading data with PlayerPrefs really is as simple as Listings 9-1 and 9-2 show. From this, the question may arise as to exactly where on the local file system the data is stored. The answer is: it depends on the user operating system. For Windows users, PlayerPrefs data is stored in the system registry, and for other systems, it's stored in local files in different locations. The Unity online documentation features more information on this. However, the PlayerPrefs class will not be used further in this chapter for storing CMOD data. This is because PlayerPrefs is intended for storing only user preferences data—that is, smaller, bite-sized pieces of data for holding brightness settings, as well as the gamer's name, game difficulty, full-screen vs. windowed mode, and more. For CMOD, we'll need to store a lot more data than this: specifically, the transform data for nearly every moveable object, including the Player and the Enemies. To achieve this, we must move away from PlayerPrefs and adopt a custom file-based solution.

> **Note**   When saving data to persistent storage, Unity often uses the *Company Name* and *Product Name* values in the Project Settings to produce a unique storage location for your data. Before saving game states, therefore, be sure to set the Company Name and Product Name to meaningful values from the Player Settings dialog, which is accessible by choosing **Edit ➤ Project Settings ➤ Player** from the application menu (see Figure 9-1).

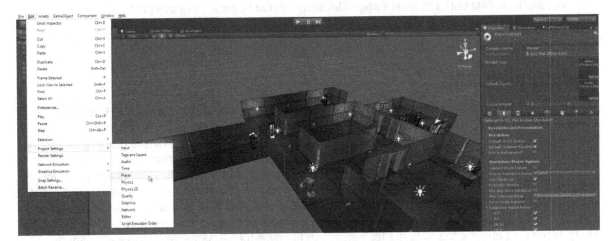

Figure 9-1.   Configuring Company Name and Product Name from the Player Settings dialog

File-Based Persistence

The second and most flexible method for storing persistent data in Unity is to resort to the Mono Framework for saving data to a file on local storage. Using this method, two main approaches are available: data can be saved to a *binary proprietary file* or to a *human-readable text-based file* like XML. Both represent file-based forms of persistent storage. The difference rests in whether the gamer can open the saved file and see and edit the contents. The traditional approach in game development is to use a proprietary file, primarily to prevent the user from breaking the game by changing the data—intentionally or accidentally—to invalid values. But it's also to prevent cheating, too, which can happen when gamers tweak the data (intentionally giving themselves extra lives, or more health, or more items).

Unity allows saving to this kind of format by using the `BinaryFormatter` class. But in this book, we'll actually choose the more open and human-readable XML route for creating saved games. There are two main reasons for this: first, a human-readable XML file allows us to easily debug not only save-game functionality, but the game in general. It lets us see the value of objects, consolidated into a single XML file; and we can also change the values and see the changes reflected in-game. And second, an open save-game file also permits other developers and third parties to easily write extensions or plug-ins for the game, adding their own data without breaking the XML scheme already in place. This means we can quickly establish a potential community of "modders" or "modifiers." So, for this chapter, we'll avoid the binary format route, and choose the XML-based saved-game file. When creating your own games, you'll need to make judgments about which method is right for you. If you're interested in saving games with the `BinaryFormatter`, a Unity video tutorial is available at `https://unity3d.com/learn/tutorials/modules/beginner/live-training-archive/persistence-data-saving-loading`.

> **Note**   File-based saving works well for many deployment types, but for web-player games and web-hosted games, persistent data becomes more troublesome due to security restrictions. There are several main options available: 1) Game data can be saved in a server-side database. 2) Game data can be stored inside a cookie file. 3) Data can be stored in a single XML string that can be passed as a query to the web player. Further details for saving data with web-based deployments are beyond the scope of this book.

Saving with XML

Saved games for CMOD will be saved in the XML format. XML stands for **EX**tensible **M**arkup **L**anguage, and it uses a hierarchical text-based structure for saving data. There are alternative text-based formats available, which are gaining popularity in games today. One is JSON (JavaScript Object Notation), which features a more abbreviated and slim-line syntax than XML, making it a particularly attractive option for streaming text-based data across networks. But currently, JSON is not supported natively by Unity or the Mono Framework (as of version 4.3). This means that you must rely on custom-made parsers or third-party parsers to read from and write to JSON files. For CMOD and this book in general, I stick to the native tools and classes that work out-of-the-box with Unity. Hence, I'll choose the XML file format, which is powerful, versatile, and long established.

> **Note**   A freely available third-party class for parsing JSON data can be found at `http://wiki.unity3d.com/index.php/SimpleJSON`. When using third-party code, be sure to read the source file comments and summary thoroughly.

Let's now take a look at the saved-game XML file structure to be used for CMOD. In sum, there are several data items we'll need to save to offer complete load-and-save functionality. Specifically, for the Player, we'll need to save *transformation* (position, rotation, and scale data), *collected cash*, *collected weapon* (if any), and *health*. For the Enemy, we'll store *transformation*, *unique ID* (to identify the Enemy type), and *health*. This data can be consolidated into a single XML file, as shown in Listing 9-3 (this sample features only one Enemy alongside Player data for the sake of brevity—though the "real" file will feature more Enemies).

Listing 9-3. Sample XML Data for a CMOD Saved Game

```
<?xml version="1.0" encoding="Windows-1252"?>
<GameData xmlns:xsi="http://www.w3.org/2001/XMLSchema-instance" xmlns:xsd="http://www.w3.org/2001/
XMLSchema">
  <Enemies>
    <DataEnemy>
      <PosRotScale>
        <X>1.94054472</X>
```

```xml
          <Y>0.019997187</Y>
          <Z>-8.58917</Z>
          <RotX>0</RotX>
          <RotY>129.9697</RotY>
          <RotZ>0</RotZ>
          <ScaleX>1</ScaleX>
          <ScaleY>1</ScaleY>
          <ScaleZ>1</ScaleZ>
        </PosRotScale>
        <EnemyID>3</EnemyID>
        <Health>100</Health>
      </DataEnemy>
    <DataEnemy>
        <PosRotScale>
          <X>8.632575</X>
          <Y>0.019997187</Y>
          <Z>-13.2708778</Z>
          <RotX>0</RotX>
          <RotY>137.86232</RotY>
          <RotZ>0</RotZ>
          <ScaleX>1</ScaleX>
          <ScaleY>1</ScaleY>
          <ScaleZ>1</ScaleZ>
        </PosRotScale>
        <EnemyID>0</EnemyID>
        <Health>200</Health>
      </DataEnemy>
    </Enemies>
    <Player>
      <PosRotScale>
        <X>12.1057281</X>
        <Y>1.05</Y>
        <Z>-17.1096153</Z>
        <RotX>0</RotX>
        <RotY>39.75003</RotY>
        <RotZ>0</RotZ>
        <ScaleX>1</ScaleX>
        <ScaleY>1</ScaleY>
        <ScaleZ>1</ScaleZ>
      </PosRotScale>
      <CollectedCash>200</CollectedCash>
      <CollectedGun>true</CollectedGun>
      <Health>50</Health>
    </Player>
</GameData>
```

You can view XML files in any text editor, including MonoDevelop. In addition, to improve readability, MonoDevelop supports syntax highlighting and code folding for XML. To make sure these features are enabled for XML files in MonoDevelop, select **Tools ➤ Options** from the MonoDevelop application menu, and then select the General tab from the Options dialog. Next, enable the Code Folding option (see Figure 9-2). Figure 9-3 shows an XML file loaded in MonoDevelop, complete with code folding and syntax highlighting.

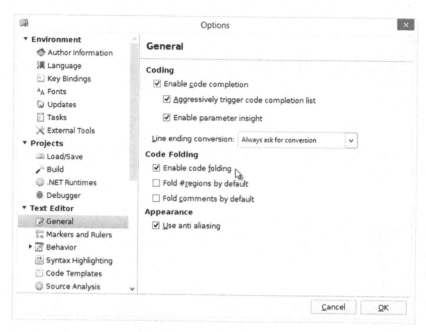

Figure 9-2. *Enabling Code Folding in MonoDevelop to view XML files*

Figure 9-3. *Editing XML files in MonoDevelop*

Getting Started with XML: Serialization

There are two main methods for saving data to XML in Unity using the Mono Framework classes. One method (the manual method) is to create an XML file in code, node by node, through looping and iteration, saving each element of data as nodes are created, using a class such as XmlDocument. The other method (used here) is to use *serialization* through the XMLSerializer class. By using serialization, you may effectively stream or snapshot a class in memory, translate it to a text-based XML version, and then write it to a persistent file—one that can be accessed later in other gaming sessions to automatically rebuild the class that was saved. Thus, by consolidating all save-game data into a single class, we can create a save-game state quickly and effectively. This method can spare us a lot of coding and extra work, *but* it only works with *specific* data types (and not all data types). This means that, before we can work with serialization itself, we'll need to code some new custom classes and structures to hold all game data, but using only data types supported by serialization. We'll then need to populate this class with valid game data prior to saving to ensure that all appropriate data is saved. Listing 9-4 lists a new LoadSaveManager class created in the file LoadSaveManager.cs. This file includes new serializable classes and structures that can be saved to an XML file.

Listing 9-4. Starting a LoadSaveManager Class

```
01 //Loads and Saves game state data to and from xml file
02 //-------------------------------------------
03 using UnityEngine;
04 using System.Collections;
05 using System.Collections.Generic;
06 using System.Xml;
07 using System.Xml.Serialization;
08 using System.IO;
09 //-------------------------------------------
10 public class LoadSaveManager : MonoBehaviour
11 {
12      //Save game data
13      [XmlRoot("GameData")]
14      public class GameStateData
15      {
16              //-------------------------------------------
17              public struct DataTransform
18              {
19                      public float X;
20                      public float Y;
21                      public float Z;
22                      public float RotX;
23                      public float RotY;
24                      public float RotZ;
25                      public float ScaleX;
26                      public float ScaleY;
27                      public float ScaleZ;
28              }
29              //-------------------------------------------
30              //Data for enemy
```

```
31              public class DataEnemy
32              {
33                      //Enemy Transform Data
34                      public DataTransform PosRotScale;
35                      //Enemy ID
36                      public int EnemyID;
37                      //Health
38                      public int Health;
39              }
40              //-------------------------------------------------
41              //Data for player
42              public class DataPlayer
43              {
44                      //Transform Data
45                      public DataTransform PosRotScale;
46
47                      //Collected cash
48                      public float CollectedCash;
49
50                      //Has Collected Gun 01?
51                      public bool CollectedGun;
52
53                      //Health
54                      public int Health;
55              }
56              //-------------------------------------------------
57
58              //Instance variables
59              public List<DataEnemy> Enemies = new List<DataEnemy>();
60
61              public DataPlayer Player = new DataPlayer();
62      }
63
64      //Game data to save/load
65      public GameStateData GameState = new GameStateData();
66
67      //-------------------------------------------------
68 }
69 //-------------------------------------------------
```

- ▪ **Lines 01–69.** Here, in total, a range of classes are defined for holding save-game data. This includes classes DataTransform, DataEnemy, and DataPlayer.

- ▪ **Lines 17–27.** The DataTransform class defines a complete transform for a game object using serializable data types, such as float, to hold data that would normally feature only in a game object's transform component, which is not serializable.

- **Lines 31–55.** Both the Player and Enemy classes use DataTransform to store their transformation data.

- **Line 65.** The GameStateData class consolidates all Player and Enemy data in the scene using serializable types. An instance of this class (GameState) is declared as a public member of the LoadSaveManager class and will be later serialized to an XML file.

Loading from and Saving to an XML File

The LoadSaveManager class is managerial, insofar as it oversees the general loading and saving process from and to an XML file. This class features a critical member, namely GameState, which consolidates all the serializable game data to be saved to a file and loaded from a file. Effectively, the GameState member will represent a game state in memory, as we'll see later. The question then arises as to how this class can be saved to XML and loaded from XML. To achieve this, the LoadSaveManager class be amended with two new functions. These are listed in Listing 9-5. Comments follow.

Listing 9-5. Adding Load and Save Functionality into the LoadSaveManager Class

```
01 //-----------------------------------------------
02 //Saves game data to XML file
03 public void Save(string FileName = "GameData.xml")
04 {
05      //Clear existing enemy data
06      GameState.Enemies.Clear();
07
08      //Call save start notification
09      GameManager.Notifications.PostNotification(this, "SaveGamePrepare");
10
11      //Now save game data
12      XmlSerializer Serializer = new XmlSerializer(typeof(GameStateData));
13      FileStream Stream = new FileStream(FileName, FileMode.Create);
14      Serializer.Serialize(Stream, GameState);
15      Stream.Close();
16
17      //Call save end notification
18      GameManager.Notifications.PostNotification(this, "SaveGameComplete");
19 }
20 //-----------------------------------------------
21 //Load game data from XML file
22 public void Load(string FileName = "GameData.xml")
23 {
24      //Call load start notification
25      GameManager.Notifications.PostNotification(this, "LoadGamePrepare");
26
27      XmlSerializer Serializer = new XmlSerializer(typeof(GameStateData));
28      FileStream Stream = new FileStream(FileName, FileMode.Open);
29      GameState = Serializer.Deserialize(Stream) as GameStateData;
30      Stream.Close();
31
```

```
32      //Call load end notification
33      GameManager.Notifications.PostNotification(this, "LoadGameComplete");
34 }
35 //------------------------------------------------
```

- ■ **Line 03.** The Save function provides a default function argument, which makes it optional. This means two call types are valid here, namely Save() and Save("*MyFileName*"). The former call will resort to the default string of "GameData.xml" as the argument.

- ■ **Lines 5–15.** The Save function begins by clearing out any Enemy data from the internal arrays, in case a previous game was saved. Then, the class XMLSerializer is instantiated, passing a valid instance to GameStateData in the constructor, indicating the class to serialize. The call on line 14 actually serializes the data in the class to a file stream. And then, finally, the data is committed to the file and the file is closed using a Stream.Close call at line 15.

- ■ **Lines 22–34.** The Load function is essentially the inverse of the Save function. This time an XMLSerializer is instantiated to Deserialize an XML file stream back to the GameStateData class, allowing the game state data to be reconstructed from a file.

- ■ **Lines 01–35.** Notice that throughout the load and save process, the NotificationsManager is updated by event calls. This will be important later, as other classes (such as the Player and Enemies) will respond to these invents to load back their data from the GameStateData object.

Completing the GameManager Class

The LoadSaveManager class is now completed. But on its own it can achieve nothing; since none of its functionality is integrated into the main game logic or mechanics. Now it's time to connect the LoadSaveManager into the GameManager to start making things work together. To start, drag and drop the LoadSaveManager script from the Project panel onto the GameManager object in the scene to add a LoadSaveManager component to the object (see Figure 9-4).

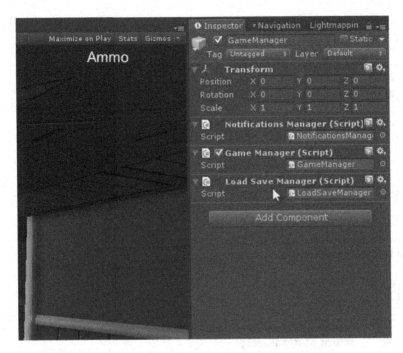

Figure 9-4. Adding a LoadSaveManager component to the GameManager object in the scene

Next, we'll amend the GameManager class first coded in Chapter 4 of this book. Consider Listing 9-6, which lists the complete and final implementation of the GameManager class, integrating with load-and-save game functionality. Comments follow.

Listing 9-6. Completing the GameManager Class

```
001 //GameManager
002 //Singleton and persistent object to manage game state
003 //For high level control over game
004 //-----------------------------------------------------------------
005 using UnityEngine;
006 using System.Collections;
007 //Game Manager requires other manager components
008 [RequireComponent (typeof (NotificationsManager))] //Component for sending and receiving notifications
009 //-----------------------------------------------------------------
010 public class GameManager : MonoBehaviour
011 {
012     //-----------------------------------------------------------
013     //public properties
014     //C# property to retrieve currently active instance of object, if any
015     public static GameManager Instance
016     {
017         get
018         {
019             if (instance == null) instance = new GameObject ("GameManager").
                AddComponent<GameManager>(); //create game manager object if required
```

```
020                      return instance;
021             }
022      }
023      //------------------------------------------------------------
024      //C# property to retrieve notifications manager
025      public static NotificationsManager Notifications
026      {
027             get
028             {
029                      if(notifications == null) notifications =
                         instance.GetComponent<NotificationsManager>();
030                      return notifications;
031             }
032      }
033      //------------------------------------------------------------
034      //C# property to retrieve save/load manager
035      public static LoadSaveManager StateManager
036      {
037             get
038             {
039                      if(statemanager == null) statemanager =
                         instance.GetComponent<LoadSaveManager>();
040                      return statemanager;
041             }
042      }
043      //------------------------------------------------------------
044      //C# property to retrieve and set input allowed status
045      public bool InputAllowed
046      {
047             get{return bInputAllowed;}
048
049             set
050             {
051                      //Set Input
052                      bInputAllowed = value;
053
054                      //Post notification about input status changed
055                      Notifications.PostNotification(this, "InputChanged");
056             }
057      }
058      //------------------------------------------------------------
059      //Private variables
060      //------------------------------------------------------------
061      //Internal reference to single active instance of object - for singleton behaviour
062      private static GameManager instance = null;
063
064      //Internal reference to notifications object
065      private static NotificationsManager notifications = null;
066
067      //Internal reference to Saveload Game Manager
```

```
068    private static LoadSaveManager statemanager = null;
069
070    //Should load from save game state on level load, or just restart level from defaults
071    private static bool bShouldLoad = false;
072
073    //public variables
074    //----------------------------------------------------------------
075    //Can game accept user input?
076    private bool bInputAllowed = true;
077    //----------------------------------------------------------------
078    // Called before Start on object creation
079    void Awake ()
080    {
081            //Check if there is an existing instance of this object
082            if((instance) && (instance.GetInstanceID() != GetInstanceID()))
083                    DestroyImmediate(gameObject); //Delete duplicate
084            else
085            {
086                    instance = this; //Make this object the only instance
087                    DontDestroyOnLoad (gameObject); //Set as do not destroy
088            }
089    }
090    //----------------------------------------------------------------
091    // Use this for initialization
092    void Start ()
093    {
094            //Add cash collected listener to listen for win condition
095            Notifications.AddListener(this, "CashCollected");
096
097            //Add game menu listeners
098            Notifications.AddListener(this, "RestartGame");
099            Notifications.AddListener(this, "ExitGame");
100            Notifications.AddListener(this, "SaveGame");
101            Notifications.AddListener(this, "LoadGame");
102
103            //If we need to load level
104            if(bShouldLoad)
105            {
106                    StateManager.Load(Application.persistentDataPath + "/SaveGame.xml");
107                    bShouldLoad=false; //Reset load flag
108            }
109    }
110    //----------------------------------------------------------------
111    //Function called when all cash is collected in level
112    public void CashCollected(Component Sender)
113    {
114            //Disable input
115            InputAllowed = false;
116
117            //Pause game
118            Time.timeScale = 0;
119
```

```
120                  //Show level complete sign
121                  GameObject MissionCompleteObject = GameObject.Find ("spr_mission_complete");
122                  MissionCompleteObject.GetComponent<SpriteRenderer>().enabled=true;
123          }
124     //-----------------------------------------------------------------
125     //Restart Game
126     public void RestartGame()
127     {
128                  //Load first level
129                  Application.LoadLevel(0);
130     }
131     //-----------------------------------------------------------------
132     //Exit Game
133     public void ExitGame()
134     {
135                  Application.Quit();
136     }
137     //-----------------------------------------------------------------
138     //Save Game
139     public void SaveGame()
140     {
141                  //Call save game functionality
142                  StateManager.Save(Application.persistentDataPath + "/SaveGame.xml");
143     }
144     //-----------------------------------------------------------------
145     //Load Game
146     public void LoadGame()
147     {
148                  //Set load on restart
149                  bShouldLoad=true;
150
151                  //Restart Level
152                  RestartGame();
153     }
154     //-----------------------------------------------------------------
155 }
```

- **Lines 39 and 68.** The LoadSaveManager is added as a private member and public property of the GameManager class. Therefore, through the GameManager, each and every other class has access to the current game state, as well as access to loading and saving games directly, through the SaveGame and LoadGame functions implemented further down in the GameManager.

- **Line 87.** The GameManager is created with the DontDestroyOnLoad property set to true, meaning the object will persist across scenes and when the current scene is reloaded. This integrates with the LoadGame function at line 146, in which the level is first *reset* to its default, and then loaded from an XML file.

■ **Lines 106 and 142.** Here, both the `LoadGame` and `SaveGame` functions are called directly for the LoadSaveManager. Notice that both calls construct a valid path on the system, using the `Application.persistentDataPath` member. The location of this folder varies from computer to computer, and from operating system to operating system. But it always points to a valid location on the file system where data may be stored persistently. It's a good idea, then, to make use of this system variable whenever saving persistent data to ensure that data is saved correctly and that your code works across multiple platforms.

Note   More information on `Application.persistentDataPath` can be found in the online Unity documentation at https://docs.unity3d.com/Documentation/ScriptReference/Application-persistentDataPath.html.

Completing the PlayerController Class

The GameManager now supports the `LoadGame` and `SaveGame` functions. Whenever an object, such as the main menu, calls these functions via the NotificationsManager, the GameManager will invoke the appropriate loading and saving behavior implicitly. In fact, if you run CMOD now and test this code, clicking the save-game button on the main menu should immediately generate a save-game XML file—a file populated with XML data. This file will be saved in the `persistentDataPath`, which could be one among a variety of folders on your system, depending on your system configuration. You can easily find where the folder is located on your computer by using the `Debug.Log` function to print the `persistentDataPath` variable to the console during Play mode. If you examine the generated XML file, however, you'll see it's just populated with *default* XML data and not any data related to the game state specifically. This is because neither the Enemies object nor the Player object ever populates the `LoadSaveManager.GameStateData` variable. These classes should effectively take action when receiving a `SaveGamePrepare` event call (to save game data), and a `LoadGameComplete` event call (to load game data). These events are generated by the LoadSaveManager, shown in Listing 9-5.

So let's now amend the `PlayerController` class first to respond to load and save events in a way that integrates effectively with the LoadSaveManager. See Listing 9-7 for two new event functions added to the `PlayerController` class. For brevity and clarity, the rest of the class is not shown here (the `PlayerController` is defined in Chapter 5). Remember to register the class as a listener for the two events with the NotificationsManager in the `Start` event. Chapter 3 features more information on the NotificationsManager, if you need a refresher.

Listing 9-7. Completing the PlayerController Class

```
01      //-------------------------------------------------
02      //Function called when saving game
03      public void SaveGamePrepare(Component Sender)
04      {
05              //Get Player Data Object
06              LoadSaveManager.GameStateData.DataPlayer PlayerData = GameManager.StateManager.
                GameState.Player;
07
```

```
08              //Fill in player data for save game
09              PlayerData.CollectedCash = Cash;
10              PlayerData.CollectedGun = CollectWeapon.Collected;
11              PlayerData.Health = Health;
12              PlayerData.PosRotScale.X = ThisTransform.position.x;
13              PlayerData.PosRotScale.Y = ThisTransform.position.y;
14              PlayerData.PosRotScale.Z = ThisTransform.position.z;
15              PlayerData.PosRotScale.RotX = ThisTransform.localEulerAngles.x;
16              PlayerData.PosRotScale.RotY = ThisTransform.localEulerAngles.y;
17              PlayerData.PosRotScale.RotZ = ThisTransform.localEulerAngles.z;
18              PlayerData.PosRotScale.ScaleX = ThisTransform.localScale.x;
19              PlayerData.PosRotScale.ScaleY = ThisTransform.localScale.y;
20              PlayerData.PosRotScale.ScaleZ = ThisTransform.localScale.z;
21      }
22      //-------------------------------------------------
23      //Function called when loading is complete
24      public void LoadGameComplete(Component Sender)
25      {
26              //Get Player Data Object
27              LoadSaveManager.GameStateData.DataPlayer PlayerData =
                GameManager.StateManager.GameState.Player;
28
29              //Load data back to Player
30              Cash = PlayerData.CollectedCash;
31
32              //Give player weapon, activate and destroy weapon power-up
33              if(PlayerData.CollectedGun)
34              {
35                      //Find weapon powerup in level
36                      GameObject WeaponPowerUp = GameObject.Find("spr_upgrade_weapon");
37
38                      //Send OnTriggerEnter message
39                      WeaponPowerUp.SendMessage("OnTriggerEnter", GetComponent<Collider>(),
                        SendMessageOptions.DontRequireReceiver);
40              }
41
42              Health = PlayerData.Health;
43
44              //Set position
45              ThisTransform.position = new Vector3(PlayerData.PosRotScale.X,
                PlayerData.PosRotScale.Y, PlayerData.PosRotScale.Z);
46
47              //Set rotation
48              ThisTransform.localRotation = Quaternion.Euler(PlayerData.PosRotScale.RotX,
                PlayerData.PosRotScale.RotY, PlayerData.PosRotScale.RotZ);
49
50              //Set scale
51              ThisTransform.localScale = new Vector3(PlayerData.PosRotScale.ScaleX,
                PlayerData.PosRotScale.ScaleY, PlayerData.PosRotScale.ScaleZ);
52      }
53      //-------------------------------------------------
```

- **Line 03.** The `SaveGamePrepare` event is called on the PlayerController just before the game state is serialized. This is the opportunity the PlayerController needs to confirm its current status to the LoadSaveManager. It does this by filling in the Player transformation data, after retrieving a reference to the serializable Player data object in the `LoadSaveManager.GameStateData` object.

- **Line 87.** The `LoadGameComplete` event is a little more intricate. The function is called automatically by the NotificationsManager just after game data has been loaded from an XML file, and so it represents an opportunity for the Player to restore its data from the serialized class back into the `PlayerController` object. It starts by restoring the Player cash and the collected weapon. In the case of the weapon, it also ensures that the weapon power-up is removed from the level if the weapon is collected (as opposed to having the fists/punch weapon), preventing the Player from collecting the gun weapon and its ammo twice. And then, finally, it restores Player health and Player transformation data.

Completing the Enemy Class

Just as we needed to update the `PlayerController` class to respond to load-and-save game events, we also need to update the `Enemy` base class, allowing all Enemies to load and save their data. The newly added functions to the `Enemy.cs` class are listed in Listing 9-8; these support load and save functionality. The full class listing (minus loading and saving) is shown in Chapter 7, if you want to see it. Remember, all source code for CMOD is included in the project files, and the completed CMOD Unity project is also included in the files for this chapter.

Listing 9-8. Completing the Enemy Class

```
01      //-------------------------------------------------
02      //Function called when saving game
03      public void SaveGamePrepare(Component Sender)
04      {
05              //Create enemy data for this enemy
06              LoadSaveManager.GameStateData.DataEnemy ThisEnemy =
                new LoadSaveManager.GameStateData.DataEnemy();
07
08              //Fill in data for current enemy
09              ThisEnemy.EnemyID = EnemyID;
10              ThisEnemy.Health = Health;
11              ThisEnemy.PosRotScale.X = ThisTransform.position.x;
12              ThisEnemy.PosRotScale.Y = ThisTransform.position.y;
13              ThisEnemy.PosRotScale.Z = ThisTransform.position.z;
14              ThisEnemy.PosRotScale.RotX = ThisTransform.localEulerAngles.x;
15              ThisEnemy.PosRotScale.RotY = ThisTransform.localEulerAngles.y;
16              ThisEnemy.PosRotScale.RotZ = ThisTransform.localEulerAngles.z;
17              ThisEnemy.PosRotScale.ScaleX = ThisTransform.localScale.x;
18              ThisEnemy.PosRotScale.ScaleY = ThisTransform.localScale.y;
19              ThisEnemy.PosRotScale.ScaleZ = ThisTransform.localScale.z;
20
```

```
21                    //Add enemy to Game State
22                    GameManager.StateManager.GameState.Enemies.Add(ThisEnemy);
23            }
24      //-------------------------------------------------
25      //Function called when loading is complete
26      public void LoadGameComplete(Component Sender)
27      {
28                    //Cycle through enemies and find matching ID
29                    List<LoadSaveManager.GameStateData.DataEnemy> Enemies =
                      GameManager.StateManager.GameState.Enemies;
30
31                    //Reference to this enemy
32                    LoadSaveManager.GameStateData.DataEnemy ThisEnemy = null;
33
34                    for(int i=0; i<Enemies.Count; i++)
35                    {
36                            if(Enemies[i].EnemyID == EnemyID)
37                            {
38                                    //Found enemy. Now break break from loop
39                                    ThisEnemy = Enemies[i];
40                                    break;
41                            }
42                    }
43
44                    //If we reach here and no enemy is found, then it was destroyed when saved.
                      So destroy now
45                    if(ThisEnemy==null){DestroyImmediate(gameObject);return;}
46
47                    //Else load enemy data
48                    EnemyID = ThisEnemy.EnemyID;
49                    Health = ThisEnemy.Health;
50
51                    //Set position
52                    Agent.Warp(new Vector3(ThisEnemy.PosRotScale.X, ThisEnemy.PosRotScale.Y,
                      ThisEnemy.PosRotScale.Z));
53
54                    //Set rotation
55                    ThisTransform.localRotation = Quaternion.Euler(ThisEnemy.PosRotScale.RotX,
                      ThisEnemy.PosRotScale.RotY, ThisEnemy.PosRotScale.RotZ);
56
57                    //Set scale
58                    ThisTransform.localScale = new Vector3(ThisEnemy.PosRotScale.ScaleX,
                      ThisEnemy.PosRotScale.ScaleY, ThisEnemy.PosRotScale.ScaleZ);
59      }
60      //-------------------------------------------------
```

■ **Lines 03–22.** As with the Player class, the Enemy class fills in the required Enemy data, and then uses the List.Add function to add the Enemy data into the GameStateData class as a serializable object.

> **Tip**   Lists and dynamic arrays were covered in Chapter 3, when considering event handling.

- **Lines 26–60.** The Load function searches through all Enemies in the GameStateData enemies list, and finds a matching Enemy entry by ID number to reload the appropriate Enemy data. This functionality therefore depends on each Enemy in the scene having a unique ID. If two Enemies have a matching ID, then confusion will arise when restoring Enemies. Notice that to restore the Enemy position in the scene, the function Agent.Warp is used instead of transform. position, which was used for the Player. Doing this is consistent with any agent that relies on pathfinding, as opposed to nonagent objects like the Player, whose position is "free" and unconstrained by navigation or physics. Chapter 7 covered pathfinding in more detail. More information on the Warp function can be found in the online Unity documentation at https://docs.unity3d.com/Documentation/ ScriptReference/NavMeshAgent.Warp.html.

Testing Save and Load Functionality

Now we've got enough for everything to work together seamlessly for loading and saving games in CMOD. In sum, we've created a LoadSaveManager that integrates with the GameManager class, and we also amended the PlayerController and Enemy classes to respond directly to load and save events through the NotificationsManager. Let's test this now from Unity. Simply press the Play button on the editor toolbar, make some changes in-game, and then display the main menu using the Escape key on the keyboard. Finally, click Save and exit the game (see Figure 9-5).

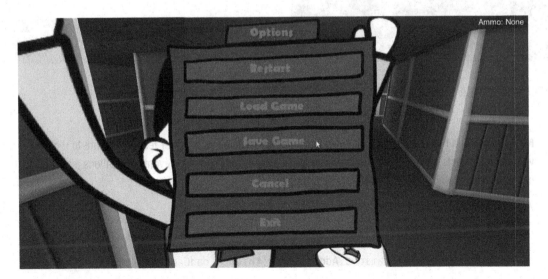

Figure 9-5. Saving a game from the main menu

Before restoring your game in Unity, jump over to the `Application.persistentDataPath` folder on your system, and you should find the save-game XML file, which is the result of the save operation. Open the file in MonoDevelop, ensuring that Code Folding is enabled in the Options dialog, and inspect the contents of the file to make sure that the data saved as expected (see Figure 9-6). Checking the file in this way is good debugging practice—it's a great way to inspect the data being saved and to check for errors and issues. It's also what you'll need to do if you ever want to tweak or change the data inside the file.

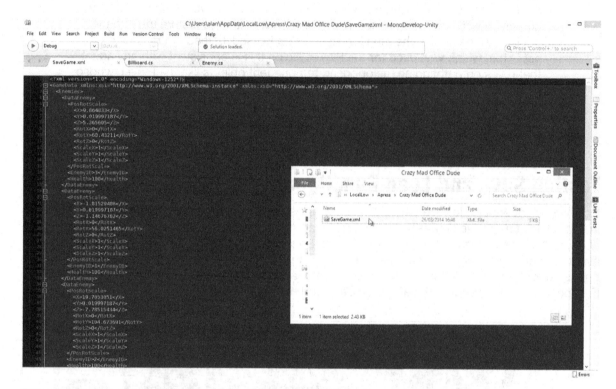

Figure 9-6. Verifying the save-game data

> **Note** If you find that your data is not being loaded or saved as expected after testing, be sure to register your enemy objects with the notifications manager to receive load-and-save event notifications (see the companion source code for more details); for example:
>
> ```
> //Add listener for saving games
>     GameManager.Notifications.AddListener(this, "SaveGamePrepare");
>
>     GameManager.Notifications.AddListener(this, "LoadGameComplete");
> ```

Now return to CMOD in Unity and restore the game using the main menu. See Figure 9-7. Voilà! Excellent work! We've created load and save functionality.

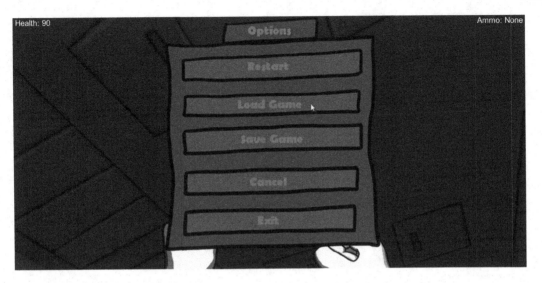

Figure 9-7. Restoring a game from the main menu

Summary

Great! You've now completed CMOD. It has everything we planned for in the earlier chapters: a complete environment to explore, an event-handling system, collectible power-ups, a First Person Controller, weapons, intelligent enemies, a GUI system, and now load and save functionality. In achieving this, we've seen a lot of C# scripting features. But, before moving onto the next chapter to round things out for this course, let's recap what we've covered in this chapter. By now, you should be able to do the following:

- Understand what persistent data is
- Use the PlayerPrefs class to store basic user preferences and settings
- Understand the limitations of PlayerPrefs
- Be aware of persistent storage alternatives, such as storing to files
- Understand the difference between binary/proprietary files and text-based files
- Be aware of some text-based file formats common in games, such as XML and JSON
- Understand serialization
- Create a LoadSaveManager with XML serialization
- Create classes with serializable data types
- Integrate your existing game with a new save-game framework
- Understand the Application.PersistentDataPath variable

Chapter **10**

Refinements and Improvements

Splendid! You've reached the final chapter of the book. CMOD is now complete and feature-filled. True, it's a relatively short game with just one level, two weapons, and three enemy types. And many gamers might even mistake the game for being "simple." But we know now that this is really more of a simplification than anything else. Despite being small, CMOD makes use of an extensive range of Unity features and C# nuances, and these in turn depend on concepts and theory that's far from obvious.

In Chapter 2, we constructed a level using the modular building technique, added lightmapping for static lighting, and configured enemies and power-up objects using Prefabs. In Chapter 3, we laid the foundations for CMOD in terms of scripting and class design by creating a NotificationsManager to support an event-driven paradigm, allowing objects to post game events when they happen, and for registered listeners to be automatically notified of the events. This class came in handy for all subsequent chapters.

In Chapter 4, we moved forward to create collectible power-up objects in the level, such as health restore, ammo restore, new weapons, and cash. In doing this, we saw the singleton design pattern, and implemented camera-aligned billboards for sprite objects. In addition, we created PingPong motion with coroutines to move the power-ups gently up and down to emphasize their collectible nature. In Chapter 5, we applied concepts such as sine waves and universal First Person Controllers to create a cross-platform `PlayerController` class that allowed the Player to move around the level in first-person mode.

In Chapter 6, we explored issues of class inheritance and polymorphism by creating a base weapon class to support a range of derived classes, implementing customized weapon functionality for the punch and the pistol weapons. Further, these weapons were coded to use physics and ray casting to attack and deal damage to enemy targets in range when fired. In Chapter 7, the native Unity NavMesh asset came to our aid as we implemented intelligent Enemy characters that not only found their way around the level, avoiding obstacles, but also exhibited patrol, chase and attack behaviors using finite state machines.

Then in Chapter 8, we added a basic but functional GUI (or *front end*) to the game, allowing the gamer to exit and restart the game. In achieving this, we explored the limitations of the native GUI class and saw alternatives, such as the 4.3 sprite features. These allowed us to create a multiresolution GUI that can position and size itself according to screen size. Finally, in Chapter 9 we added load-and-save game functionality to CMOD. With this, gamers can save and load game sessions from XML files that persist between game sessions.

In sum, we've come a long way and seen C# applied practically in many ways. But, there's still so much more to know and see. No single book could possibly cover it all. In fact, you could spend weeks and months, and even years searching through books and online tutorials, and still find new concepts and ideas you'd never encountered before, because there's always more to learn. That's the nature of the games industry—and probably every other industry, too! So the aim of this chapter, which is about looking ahead, is comparatively modest. Its aim is to consider specific ways CMOD could be reasonably improved or changed using *only* other concepts and techniques that we've not covered in much detail already, to give you a feel for some additional features and ideas "out there" in the field. So let's go!

Level Changing

As it stands, CMOD features only one level or scene. Consequently, the most obvious way in which CMOD could be expanded is by adding more levels. The general idea would be that, on collecting all cash power-ups in one level, the Player would progress to the next. And this process would repeat for as many levels as there were in the game. Or maybe, you'd even create procedurally generated levels (levels autogenerated at runtime), potentially allowing the game to progress indefinitely—or until the gamer's patience expired! Whichever route you choose, you'll likely want the ability to change levels in-game, moving from the Player from one level to the next. Thankfully, Unity makes this task easy with the Application class. This class supports several level loading methods. The most commonly used is LoadLevel, which looks like Listing 10-1.

Listing 10-1. Loading a Level Using Application.LoadLevel

```
Application.LoadLevel(1);
```

> **Note**   More information on the Application class can be found in the online Unity documentation at https://docs.unity3d.com/Documentation/ScriptReference/Application.html.

Levels can be loaded either by number (ID) or by name (that is, the scene name, excluding the .scene file extension). However, for LoadLevel to work as intended, all levels in the game must be included in the *levels list*. This list can be accessed by choosing **File ➤ Build Settings** from the application menu. From there, scene files can be dragged and dropped from the Project panel into the levels list. You can also rearrange the order of scene files within the list by dragging and dropping items. Each level is assigned a unique number or ID, shown in the right-hand column (see Figure 10-1). This ID can be passed to the LoadLevel function to load the appropriate level.

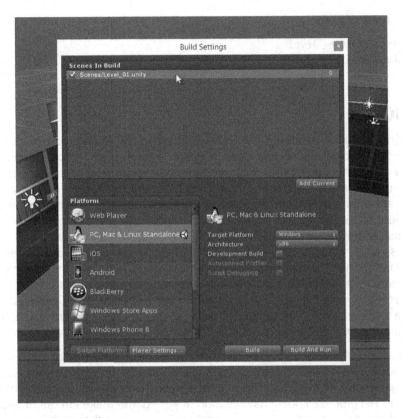

Figure 10-1. Adding levels to the levels list

If you were being really ambitious and made a huge level, one that sprawled on for a long time and included many more meshes and enemies, it may take a long time to load. Generally, it's not a good idea to keep the gamer waiting. Today, we're acclimatized by so many time-compressing technologies offering *instant* access to media and *on-demand* services, that waiting times *feel* longer than they ever have. To alleviate waiting times and avoid gamer frustration, Unity allows you to load levels asynchronously, too—that is, to load levels *in the background* while the gamer is still playing the game. To do this, the `Application.LoadLevelAsync` coroutine can be used (see Listing 10-2).

Listing 10-2. Loading a Level Asynchronously

```
yield return Application.LoadLevelAsync("ABigLevel");
```

The type of level loading that we've considered so far works well when you need to completely move from one level to the next in the traditional sense—that is, exiting level X to move to level Y. But sometimes you'll make games, like large, open-ended RPGs or flight simulators, in which the environment should be experienced as one continuous and enormous world that stretches on, seemingly forever. In such games, you don't want a transition or change from one discrete level to the next. You don't want the user to notice a transition at all. You just want the world to seem complete and integrated, even though you may have developed it across multiple scene files. In essence, you want to load in a different scene and *add it* to the existing one, creating the appearance of a complete and integrated environment. In this case, you can use the function `Application.LoadLevelAdditive` or `Application.LoadLevelAdditiveAsync` (see Listing 10-3).

Listing 10-3. Loading Levels Additively

```
//Loads level 2 into existing level
Application.LoadLevelAdditive(2);
```

Event Handling

The event-handling system created in Chapter 3 was termed the *NotificationsManager*. It was created as a Singleton object. Using this class, a *Poster* may dispatch a notification about an event as it happens, such as an enemy-destroyed event, and the NotificationsManager responds by immediately invoking event calls in any registered *Listeners* for that event, allowing them to act as required. By centralizing event handling through a single managerial class, every other class has an independent and effective way to respond to almost any event without directly affecting the implementation of any other class. In Chapter 3, the event framework was implemented by using the SendMessage function of *GameObject*. This function can be called on a per object basis and invokes any functions of a matching name on any components attached to the object. See Chapter 3 for a refresher if required, and also the relevant Unity documentation at http://docs.unity3d.com/Documentation/ScriptReference/GameObject.SendMessage.html. The SendMessage function works like the BroadcastMessage function, except that BroadcastMessage cascades invocation downward through all child objects in the scene hierarchy.

In many situations, as with CMOD, you can get away with using SendMessage and BroadcastMessage without any problems. But both of these functions rely on deeper underlying code that *can* be computationally expensive, leading to performance issues. This primarily (though not exclusively) results from an internal process known as *reflection*. If your game makes frequent and extensive use of either SendMessage or BroadcastMessage, and you're experiencing performance issues, then it's time to seriously rethink your code and to consider alternatives. And indeed, there are many alternatives.

The biggest problems that we faced when coding the event-handling system was how to invoke events on listeners that could potentially be of any data type. A Listener could be any kind of class, and because we can't know in advance which type it is, then we don't know which functions it supports and which functions we can call. The SendMessage and BroadcastMessage methods allow us to easily get around this problem, because they simply require us to provide a function name *by string*, and they execute that function for us across all components in an object, regardless of object data types—provided the function exists in the first place. So, when considering alternatives for event handling, we need solutions that will allow us to achieve a similar kind of behavior. There are at least two possibilities in C: *interfaces* and *delegates*.

Interfaces

Interfaces are a powerful feature native to C#, and not Unity specifically. They let you create a special kind of runtime polymorphism and they offer a solution to effective event handling. Let's see how in practice. In short, with a C# interface you start by defining one or more functions together, as shown in Listing 10-4.

Listing 10-4. Declaring an Interface in C#

```
public interface IListener
{
        //Event called through listener interface
        void OnEventOccured(EVENT_TYPE EType, int Param);
}
```

At this point, we've defined an interface for a potential event listener. Next, *any* class can implement this interface. This means the class *guarantees* it will implement an OnEventOccured function, as specified in the *IListener* interface, as shown in Listing 10-5.

Listing 10-5. Implementing an Interface in C#

```
public class Listener : MonoBehaviour, IListener
{
        //[... other stuff here]

        //Implement interface - called on event
        public void OnEventOccured(EVENT_TYPE EType, int Param)
        {
                Debug.Log ("My Event Called");
        }
}
```

Now here, *any* other class can interface with Listener directly through the IListener interface, without ever needing to know its *true data type*. It just needs to know about the IListener interface. Consider Listings 10-6 and 10-7. These two samples represent two completely separate script files, together defining a sample event-handling system and a sample Listener, simply for demonstration purposes, using interfaces. Both of these scripts should be attached to the same object in the scene to test its functionality in Unity. When you do this, a NotficationsManager will post a notification to a registered listener on every key press, via interfaces. Notice how this class achieves exactly the same behavior as the SendMessage and BroadcastMessage functionality we used in Chapter 3, but without the extra performance cost. Go ahead and try it!

Listing 10-6. NotificationsManager.cs: Defines an Interface and Notifications Manager

```
//-----------------------------------
using UnityEngine;
using System.Collections;
using System.Collections.Generic;
//-----------------------------------
public interface IListener
{
        //Event called through listener interface
        void OnEventOccured(NotificationsManager.EVENT_TYPE EType =
        NotificationsManager.EVENT_TYPE.ON_ENEMYDESTROYED, int Param = 0);
}
```

```
//-------------------------------------
public class NotificationsManager : MonoBehaviour
{
        //Define even types here...
        public enum EVENT_TYPE {ON_ENEMYDESTROYED = 0, ON_LEVELRESTARTED = 1,
        ON_POWERUPCOLLECTED = 2, ON_KEYPRESS=3};

        //Collection of listeners
        private List<IListener> Listeners = new List<IListener>();
        //-------------------------------------
        //Function to add listener
        public void AddListener(IListener lObject)
        {
                //Add listener to list
                Listeners.Add(lObject);
        }
        //-------------------------------------
        void PostEvent(EVENT_TYPE EType = EVENT_TYPE.ON_ENEMYDESTROYED, int Param = 0)
        {
                //Notify all listeners
                for(int i=0; i<Listeners.Count; i++)
                        Listeners[i].OnEventOccured(EType, Param);
        }
        //-------------------------------------
        void Update()
        {
                if(Input.anyKeyDown)
                {
                        //Post key press event to all listeners
                        PostEvent(EVENT_TYPE.ON_KEYPRESS,0);
                }
        }
        //-------------------------------------
}
//-------------------------------------
```

Listing 10-7. Listener.cs: Sample Listener Object

```
using UnityEngine;
using System.Collections;

public class Listener : MonoBehaviour, IListener
{
        private NotificationsManager NM = null;

        void Start()
        {
                //Get notifications manager
                NM = GetComponent<NotificationsManager>();

                //Add as listener
                NM.AddListener(this);
        }
```

```
//Implement interface - called on event
public void OnEventOccured(NotificationsManager.EVENT_TYPE EType = NotificationsManager.
EVENT_TYPE.ON_ENEMYDESTROYED, int Param = 0)
{
        Debug.Log ("My Event Called");
}
}
```

> **Note**   A sample project demonstrating interfaces can be found in the book's companion files at
> `Chapter10/Interfaces/`.

Delegates

Interfaces simulate polymorphism among classes of different types. Delegates, in contrast, work at
the function or method level, as opposed to the class level. Imagine that you can treat a function
like a variable: you can create a *variable* and store a reference in it to a *function* elsewhere, even to a
function in a *different* class. And then imagine that you could later *execute* that variable, *invoking* the
function it references. This is effectively what delegates let you achieve. A delegate is a special object
referencing a function. This means that we can create a NotificationsManager by maintaining an array
of delegates, referencing the functions for many different listener objects. The only standard or rule
the listeners must obey for this to work effectively is that their event functions maintain the same
prototype—that is, has the same argument list and return type. Let's see this in action across two
different script files: one for the NotificationsManager and one for the Listener (see Listings 10-8 and 10-9).
Then give it a test in Unity.

Listing 10-8. NotificationsManager.cs: Defines an Interface and Notifications Manager Using Delegates

```
using UnityEngine;
using System.Collections;
using System.Collections.Generic;

public class NotificationsManager : MonoBehaviour
{
        //Define even types here...
        public enum EVENT_TYPE {ON_ENEMYDESTROYED = 0, ON_LEVELRESTARTED = 1, ON_POWERUPCOLLECTED = 2,
        ON_KEYPRESS=3};

        //Declare listener delegate
        public delegate void ListenerDelegate(NotificationsManager.EVENT_TYPE EType, int Param);

        //Array of listener delegates
        private List<ListenerDelegate> Listeners = new List<ListenerDelegate>();
```

```
        //Add listener
        public void AddListener(ListenerDelegate Listener)
        {
                Listeners.Add(Listener);
        }

        void PostNotification(NotificationsManager.EVENT_TYPE EType, int Param)
        {
                //Notify all listeners
                for(int i=0; i<Listeners.Count; i++)
                {
                        //Call delegate like function
                        Listeners[i](EType, Param);
                }
        }

        void Update()
        {
                //Notify event system on keypress
                if(Input.anyKeyDown)
                        PostNotification(EVENT_TYPE.ON_KEYPRESS,0);
        }
}
```

Listing 10-9. Listener.cs: Creates a Listener with Delegates

```
using UnityEngine;
using System.Collections;

public class Listener : MonoBehaviour
{
        private NotificationsManager NM = null;

        void Start()
        {
                //Get notifications manager
                NM = GetComponent<NotificationsManager>();

                //Add as listener
                NM.AddListener(OnEventCall);
        }

        //Function prototype matches delegate
        public void OnEventCall(NotificationsManager.EVENT_TYPE EType, int Param)
        {
                Debug.Log("Event Called");
        }
}
```

> **Note** You might also want to check out the .NET/Mono delegate framework through the System.Action class.
>
> A sample project demonstrating delegates can be found in the book's companion files at
> Chapter10/Delegates/.

Write Shorter Code

The famous computer scientist Ken Thompson is often attributed as saying, "One of my most productive days was throwing away 1000 lines of code." And another computer scientist, Edsger W. Dijkstra, echoed a similar idea when he said, "Simplicity is a prerequisite for reliability." Here, there's the idea that simplicity is preferred wherever possible. In programming, this often means not resorting to needless complexity and excess; and keeping your code shorter, tidier, and more readable, while still being reliable and efficient. Achieving this in practice is actually harder than it sounds, and it's often something you develop with experience. But there are tips and techniques you can use right now to write shorter and clearer C# code that's often easier to read and maintain. Some general tips follow.

Ternary Operator

The term *ternary* is Latin, meaning "composed of three parts." This name describes the three-part nature of the ternary operator in C#, which is essentially a form of abbreviation. It is sometimes call the *conditional operator*. Often, when coding games, you'll need to check a specific condition using an if-else statement. Then, based on the outcome of the check, you'll need to assign a variable some specific value, in both the if and the else blocks; something like what's shown in Listing 10-10.

Listing 10-10. Assigning Variables Based on Conditions

```
if(DoorClosed == true)
{
        MonsterState = MONSTER_STATE.Idle;
}
else
{
        MonsterState = MONSTER_STATE.Attack;
}
```

The ternary operator lets you shorten code like this into only one line using the ? and the : symbols. Using the ternary operator, Listing 10-10 could be abbreviated into Listing 10-11.

Listing 10-11. Using the Ternary Operator

```
DoorClosed = (DoorClosed == true) ? MONSTER_STATE.Idle : MONSTER_STATE.Attack;
```

Null-Coalesce Operator

In programming, the value null means nothing, emptiness, oblivion, nothingness. It expresses invalidity. One common task in programming is to assign a value to a variable on the basis of a null check, to ensure we're working only with valid data. Consider Listing 10-12.

Listing 10-12. Check for Null Values on Assignment

```
if(DroneEnemy != null)
        EnemyReference = DroneEnemy;
else
        EnemyReference = BossEnemy;
```

This kind of statement could, of course, be shortened using the ternary operator that we've seen already, but for null checks specifically, it can be shortened even further with the null-coalesce operator, as shown in Listing 10-13.

Listing 10-13. Shortening with Null-Coalesce

```
DroneEnemy = DroneEnemy ?? BossEnemy;
```

Automatic Properties

C# properties are useful because they give you the chance to perform additional functionality, such as validation, when specific variables are set or read in a class. Sometimes, however, you don't really need to perform any functionality on setting or getting variables, apart from basic assignment. In these cases, you could just use a public variable directly instead of a property. But, you may also want to keep the variable wrapped behind a property anyway, so you can later implement validation without breaking any existing code. You could do this the long way, as shown in Listing 10-14.

Listing 10-14. Properties as Accessors

```
class MyData
{
        //Private member
        private string sName;

        //Public property
        public string Name
        {
                get{return sName;}
                set{sName = value;}
        }
}
```

However, a shorter alternative to write accessor methods like this is using *automatic properties*. The equivalent code can be written as shown in Listing 10-15.

Listing 10-15. Automatic Properties

```
class MyData
{
        //Public property
        public string Name{get; set;}
}
```

We could take this even further and create read-only and write-only automatic properties. Although the access levels apply only to *other* classes accessing the properties, and not to the owner class itself. Listing 10-16 creates a read-only property, and Listing 10-17 creates a write-only property (if you'd really need such a thing!).

Listing 10-16. Read-Only Automatic Properties

```
class MyData
{
        //Public property
        public string Name{get; private set;}
}
```

Listing 10-17. Write-Only Automatic Properties

```
class MyData
{
        //Public property
        public string Name{private get; set;}
}
```

C# Features or Quirks?

Let's now consider some other, more controversial, features of C# that are helpful for coding games, such as when expanding on CMOD, or are at least useful to know, if nothing else. These features are controversial in the sense that some developers cannot see or don't accept their usefulness in any circumstances, except for the most obscure or remote cases, while others declare their usefulness in many circumstances. Let's see what these are.

Private Does Not Mean Inaccessible

Let's say you declare a class with a `private` variable, as shown in Listing 10-18. You may think that the variable is protected in that no other instances could ever access it, but for the instance to which it belongs. The variable is not public but private, and so surely no other instances can access it, right? Wrong.

Listing 10-18. A Class with a Private Variable

```
public class MyClass
{
        private string Name = "DefaultString";
}
```

Listing 10-19 shows a case where an object can access and edit the private variable of another instance, as freely as if it were its own variable.

Listing 10-19. Accessing a private variable

```
public class MyClass
{
        private string Name = "DefaultString";

        void TestFunction()
        {
                MyClass C = new MyClass();
                C.Name ="ah ha";
        }
}
```

This happens because the privacy variable obtains between *classes* and not *instances*. Multiple instances of the *same class* can access each other's private variables. Thus, private variables are inaccessible *only* to instances of different classes.

goto is C# Teleportation

There's one statement in programming that nearly every programmer seems to dislike. It's been termed "bad practice" and has received such wide condemnation that it's easy to wonder why newer languages like C# even added the feature in the first place. That feature is the infamous goto statement (pronounced *go to*), which allows program execution to suddenly divert from its normal course and jump to a different, specified location in the source file. Thus, it's a kind of teleport feature. Some people recommend never using goto at all, because its teleporting nature obfuscates code, making it difficult to follow and understand. And yet, in moderation, goto can prove useful and sometimes cleaner for breaking out of loops early (see Listing 10-20).

Listing 10-20. Using goto

```
void Search(int Index)
{
        int[,] IntArray = new int[4, 2] { { 2, 2 }, { 5, 5 }, { 5, 1 }, { 2, 8 } };

        for(int i = 0; i < IntArray.GetLength(0); i++)
        {
                for (int j = 0; j < IntArray.GetLength(1); j++)
                {
                        if (IntArray[i, j].Equals(Index))
                        {
                                goto Found;
                        }
                }
        }

        Found:
                Debug.Log("GameObject Found");
}
```

Static is Omnipresent

The *static* keyword was considered in Chapter 4, when creating Singleton objects. In short, using the static keyword, you can add variables that completely cut across instance scope boundaries—that is, variables that retain their value not for a *specific* instance of a class, but for all instances. If you need to create a value that applies to *all* instances of a class, as though it were a *shared* variable, then static variables can come in handy (see Listing 10-21 for use of a static variable in a class).

Listing 10-21. Using Static Variables

```
using UnityEngine;
using System.Collections;

public class MyClass
{
        //Variable will be shared for all instances
        static public int MyVar = 50;

        //Variable will differ among instances
        public string Name = "";

        //prints static variable to console
        public void PrintMyVar()
        {
                Debug.Log (MyVar);
        }
}

public class Sample : MonoBehaviour
{
        void Start()
        {
                //Delcare instances of MyClass
                MyClass C1 = new MyClass();
                MyClass C2 = new MyClass();

                //Static variable set to 100
                MyClass.MyVar = 100;

                //Both classes will print 100 because they share the variable
                C1.PrintMyVar();
                C2.PrintMyVar();
        }
}
```

Note   Take care with memory management when using static objects. Unity will not automatically clean or delete static references, even between scene switches.

Braces Define Scope

When thinking about variables and scope, it's easy to think in terms of global variables living application-wide, class variables as being class-wide, local variables as being function-wide, and block variables as existing inside loops and if statements. But the braces symbols { } can be used inside any function on their own, without the presence of a surrounding loop or if statement in order to control variable scope, if required (see Listing 10-22).

Listing 10-22. Unconventional Block Scope

```
void Start()
{

    {
            //Scope inside braces
            string Name = "Bob";
            Debug.Log(Name);
    }

    //Variable not accessible here - will generate a compile error
    Name = "John";
    Debug.Log(Name);
}
```

Summary

So now we've reached the end of this intensive C# course in professional game development with the Unity engine. We've covered a lot of ground. CMOD is completed, and having read this chapter, you're now better positioned to make potential improvements and refinements, such as adding more levels and refining the event system using either interfaces or delegates. In addition, you've seen potential tips and tricks to keep in mind when using C# that can really help boost your productivity.

Now, although there's lots more to see and learn (as there always will be), you can still use and reuse the concepts here, with practically limitless potential. Using only the code and ideas presented in this book, you can produce amazing results. And I hope that this book brings you game-development success. So with that said, let me congratulate you on completing the book and creating a cartoon first-person shooter that rests on solid code—with the potential to be expanded even further. This is Alan Thorn, signing off.

But before I do so, let's recap what this chapter has offered. After completing this chapter, you should be able to do the following:

- Understand ways in which CMOD can be expanded
- Know how to load new levels with Application.LoadLevel
- Load levels asynchronously and additively
- Improve the event system with interfaces

- See the potential for events and other callbacks by using delegates
- Appreciate the benefits of shortening code and improving its readability
- Use automatic properties
- Understand the ternary operator and the null-coalesce operator
- Understand the limitations of private variables
- Use goto effectively
- Understand the usefulness of static variables
- Understand how braces relate to variable scope

Index

X, Y, Z

Get the eBook for only $10!

> Now you can take the weightless companion with you anywhere, anytime. Your purchase of this book entitles you to 3 electronic versions for only $10.

This Apress title will prove so indispensible that you'll want to carry it with you everywhere, which is why we are offering the eBook in 3 formats for only $10 if you have already purchased the print book.

Convenient and fully searchable, the PDF version enables you to easily find and copy code—or perform examples by quickly toggling between instructions and applications. The MOBI format is ideal for your Kindle, while the ePUB can be utilized on a variety of mobile devices.

Go to www.apress.com/promo/tendollars to purchase your companion eBook.

Apress®
THE EXPERT'S VOICE™